Weekend CYCLING

Christa Gausden

Hamlyn Paperbacks

WEEKEND CYCLING
ISBN 0 600 20444 8

First published in Great Britain 1982
by The Oxford Illustrated Press
Hamlyn Paperbacks edition 1982

Text and routes copyright © 1982 by Christa Gausden
Maps and illustrations copyright © 1982 by The Oxford
Illustrated Press

Line illustrations by John Gilbert Rankin

Hamlyn Paperbacks are published by
The Hamlyn Publishing Group Ltd,
Astronaut House, Feltham,
Middlesex, England

Reproduced, printed and bound in Great Britain by
Hazell Watson & Viney Ltd, Aylesbury, Bucks

CONTENTS

DEDICATION

This book is dedicated to the many folk who showed me such kindness when, during my Weekend Cycling ride-testing tour, I asked to camp on their land.

The ex-colonial tea-planters turned West Country vinegrowers, whose high teas were of the best.
The lady who tended her garden in Sunday best dress and wellingtons.
The couple who refused me a tent pitch — insisting I use their luxurious caravan instead.
The farmer's wife with her cage of ferrets beside the outside loo.
The family who fed me up with delicious pasties made with only their own produce.
The gentleman who presented his wife with a scruffy camper for the lawn – one present for her 70th birthday.
The jovial farmer – and especially his horse – who shared their field good-naturedly with me.
And many others too.

My thanks to them all. Their warm welcomes, lively interest and comfortable conversations made the tour an unforgettable adventure.

INTRODUCTION

As you leaf through this volume in a city bookshop or in an armchair, a weekend cycling venture in the country might seem a pleasant but idle dream. It needn't be, for as long as you can ride a bike, you can do it. Leaving the hustle of work and town life behind on a Friday night, your return on Sunday will find you relaxed and stimulated by a weekend of exercise in the fresh air in a beautiful part of the country.

Britain is ideal for weekend cycle rides. We have such a rich legacy of historic, pretty or peculiar buildings that even the shortest rides pass places worth exploring. Then too, it is our good fortune to have inherited those long-established paths and cartroads which once linked cottage to church, farm to market, and village to firewood forest. Many of these old ways have now become the tarmaced lanes which form Britain's dense network of unclassified roads. With too many bends and junctions to appeal to most motorists, they are quiet and therefore ideal for the cyclist.

Enjoyment of nature and sight-seeing combine almost as a matter of course with cycling, and those of you who normally travel by car will be delighted and surprised by the amount of detail to be discovered as you travel more slowly and are so easily able to stop and investigate something that has caught your attention. Cycling also combines well with many hobbies: photography, lepidoptary, collecting wild flowers for example all benefit from easy access and the lack of parking problems.

Some Fears Allayed

Misgivings which can beset a newcomer to cycling in the countryside mostly boil down to fears of the unknown, which when looked at closely, can be quickly allayed.

Age: If you ride at your own pace and cover a distance to suit you, age need not be a limiting factor. The rides in this book give short and long alternatives, and they are designed so that you do not have to choose an additional loop to the basic route until you have covered some distance and found your pace for the day. Should you find the going harder than you expected, you can just complete the basic circular route, or you can simply turn back, and enjoy the views the other way round.

Hills: Beginners are often unnecessarily apprehensive of hills, under-estimating what they can do, and forgetting that it can actually be pleasant to walk a bike uphill with pauses to rest and admire the views, as long as there is no need to hurry.

On the other hand, long slopes in Britain's higher areas can sometimes take even fit riders half-an-hour of ascent. If you have never tackled slopes of any size, make the first area you explore one with smaller gradients, such as the Northumberland Coastlands or the Wessex Downs. Don't be put off by hills if you are small: you may have less muscle but you also have less body weight to carry up. Rest assured, also, that hill-climbing gets very much easier with practice.

Busy traffic: If you live in a town or city you can certainly be forgiven for worrying about traffic, but the routes have been carefully planned to take you mainly along quiet lanes, where you can hear the occasional cars approaching from a long way off. A few local motorists, familiar with the twisting lanes go faster than they should, and so it is wise for you to ride single file at bends, keeping well in to the left. It can also sometimes happen that a motorist in a hurry will try to overtake you where the road is too narrow for safety. Prevent him from so doing by keeping a position near the road's centre, but pull in to let him pass at the first possible field gateway.

Getting lost: The purpose of the detailed route directions in this book is to guide you through the maze of country lanes and to ensure you do *not* get lost! But if by some misfortune you still get lost, do not panic. Remember that Britain is thickly populated, and even in Scotland it is not possible to carry on very far without passing a village or farm where you can ask your way.

Bad weather: Britain's temperatures are kind to cyclists: the summer heat is rarely so great as to sap your energy, and the winter cold is rarely so bad that the exercise and sensible clothing won't keep you warm. However some of the routes do cross high land, so read the texts carefully and avoid those exposed routes that suffer extreme weather unless you are experienced and have good equipment.

Rain is a far more likely cause of discomfort than extremes of temperature, but during ten weeks of ride-testing for this book in the awful early summer of 1980, I still suffered only one day of continuous rain. More often I had to put up with showers, but even these could be anticipated in time to find a big tree, a church porch, or permission to use a farmer's outhouse to shelter in. If the rain is really persistent, then seek out a stately home, museum or other building to look around until it eases off.

Animals can be a nuisance and alarming if you are not prepared. The vital point to grasp is that the sheep and cattle which graze by unfenced roads, or the dogs lounging in farmyards quite often—and understand-ably—see a cyclist not as a person on a machine but as some new, fast-moving and possibly challenging beast. Different animals react in different ways. Sheep may suddenly dash into the road in front on you; cows may sometimes crowd you out of curiosity and sheep dogs may chase you off their territory. Therefore, be ready to brake suddenly when passing sheep, move slowly and purposefully through a herd of cows (taking care to avoid passing close to their back legs), and if you can't outstrip a sheep dog then dismount and walk calmly past so it can see you are not a threat.

Accommodation: If you haven't booked your accommodation in advance and find all the recommended accommodation full, then try the tourist information bureau for more addresses, or find a telephone box and look in the yellow pages under 'hotels', 'guesthouses' and 'inns'. Alternatively ask around in the local library, pub, post office or newsagent. If you get really stuck, ask at the police station.

Choosing Your Trip

Britain enjoys a wonderful variety of landscapes, and the twenty-four sets of rides sample a wide selection of them. To help you make your first selection, read through the area descriptions and information about cycling conditions. Then see how accessible the centre is and look at the maps (with their alternative loop rides) to find a route that suits your needs and ability.

Your chosen area may enjoy seasonal events, like fell sports in the Lake District, or you may particularly want to visit a tourist attraction such as a narrow gauge railway that might close in the low season. Contact the relevant tourist information bureau for the current year's information and dates.

Once you have browsed through the book and decided on the areas which interest you, give a thought to the choice of centres. For a family it may be important that there is a swimming pool and entertainments for the children. Those especially worried about bad weather may prefer somewhere with museums and a cinema as alternatives to cycling. There is no need to shy away from a 'touristy' centre even in summer: Bourton-on-the-Water, for instance, earns its nickname of 'Blackpool of the Cotswolds' during the day, but you will be out cycling then anyway, returning when the coaches and day-trippers have left.

The timing of your weekend away is also important. If you particularly want to follow a long ride option, or visit lots of points of interest, try to go in June when the hours of daylight are longest. If however, you want to visit a popular area and not cover too many miles, then September is a good month, for it is usually still warm, the autumnal colours can be beautiful, and with the peak holiday season over, the routes are quieter.

Getting Ready for the Trip

To enjoy cycling you need spend neither money on specialist equipment

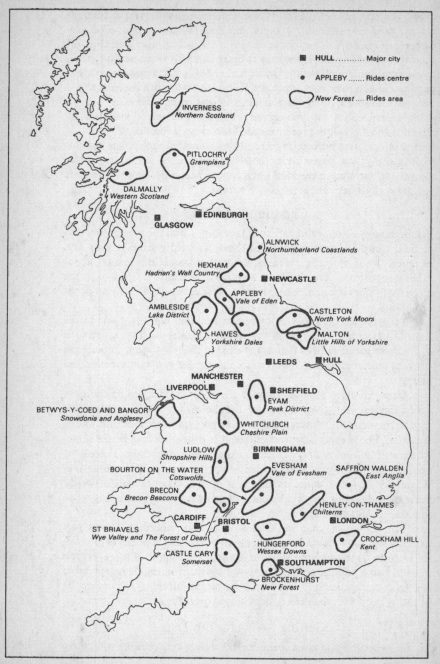

HULL .... Major city

● APPLEBY .... Rides centre

New Forest .... Rides area

INVERNESS
Northern Scotland

PITLOCHRY
Grampians

DALMALLY
Western Scotland

■ EDINBURGH

GLASGOW ■

ALNWICK
Northumberland Coastlands

HEXHAM
Hadrian's Wall Country

■ NEWCASTLE

APPLEBY
Vale of Eden

AMBLESIDE
Lake District

CASTLETON
North York Moors

HAWES
Yorkshire Dales

MALTON
Little Hills of Yorkshire

■ LEEDS

■ HULL

■ MANCHESTER

LIVERPOOL ■

■ SHEFFIELD

BETWYS-Y-COED AND BANGOR
Snowdonia and Anglesey

EYAM
Peak District

WHITCHURCH
Cheshire Plain

LUDLOW
Shropshire Hills

BIRMINGHAM ■

BOURTON ON THE WATER
Cotswolds

EVESHAM
Vale of Evesham

SAFFRON WALDEN
East Anglia

BRECON
Brecon Beacons

CARDIFF ■

BRISTOL ■

HENLEY-ON-THAMES
Chilterns

■ LONDON

ST BRIAVELS
Wye Valley and The Forest of Dean

HUNGERFORD
Wessex Downs

CROCKHAM HILL
Kent

CASTLE CARY
Somerset

■ SOUTHAMPTON

BROCKENHURST
New Forest

nor time on learning new skills. It is, after all, only like riding down to the shops except the distances are longer and the roads and scenery are more pleasant. Given that you already have a bicycle, your preparation need only be a few common sense checks and choosing the right things to pack: so easy that you could decide to go on Thursday and be off after work on Friday evening.

Choosing your bicycle

These comments are intended to help you choose a cycle to hire or borrow wisely, or to point out the limitations of your own machine. If you intend to buy a new bicycle, try to get the advice of experienced cyclists, for the choice is bewildering and pitfalls are plenty. Some expensive bikes, for instance, look good only because of the smart parts put onto second-rate frames. Good books which can help you understand and choose cycles are mentioned on page 25. Three basic types of bicycle are common today. None is absolutely 'the best' but each is suited to certain purposes.

The 'roadster' (policemen's and postmen's bicycles are examples), usually has three hub gears, is heavily built and gives a fairly upright posture. It is fine for gentle terrain but would be hard work in hilly areas.

The drop-handlebar bicycle (often wrongly called 'the racer'), gives a posture which makes your body an efficient cycling engine. Not only do more of your muscles naturally come into play than on a roadster (on which your legs have to do nearly all the work), but your body also presents less area and hence resistance to the wind. It also offers a choice of hand position: the 'down' position or the more leisurely 'up' position, which in turn allow a welcome change in body position. These bikes are usually 5 or 10 speeds with derailleur gears, and can therefore deal more easily with steeper slopes.

The small-wheel bicycle usually has three gears but its design and the posture needed to ride it sacrifice a degree of cycling smoothness and efficiency in the interests of convenience in towns.

If you already have a bicycle, rest assured that you can find a route in this book to suit it—people have even ridden penny-farthings across America! However, if it is one of the less efficient types then be content with flatter areas and shorter rides—at least until you have discovered your capabilities.

Gears are simply a device whereby you can adapt the speed and 'push' of your pedalling to the conditions. The simple rules are: if the going feels hard change to a lower gear, and if it feels too easy, change to a higher gear. When borrowing or hiring a cycle for exploring hilly country, try to get one with a wide range of gears, including a bottom gear of, in cyclists' jargon, about 40 inches or less. The 3-speed roadsters and small-wheeled cycles only rarely have a wide range of gears.

Preparing your bicycle

Much more important than the type of your bicycle is its road-worthiness, not only because a silly problem could spoil your weekend, but because you must consider the safety of yourself and others. You are unlikely to have mechanical problems on the road if you follow the golden rule to 'never leave with a known fault'.

You will always run some risk of punctures, but they are quickly mended (see page 14), and in the ten weeks it took to cover some 3500 miles (5500 km) to test the routes for this book, I had only three punctures and one other fault of a type I could not mend myself.

The bicycle has the great advantage that most of its parts are both simple in principle and at least partly open to view so that you can check them. A quarter of an hour should be enough for a thorough check, even if you are new to the task. The following list of things to do may look daunting, but they are quicker to carry out than to read, especially if the bicycle has been recently checked. It is only a check list though—the righting of faults is not explained in detail, as you will be doing this at home where help is still at hand.

Cycle maintenance checklist

Frame: Little is likely to go wrong with the frame so it is more a question of making sure it is a suitable size for you. Although adjustment of handlebar and saddle height can make a slightly wrong-sized frame serve, never borrow or hire a cycle of markedly wrong size, and certainly never buy one without talking it over with an experienced cyclist.

Is the saddle height correct? Beginners often find cycling hard work simply because their saddles are too low and they push with the wrong part of the foot. Adjust your saddle so that your leg is very nearly straight with the ball (not the arch) of your foot on the pedal in its lowest position. For safety reasons however, at least 3'' (8 cm) of the saddle post must be left inside the frame. If you cannot do this the frame is too small for you. Then check that you can sit on the saddle whilst keeping yourself and the bike upright by 'standing' on your toes: if you cannot it is too high for safety.

Is the handlebar height correct? The handlebar height should make you comfortable. It is largely a matter of personal preference (and body shape) but the handlebar's cross tube on a drop handlebarred cycle should be at roughly the same height as the saddle to give you an efficient cycling posture. At least, about 3'' (8 cm) of the handlebar stem should be left inside the frame.

Are the stem positions firmly fixed? After adjusting either saddle or handle-bar height be sure to tighten the screws well, or you might suffer on crossing a bump in the road! Check by leaning on each in turn with your hands and suddenly thrusting down with as much force as you can muster.

Are the handlebars and front wheel firmly connected? Stand in front of the bike and facing it. Move forward to grip and hold the front wheel still between your legs, then try to turn the handlebars as if you were steering around corners. If the handlebars move then the vital 'expander bolt' inside will be loosening, shortly to leave you with no steering control.

Are the wheels true? To test this, turn the bike upside down, spin the wheels, and watch the metal wheel rim (not the tyre) where it passes the frame near the brakes. If you see a wobble, either up and down or side to side, the wheel is no longer in true shape and is consequently weak. It may also rub against the brake blocks and slow you down.

Are the spokes in order? With the bike upside down, go round each side of each wheel, pinging every spoke with your fingers like a harp-string. You will soon discover any that are broken or slack. The spokes give the wheel its shape and strength, and if one goes then more often follow, so never think that 'just one spoke' doesn't matter.

Are the tyres in good condition? Check that the rubber is neither perished nor too worn down. Make sure that the tyres are pumped up hard since it makes the going much easier and punctures less likely.

Are the cones well-adjusted? Each wheel turns on a spindle on races of ball-bearings held in cup-shaped spaces inside the hubs called 'cones'. If they are too tight (so that the ball-bearings do not have enough space) the wheel, when the bike is upside down, will not turn as easily and smoothly as it should. If, on the other hand, you can take hold of the wheel's rim at any place and waggle it from side to side, the cones are too loose.

With the bike still upside down, gently spin each wheel, and listen. If there is a 'graunching' sound from the hub, it could either mean that here is dirt in the ball-races, or that a ball-bearing is pitted or even cracked. Left to come to rest of its own accord, a nicely adjusted wheel should stop with the valve at the bottom, since the valve makes that part slightly heavier.

Are the pedals running smoothly? Check that the pedals spin with ease, and that they do not jiggle if you try to twist them in any other directions with your hands. Any problems here mean that the cones or equivalent (not all pedals having races of ball-bearings) are too tight or too loose.

Are the pedal cranks in order? The cranks are the metal arms connecting the pedals to the spindle, itself passing through a hole in the frame called the 'bottom bracket'. Put the cranks in a horizontal position, then take hold of each pedal in one hand. Try to pull them both upwards simultaneously. If there is any 'play', then one or both cotter pins will need adjusting or replacing.

Is the bottom bracket in good condition? Turn the pedals and listen for any horrible noises from the bottom bracket. If you hear anything there is probably dirt or damaged ball bearings in the races. A stiff or loose spindle is probably due to bad adjustment of the bottom bracket cones.

Is the chain stretched? To test whether the chain is stretched, take hold of the chain where it lies over the front of the chainwheel and try to pull it forwards. If it moves more than just a fraction it has stretched a bit, and if you can see daylight between the chainwheel and chain, even without pulling, you will need a new chain and perhaps, because new chains and worn cogs or chainwheels don't get on together well, new cogs or a chainwheel too.

Is the chain slack? Put your finger on top of the top stretch of chain, about midway between the chainwheel and rear sprocket. If you can easily press it down through more than about ½'' (1 cm), the chain is too slack and liable to jump off one or other cog as you cycle over bumps. If the slackness is due to chain-stretching you will know it already from the above check. Otherwise it will be due to the chain having too many links, or to the back wheel being set too far forward in the bicycle frame.

Is the gear cable in good condition? Follow the cable along from the trigger end to the other, checking that it runs smoothly around all its bends as you change gear (cleaning away dirt and applying a little oil usually solve any problem here). If you spot any fraying, put in a new cable, since a snapped cable on a trip means you will have to limp home with top gear only. If your cycle has a double chainwheel you will have two gear cables to check.

Can you get all the gears? You may not need all your gears in your home city, and it could be devasting to realize only when faced with the first hill of your trip that you cannot connect into the low gears, so go for a test ride around the block. Hub gears can start to slip moderately frequently 'on the road', usually as the gear cable stretches with use. The infuriating fault takes literally only seconds to right with know-how so get someone to teach you the technique even if your gears are currently in order.

Brakes: are the blocks worn down? Most brake blocks have studs on them, allowing rain water to flow away through the gaps between. If the studs are nearly worn away, fit new blocks. It is, in any case, wise to carry spare blocks on a trip, as the wear on long, steep slopes can be surprisingly fast.

Brakes: are the shoes the right way round? Brake blocks are set in metal holders called 'shoes'. Some are closed with metal walls on all four sides and ends, but others have one end open so that old blocks can be taken out and new ones fitted. To test that they are on the right way round check that the open end faces the rear of the bike.

Brakes: are the cables in order? Check the front and back cables from one end to the other whilst constantly pulling and releasing the brakes, looking out for fraying and lack of smooth running especially around bends.

Brakes: are the cables the right length? Go for a test ride, trying out both brakes. If you need scarcely to pull the levers to brake, you may end up going into a skid or over the handlebars. The length of cable wire from lever to calipers (the curved arms which carry the brake shoes) is a little too short, and it can be adjusted where the cable wires passes through a bolt with a hole fixed to the calipers. If, on the other hand, you have to pull the levers nearly right to the handlebars to brake, then you will have no extra leeway with which to brake harder on a steep hill or in rain. The cable wire is too long, and needs pulling through the bolt hole a little. After adjusting the cable wire length in either direction, be sure to close the bolt hole with its nut thoroughly, and then to check braking sharpness again.

Brakes: are the levers and calipers properly fixed to the frame? You would probably notice any loosening of the levers from the handlebars whilst riding anyway, but the calipers could loosen dangerously without your knowing. Check the front and back brakes separately, pulling the brake whilst wheeling the bike forwards. If the calipers are dragged round more than just an unavoidable fraction by the wheel before it stops, the nut and bolt fixing them to the frame is too loose. If the calipers do not spring open quickly and smoothly when you release the brakes then there is too much friction between them, perhaps because the nut and bolt are too tight. Sometimes a little oil where the calipers rub each other does the trick, but on no account let any oil get onto the brake blocks or wheel rim, as this will make them ineffective.

Lights: In British law you need not carry lights unless cycling in the dark or in very gloomy weather, although you must have a rear reflector. If you need lights, check them often as bumps in the road can disturb loose contacts or break fragile bulb filaments (it is wise to carry spare bulbs too).

Bell: British law requires a pedal cyclist to have an 'audible warning of approach', and even the human voice fits the bill. However, a bell has the advantage that everyone knows what it means, so it is a good idea to have one.

Carrier: Check that all the carrier stays are still straight and firm, and that all screws are still tight, as vibration under a load during cycling can loosen them. Carriers of some designs can gradually slip down from where they are fixed to the frame below the saddle, eventually interfering with proper working of the back brake.

Mudguards: Full-length mudguards will be appreciated when you ride in the rain or on muddy country roads. Check that none of their screws have worked loose.

Oil: An inadequately oiled bicycle is not only hard work to ride, but its parts will have much shortened lives. Put a little oil in or on all the moving parts, namely: *wheel spindles* (with the bicycle laid on its left-hand side, so that the oil can trickle through from one end of the spindle to the other, but with no risk of the derailleur gears on the right-hand side being scraped on the ground), *gear hub* (relevant only if your bicycle has hub gears. Put oil in through a little lidded hole in the hub.) *bottom bracket* (also through a small lidded hole on its top side), *pedal spindles, chain, gear and brake triggers and cables* if necessary, *brake calipers* if necessary. Take great care never to get oil on the brake blocks or wheel rims; either would make the brakes ineffective.

Mending a Puncture

There is no substitute for learning how to mend a puncture from someone before you set out, but here is a step by step guide:

1. Lay all tools, nuts etc in one place.
2. Take the wheel out of the bicycle frame.
3. Take off the valve collar.
4. Let the air out of the tube.
5. Lever one side of the tyre off, starting opposite the valve.
6. Take the tube out, taking the valve carefully through the hole in the rim.
7. Inflate the tube a little and listen for a hissing noise that will guide you to the hole. If you can't hear any hissing then the hole will be tiny and the best way to locate it is to move the tube slowly past your lips until you can feel the escaping air. If that fails then the hole is so small that you just have a slow puncture and the tube will take you miles before getting soft.
8. Patch the hole according to the puncture kit instructions.
9. Run your fingers along the inside of the tyre to find any thorn or sharp stone lodged in it.
10. Put the tube back in, starting with the valve, which must poke straight through its hole in the rim.
11. Ease the tyre back on, starting at the valve, and using levers only at the end if you have to.
12. Inflate the tube by a few pumps.
13. Push the tyre back from the rim edge, all the way round the wheel on both sides, to check that the tube is not pinched between the tyre and the rim.
14. Put the collar back on the valve.
15. Pump the wheel up hard.
16. Tighten the valve collar again.
17. Put the wheel back in the frame, checking that the rim is equidistant from the two sides of the frame near the brake, and that the brake blocks still meet the wheel rim as they should when the brake lever is pulled.

Equipment for the Bicycle

You will need some means of carrying things on your bicycle. On no account think that you can make do with a bag on your back. Your cycle may well already have a saddle-bag or basket adequate for the job, but if it has not, or if you need more carrying capacity because, for example, you are taking camping equipment, the most versatile and cheap answer is to fit a sturdy metal carrier above the back wheel. There is no need to buy the special bags designed for use with such carriers (although they will make life much easier if you make frequent cycle trips). Any tough bag strapped firmly to the carrier will serve, provided you follow these rules:

1. Keep the heavy things low down (high-up they will make you wobble or loose your balance).
2. Make sure that nothing is dangling, as it could get wound up in the spokes.
3. Strap the bag on securely so that it can neither slip in any direction, nor bounce about if you ride over bumps.

Try to arrange your packing so that the things you need quickly and often, such as a camera or an extra jumper, are easy to get at.

Cycle kit

Although mechanical problems are unlikely to occur, you should always carry a cycle kit. Even if you cannot do the repairs yourself, you will at least have the tools and spares in the likely event of someone helping you. This is a list of things I have found adequate on virtually all weekend trips:

1. Spanners fitting all the nuts and cones on your bike.
2. Screwdriver
3. Allen keys (if the bike needs them).
4. Rag for wiping hands after repairs.
5. Tyre levers
6. Puncture repair kit
7. Inner tube (this is not an essential, but it is so much easier to change on the road, especially in rain, than to mend the puncture which can be tackled at leisure in the evening).
8. Long brake cable (which can be pressed into service as an interim short brake cable).
9. Gear cable (if the spare brake cable can be adapted to this purpose, so much the better).
10. Spare bulbs for both lamps.
11. Spare brake blocks
12. Some thin glavanized steel wire and string (for makeshift, temporary repairs such as substituting for a broken saddle-bag strap).
13. Pump
14. Lock

If you have £1 or so to spare, invest in a water bottle and cage. Thirst can make an otherwise pleasant ride a torture, and although a bottle could be carried in your bag, it might leak, and is not so handy to get at.

Equipment for Yourself

Remember that you are not just the cycle's passenger, but its engine too, and so you will need plenty of 'fuel' or calories on a cycling outing. Even if you intend to find a pub or café lunch, carry at least some water and some biscuits or chocolate.

You will almost certainly be able to make a good choice of clothes for cycling from those who have already, bearing certain principles in mind. In the interests of visibility to other road users, try always to have at least one of your outer garments of a light colour. An alternative is to have a brightly coloured rear bag.

Several thin layers, such a three thin jumpers, will give you far more control of your warmth than one thick layer, such as a padded jacket. You need to be able to adjust the amount of clothes you wear as you get a bit hotter from riding into a headwind, for example, or colder from a long free-wheel.

You will probably be out in the open for many hours, and so to avoid the possibility of a chill through taking too little clothing, it is better to err on the side of taking too much until you learn your needs from experience. In cool weather the exercise of cycling will help to keep your body warm, but your inactive extremities could suffer. Wear roomy shoes with thick socks, and a woolly hat really is an essential. Gloves are important too, because you need your hands to be warm and supple for working the brakes and gears.

Bad weather clothing is vital in Britain's changeable climate, as protection against both rain and penetrating wind. The conventional cycle-cape has the advantage of allowing enough air circulation under it to prevent condensation, but it does catch the wind like a sail, making cycling with head or cross winds hard work indeed. A nylon jacket or cagoule offers much less resistance to wind, but can make you damp by not allowing perspiration to escape (unless you can afford one made of Gortex whih 'breathes'). You can get waterproof trousers but if it is warm enough, stick to shorts and bare skin which dries more quickly than any garment.

Shoes with fairly stiff soles make pedalling more efficient. Training shoes are suitable, but after rain, the rapid evaporation of water soaked into the material can make your feet cold. Closed, flat-soled sandals are fine, but they must have rough soles otherwise your feet could slip either from the pedals or when you put them down on a wet road.

When you make your choice of what to take, remember that you have to carry every extra ounce up every hill. Save weight wherever you can, taking a nearly empty tube of toothpaste, for example, or a thin paperback instead of *War and Peace*. Below is my checklist for a summer weekend staying in accommodation with meals provided. Use this as a guideline until you develop your own list.

Worn: Sandals, socks, underwear, shorts, bikini top, T-shirt, thin jumper, watch.

Essentials: Waterproof clothes, hat, gloves, extra jumper, first aid kit, cycle kit, pump, lock and key, water, food, maps or guide book, compass (not strictly necessary, but it can sometimes provide a rapid answer to an otherwise tricky route-finding problem), money, paper and pencil, hairbrush, hanky, penknife, big plastic bag (handy for all sorts of things like sitting on damp grass or collecting chestnuts). I take the following but try to leave them at my accommodation during the day: complete change of clothing, toilet kit, biscuits.

Non Essentials: Camera and film, book, needlework, letter paper.

Preparing Yourself

As you will be sharing roads with others, it is a good idea to refresh your memory as to road regulations and your rights and duties with a browse through the Highway Code. Try to discover any information you want from the tourist information offices or publications in your local library in advance of your visit. Then you can plan your outings sensibly around the opening times of any tourist attractions you wish to see.

Getting There

Trains: offer a quick way to reach your chosen centre, given convenient stations and good connections. Transporting a bike by train is comparatively easy, as there is no need to dismantle or unload the cycle. Train fares are expensive, but accompanied cycles generally go free. Some trains such as the high speed 125s and certain commuter trains will not accept cycles, so check that there are no restrictions on your chosen trains before travelling. Before leaving home attach a label to the bike stating your name and destination.

Arrive at the station with at least ten minutes to spare, as you may have to either carry the bike up and down steps to the platform, or find someone to help you get to the right place.

Try to discover where is the guard's van is likely to stop on the platform so that you don't have to push through all the other passengers to reach it. When you have the bike safely aboard, remove any valuables, and secure it to the wire mesh with an elastic cord. Do not lock it to anything as the guard might have to move it during the journey to take in more parcels or drop others off. Return to the guard's van a little before reaching your destination, so that you can be ready to get off as soon as the train pulls in.

The transporting of bikes on trains is a concession, not a passengers' right, and British Rail reserves the right to refuse you cycle-carriage in the event, say, of the guard's van being too full of Red Star parcels. In practise, however, refusals are rare. You must never bank on being able to take your preferred train, though, especially if there are several of you with bikes, so try not to leave your travel to the day's last train.

Car: Travel by private car is cheaper than train, especially if two or more people share petrol costs, but some dismantling of the bicycles will be necessary. Taking the front wheels off is a quick way to fit bikes into the backs of estate cars, but don't forget to take the wheels and their nuts too! Roof-racks designed for carrying up to four cycles are advertised in cycle magazines, and they are easy to use, usually requiring only that the front wheels be removed. Although initially expensive, they quickly pay for themselves after the first few trips.

Coach: Coaches and buses in Britain do not carry bicycles, but you can make use of them if you hire a bike at or near the centre rather than taking your own. Long distance coaches are cheap, and can offer a fast and direct route to your destination.

Cycle Hire

Cycle hire allows you to explore an area to which you cannot easily take your own bike, or to try out cycling whilst you are still deciding whether to buy a bicycle. However, a hired bike will rarely 'fit' you so well as a bike you buy especially for yourself, so allowances must be made.

Cycle hire shops that were at or near the centres in 1980 are mentioned in the book, but shops open and close quite frequently. It is a good idea therefore to ring and organise the hire of your bike before the weekend. If you have difficulty, regional tourist offices can usually send you an area list of shops, but a more local office at or near the centre will be more up-to-date, and is more likely to know about smaller concerns.

Cycle hire is a bit of a gamble, some machines being carefully maintained and others being just the right side of the law so always give a hired bike a quick check-over before setting out. When you ring to book your bike, ask about hire rates, which vary enormously, and make sure that you can hire the type of cycle you want. Except with small wheel cycles, a good hire shop should ask you roughly what frame size you want. If you don't know the frame size, then simply tell them your height and they will be able to judge what should be approximately right for you.

Ask also about the opening times of the business. You don't want to plan a long ride for Sunday and then find the cycle must be returned by noon. Discover whether a cycle repair kit is lent out with the bike or not. Do consider hiring a cycle at places other than the rides' centre, either going on to the centre by train, or adapting the rides to start and end at the hire point by using accommodation elsewhere *en route*.

Accommodation

Hotels are the most expensive option, but have the obvious advantages of a welcome degree of luxury at the end of a hard day's cycling: hot water, food and drinks, and privacy, although rarely shelter for your bicycle. It is worth remembering though that cycling increases your appetite and you may want to buy some snack foods to supplement the meals. The meal times are often fixed so check them before you go out in the morning.

Holiday Fellowship and Countryside Holidays Association Houses exist at or near a few of the centres. 'Outdoor' guests are welcome and there are often communal activities (which are not compulsory) to encourage people to mix. They can be a bit 'hearty', but hot baths are available and the meals are large. The rooms usually have two or four beds and you may well have to share with strangers, but overall, the accommodation is good value.

Bed and breakfast accommodation tends to be run by friendly people who enjoy meeting their guests and dealing with individual needs such as finding shelter for your bike. These small establishments are reasonably priced but evening meals are not always provided.

Youth Hostels are the cheapest sort of accommodation (excluding camping) not only because the overnight fee is low (about £2 compared with about £5 for B & B in 1980), but also because they have self-catering facilities. Many hostels also serve meals which although a little more expensive than doing your own, do mean that you don't have to shop or carry the extra weight of food on your bike, and of course you don't have to cook it! On the other hand meal times are usually fixed.

Youth Hostels are open to all from the age of five upwards. One of the pleasures of hostelling is the companionship gained from meeting other fellow-travellers and the exchange of stories. Accommodation is never spacious, and there is little privacy. Nearly all British hostels have cycle sheds, but many lack showers or baths. They close between 10.00 am and 5.00 pm during the day (the hours are different in Scotland). Lights out is at around 11.00 pm, meaning that you might have to forego a last drink at the pub but also that a peaceful night is assured.

If you want to try out hostelling before becoming a member, you can do so under a guest pass scheme whereby you pay the normal overnight fee plus one third of the membership fee, deductable from the fee you pay later if you decide to join.

Site Camping allows you to come and go as you please but you have to adapt to the amount of camping equipment that can be carried on a bike by, for instance, foregoing an air mattress and keeping cooking equipment to a minimum. The disadvantages are that in bad weather the lack of space in a small tent can become irritating, and not being able to dry out wet clothes can be dispiriting.

Initial outlay on camping equipment is expensive, unless you can borrow it, but the overnight charges at even the most expensive sites are cheap relative to hotels and B & B. Once you are equipped you are much better able to go away for a weekend on impulse, sites usually having space even when all beds in a town are taken, and the extra packing and organisation needed for a camping trip soon become second nature. Camp-sites vary greatly in size, cost and facilities, from the farmer's field, tap and loo, to the acres of trim caravans and frame tents with shops and showers etc.

If you buy your own equipment, ask for advice and demonstrations, if possible from experienced lightweight campers. There is an enormous range to choose from but I have found the following to be practical and reliable:

Saunder's Backpacker tent
Black's Tromso sleeping bag
'Karrimat' closed cell mat
Trangia co-ordinated meths stove and cooking pots
Sigg metal bottle for carrying meths
Water container of the collapsible, tough plastic bag type

Wild Camping means camping on private land with the owner's per-mission. Most owners are obliging if asked first, but can be understandably angry if not. It is possible to camp on rough land in mountain areas (especially parts of Scotland) without permission but prudence is required and until you get a feel for where camping will neither damage the land nor upset anyone, it is best to be guided by where others are camping wild.

When choosing a site, bear the following four 'Ws' in mind: *Wind*, even if slight on your arrival might freshen later, so a pitch in the lee of a hedge or a rise in the ground is an advantage. If you do have to use an exposed site, orientate the tent so that its long axis parallels the wind direction. *Wet*: Avoid pitching directly under a tree for although it might offer shelter at first, water will drip on to the tent for a long time after-wards. Avoid too, pitching in even a little depression in the ground for you might find yourself sleeping in a puddle! *Water:* A good sized water carrier is important equipment for wild camping, not only for your own con-venience but so that you don't have to bother the land owner too often. If you are camping on rough ground you must pitch near a river and carry sterilization tablets (available from chemists). Fill up the carrier and add tablets as one of your first jobs on arrival so that you have a ready supply of safe water. *Warmth:* Morning sun on a tent is not merely pleasant: it dries off any rain or dew from the night, making the tent easier to pack and lighter to carry. (A small chamois leather adds but little weight to your pack, and enables you to sponge off wet equipment fairly thoroughly.)

The perfect site is rarely found, and in practice, you will probably have to compromise on one or more of the above four 'Ws'.

Accommodation availability should be checked with the local tourist information bureau or the accommodation itself before the weekend, especially in peak holiday seasons or if you mean to stay in a village where alternatives are few. The tourist information offices are given for each centre, but other useful addresses are on page 25.

The rides are described as starting and finishing at the centres, but you can follow them as a figure of 8, beginning wherever you please, in order to stay in your preferred type of accommodation.

Food and Drink

The exercise of cycling out-of-doors will make you unusually hungry and thirsty. It is only too easy for the town dweller who can always find an open food shop or restaurant to forget that although you can normally find some source of food on a country cycle-ride on a Saturday morning, you cannot count on it in the afternoon or on a Sunday. Always carry some food and water.

Pubs and cafés serving food are mentioned in the rides, but take the information as a rough guide only. Standards and prices vary widely, concerns can close or change hands, pubs may not bother with food on Sundays and cafés may be closed then. Even if you do eat out, the meal might not satisfy your cyclist's appetite. So again, even if there seem to be several pubs or cafés on the route, be prudent and take food and water with you.

Finding Your Way

There are people who feel ill at ease unless they can follow where they are going on a commercial map, whilst others wish neither to spend money on maps nor to rely on their map-reading ability. The rides in this book can be followed in one of two ways: choose the system which suits you best.

The signpost directions

The written descriptions of how to follow each ride give an instruction for every road junction you pass. The majority simply state what it says on the signpost and you should follow, but those junctions which have no signposts are described more fully. Ignore no through roads and side roads within towns as they are not included in the directions.

On the whole, signposts are an enduring feature of the countryside, but they are occasionally changed, broken or removed, and the possibility of new roads or junctions having been built, cannot be ruled out. If you find a discrepancy between signposts 'on the ground' and in the book, go the way that seems likeliest, checking the next junctions against their descriptions. Should they seem wrong, either go back to the first trouble spot and try again or cycle to the nearest house or signposted village and ask for new directions.

Most of the rides are best followed a particular way around; either because they are physically easier that way, or because it allows you to make your final choice of ride options later in the day when you are less likely to either under- or over-estimate the rides you want to cover. The

KEY TO SIGNPOST DIRECTIONS

R (Westerham).	Turn or fork right to follow the road signposted Westerham.
L	Turn or fork left.
Toys Hill	Place passed through or near.
Emmetts	Places that appear in bold type have been specifically mentioned in the text and therefore have also been set in bold in the ride directions and map for easy reference.
b	Letters of the alphabet set in italics denote a point where two or more rides meet. They are set in italics in the text, ride directions and map for easy reference.
Cont.	Continue. Where the instruction just tells you to 'Cont at next junction', either follow with the dashed white lines that sometimes mark side roads off from relatively main roads, or, if there are no white lines, take the road which continues in the direction you are following anyway.

directions are generally given for one way only but occasionally they are given for both when there is a particular reason for doing so.

Whether you follow the rides by the signpost directions or the maps, you must be wary of private farm roads. Although they usually bear the farm's name, they can sometimes be long, tarmaced and unlabelled, and hence confusingly like small public roads. Take care not to apply the direction for the next road junction to the farm road turn-off. There is no fool proof way of avoiding this mistake but I have tried to reduce the risk by warning you in the text where they occur frequently—such as in the Brecon Beacons. A small consolation is that you can rarely go far wrong—for you will simply arrive at a dead end in front of the farm house and then have to turn back!

The ride maps

The alternative method of finding your way is to marry up the map in the book with a good commercial map, turning the book so that north is 'up' if it helps, and then navigate by the commercial map. Although this takes more time and effort, it is more flexible as you can go whichever way round you choose, or even short-cut or adapt the rides if you like. Turn-offs from the rides which are A, B or unclassified roads, are shown, on the ride maps, but 'No Through Roads', farm drives and side roads in towns are not shown. The key to the ride maps is as follows:

RIDE MAP KEY

classified road		railway	+++++
Main Route	——————	river	~~~~
First Loop	– – – –	sea or lake	░░░░
Second Loop	··········	built-up area	▰▰
unclassified road		railway station	≩
Main Route	———	youth hostel	▲
First Loop	– – – –	campsite	△
Second Loop	············	on-route place	•
path or track	—·—·—·—	off-route place	○

name of route centre (bold capitals)	**HAWES**
geographical feature (italics)	*North Downs*
name of village, building, or other man-made feature	· Lymore
place of interest, mentioned in the ride text (bold type)	**Grasmere**
point where two or more rides meet (italic letters)	*a, b, c*

Commercial maps

There are three series of commercial maps well-suited to cyclists.

Ordnance Survey 1:250 000. These are the smallest scale maps a cyclist can manage. All the lanes except for dead-ends are shown, but there is no room for features like churches or tracks, nor can all small villages be marked. Route-finding with these maps needs patience but it is reliable, as the junctions are shown with accuracy. If you look closely enough you will, for example, find that staggered cross roads are actually drawn staggered. Height is shown by both contours and shading, giving an excellent overall impression of the terrain, but as the contour interval is 200 ft (about 65 m) a road seeming to be flat on the map can have plenty of tiring smaller hills. Great Britain is entirely covered by 9 sheets of this economical series, and several centres in this book are covered by the same sheets.

Bartholomew's 1:100 000: This series covers Great Britain in 62 sheets, the extra space given by the larger scale being used to show a few features like churches and windmills, making route-finding easier. Some tracks and private roads are also shown, but as the symbols do not make the difference between these and small lanes clear, this is as likely to confuse as to help. Height is shown by shading.

Ordnance Survey 1:50 000: These maps are expensive but a delight to use. Route-finding is made easy by accurate marking of many features in their precise positions, such as railway embankments, chapels, woods, isolated pubs and youth hostels. You will be especially glad of this accuracy if, for example, you want to quickly find a church porch to shelter in. Private roads, tracks and Rights of Way are all shown. Contour lines at 50 ft (15 m) show the heights. Most centres in this book require two or more of these maps, but if you mean not to follow the longer ride options, check before buying that you actually need all the maps.

The Ordnance Survey 1":1 mile tourist maps, produced especially to cover areas popular with walkers and other visitors to the countryside, are essentially the same as the OS 1:50 000 series. The scale is slightly smaller, and height is shown by shading as well as contours.

Route-finding on roads using commercial maps rarely requires a compass, but one can be useful especially in areas like woodlands where you can see no landmarks to help you out. If you possess a compass, take it with you.

Rights of Way

A few of the rides use rights of way. They are paths or tracks which the public has used for years, and which are now protected in law so that the landowner may not prevent their use except in very special circumstances. Right of way footpaths can be used by pedestrians only, but the Countryside Act of 1968 gave pedal cyclists the right to use bridleway rights of way, although some landowners are unaware of this. You should always give way to walkers and horse-riders on bridleways.

Other tracks may not be legally defined rights of way, but the landowners may yet allow their 'permissive use', whilst nevertheless retaining the right to withdraw that permission. In the unlikely event of your being challenged whilst using one of the few 'permissive use' tracks and paths in the rides, you must give way with grace.

RIDE TEXT KEY

NT	National Trust
NTS	National Trust for Scotland
DoE	Department of the Environment
open	places open to the public at certain times.
	Castles, gardens and houses mentioned without the 'open' comment can be seen from the outside only. Churches and museums can be assumed to be open to visitors.
Emmetts	a point of interest which also appears in bold type on the ride map and in the signpost directions

Useful Addresses and Publications

Historic Houses, Castles and Gardens: A comprehensive listing of places to visit which is published annually, and gives a description of each place, the facilities it offers, the opening times and entrance fees. Available from booksellers.

Museums and Galleries: Published annually, this comprehensive listing gives brief descriptions of each museum and gallery, its opening times and its entrance fees, if any. Available from booksellers.

The National Trust, 42 Queen Anne's Gate, London SW1H 9AS. Set up to protect places of historic interest and natural beauty, the National Trust owns many properties passed on the rides in this book. If you become a member of the Trust, your card will admit you free to all of them. An annual booklet describing all National Trust properties is available from the above address.

The National Trust for Scotland, 5 Charlotte Square, Edinburgh 2. This body does for Scotland what the National Trust does for England and Wales. Membership of one of them admits you to properties of the other free of charge too.

Monuments in the care of the Department of the Environment. The booklet lists properties such as ruined castles and prehistoric monuments in the care of the Department of the Environment and open to the public. Many such properties are passed on the rides and a season ticket can be bought giving admittance to them all. The booklet is available from HMSO bookshops, whose London address is 49 High Holborn, London WC1V 6HB, and which has branches in Cardiff, Edinburgh, Manchester, Bristol and Birmingham.

Railway and coach timetables covering the entire country can be referred to in public libraries, which are likely to hold the above-mentioned publications too.

Youth Hostels Association (England and Wales), National Office, Trevelyan House, 8 St Stephen's Hill, St Albans, Herts, AL1 2DY, tel: (0727) 55215.

Scottish Youth Hostels Association, National Office, 7 Glebe Crescent, Stirling, FK8 2JA, tel: (0786) 2821.

The Holiday Fellowship, 142 Great North Way, London NW4, tel: (01) 203 3381.

The Country-wide Holidays Association, 24 Birch Heys, Cromwell Range, Manchester M14 6HU, tel: (061) 224 2887.

British Tourist Authority, Tourist Information Centre, 64 St James's Street, London SW1, tel: (01) 730 0791. Most of the information will be of too broad a nature to be useful to you, but lists of coming events and addresses of regional offices and information centres are available.

The following three Tourist Boards have guides for accommodation and eating out facilities, although on the whole their other information will be too general to suit you.

English Tourist Board, 4 Grosvenor Gardens, London SW1, tel: (01) 730 3400.

Wales Tourist Board, 3 Castle Street, Cardiff, tel: (0222) 27281.

Scottish Tourist Board, 23 Ravelston Terrace, Edinburgh 4, tel: (031) 322 2433.

The regional tourist offices, are too numerous to list. Most of the information you could require can be obtained from the local bureaux mentioned under the ride centres, but should you want broader information such as cycle-hire or accommodation lists before deciding precisely which centre to visit, these regional tourist offices can help. The addresses are available from the British Tourist Authority, and the three national Tourist Boards.

Local Tourist Information Bureaux are mentioned in this book under the ride centres. However, there are many others, and some such as those near the extremities of the rides might be useful to you. A booklet listing them all is available from any one of them.

Edward Stanford Ltd, 12–14 Long Acre, London WC2E 9LP. An excellent map and guide book shop with a mail order service.

Field and Trek Equipment Ltd, 23–5 Kings Rd, Brentwood, Essex CM14 4ER, tel: (0277) 221259. A mail order supplier of good camping and outdoor equipment.

YHA Shops, 14 Southampton Street, London WC2E 7HY, tel: (01) 836 8541; 35 Cannon Street, Birmingham B2 5EE, tel: (021) 643 5180; 166 Deansgate, Manchester M3 3FE, tel (061) 834 7119. The shops are open to non-YHA-members and stock a wide range of outdoor equipment.

Richard's Bicycle Book by Richard Ballantine, Pan, 1979. A clear and well-illustrated guide to cycle maintainance.

Adventure Cycling in Britain by Tim Hughes, Blandford, 1978. An all-round cycle-touring book dealing with both the bicycle and the country of Britain, which could be useful to you if you decide to take up more cycling.

The CTC Route Guide to Cycling in Britain and Ireland by Christa Gausden and Nicholas Crane, Oxford Illustrated Press, 1979. An extensive guide book of cycling routes, adaptable to form rides lasting from one day to many weeks.

If you think you would like to take part in other cycling activities, consider joining either of these two clubs:

The Cyclists Touring Club, 69 Meadow Godalming, Surrey GU7 3HS, tel: (04868) 7217; *The British Cycling Federation*, 70 Brompton Road, London SW3, tel: (01) 584 6707.

KENT

Penshurst

Although these routes touch upon Surrey and Sussex, they lie mostly in Kent, the aptly-named 'Garden of England', with its well-tended landscape of little fields, orchards and hop-fields, its cottages and oast houses. In May there are blossoms on the fruit trees and in the long-established hedgerows. Patches of woodland soften the scene: the area is still called 'The Weald' from the old word 'Wald' meaning 'wood'.

The routes take you through several distinct areas. The Hever routes are easy, as they cross flattish land towards the low sandstone hills around Tunbridge Wells. The harder Westerham routes take you through the Greensand Ridge, a range of sandstone hills of which Crockham Hill is itself one, then to the chalklands of the North Downs. Both hill ranges afford superb views, and you will see that many opulent houses, including Churchill's Chartwell, have been strategically built to enjoy them. A variety of materials have been used in the houses including red-bricks, tiles, sand-stone and sometimes flints from the chalk downlands. Other buildings are of fresh, white-painted weatherboarding, or are half timbered.

Because this pretty area lies near London you will pass dull areas of recent housing and busy trunk roads, but the routes themselves are quiet and there are a lot of pubs and cafés en route.

Moderate cycling. Quiet, with some short, fairly busy stretches.

CROCKHAM HILL

Location: 7 miles (12 km) south-west of Sevenoaks, and 2 miles (3 km) south of Westerham.

Trains: Oxted Station is 4 miles (6 km) away, Sevenoaks Station is 9 miles (15 km) away, being on lines from London Victoria Station and Charing Cross respectively. London 45 mins. Marlpit Station is 2 miles (3 km) away, on a line through Guildford and Reading, thus linking to other parts of the country.

Tourist Information Bureau: Town Hall, Tunbridge Wells, Kent, tel: (0892) 26121.

Accommodation: Hotel and bed and breakfast accommodation is available in Westerham and at the inn at Four Elms. There are YHs at Crockham Hill and at Kemsing on the Ightham Mote Loop. Camping is allowed at both.

Cycle-hire: The nearest are: F. C. Couchman, 8 Station Road Approach, Tonbridge, tel: (0732) 353569 and Smiths, 5 Sevenoaks Road, Otford tel: (095 92) 2517.

Cycle Shop: There is a good cycle shop in Edenbridge.

Maps: OS 1:50 000 (nos 187, 188 and 177 for the Eynsford Loop); Bartholomew's 1:100 000 (no. 9); OS 1:250 000 (no. 9).

Crockham Hill

Crockham hill is a village with the typical facilities of 'one church, one pub, one post-office and stores'. Its expansive views were 'discovered' in the nineteenth century, when several great houses were built above the village, although Mariners has been there at least since the writing of the Domesday Book.

Octavia Hill, one of the three founder members of the National Trust (which protects much land in the area) is buried here, and a monument is dedicated to her in the church. Should the weather be very bad, you need go only 2 miles (3 km) to explore either Chartwell or Westerham.

THE WESTERHAM ROUTE

As far as Emmetts you will have to do some hard cycling, probably getting off to walk at times, but it is all in the good cause of enjoying magnificent views from the Greensand Ridge, those from **Toys Hill** being renowned. Later on, the route follows a fairly level course below the North Downs: indeed, this is the ancient Pilgrims Way, and pilgrims with still many miles to walk to Thomas à Becket's shrine at Canterbury would have been as glad as you of the level going! The scenery changes, too, from pockets of farmland amid fine woods on the Greensand, to views of the clean, curving lines of the chalk downs.

Chartwell (NT, open) was Winston Churchill's home for many years. The house contains Churchilliana and, in the grounds complete with the black swans which were a gift from the Australian government, is a studio built partly by him which houses his paintings. There is a café and restaurant.

Emmetts (NT, open) is a garden of rare trees and shrubs which show lovely colours in both spring and autumn.

Near the green at **Westerham** stand some picturesque buildings, tea-rooms, pubs serving food, and a church with interesting features. It is dominated by the statue of General James Wolfe, the victorious leader of the English over the French in Quebec, Canada, in 1759. Wolfe was born in Westerham, and Quebec House (NT, open), a pleasant seventeenth-century red-brick house, was his home. Wolfe received his commission in the grounds of **Squerryes Court** (open), a William and Mary manor house with a collection of Dutch paintings.

The Ightham Mote Loop

This loop follows the general pattern of the Westerham route, with some hard riding on the Greensand in the south before a superb freewheel down into **Sevenoaks Weald**, and fairly easy terrain below the North Downs.

You will see many of Kent's building styles. There are oast houses, of course, those at **Ightham Mote** having moving caps, and one at **Ide Hill** has a horse on its vane. The red brick and tile Long Barn (open) at the entry to Sevenoaks Weald rambles enchantingly. Reputedly the birthplace of William Caxton, the first English printer, it was an early home of Harold Nicholson and Vita Sackville-West, who created the garden. Six-hundred year old Ightham Mote (open) is built in brick, sandstone and half-timbering and is one of England's few remaining moated manors. It is a delightful place, the beauty of the building enlivened by swans and goldfish in the moat, swallows diving for insects above the water, and white doves and peacocks on the grass.

There is twentieth century housing on Kemsing's outskirts, but at **Heaverham**, buildings of many periods right up to the present day blend harmoniously. There are some attractive places at **Otford**, and a footpath by the church leads past remains of a sixteenth-century archbishop's palace. There are tea rooms and pubs serving food there too. Later, curiosity may make you detour the half-mile to **Chevening**, the estate village to Chevening House, once Prince Charles's home. Rights of way on foot go through the splendid park set out on the North Downs edge.

The Eynsford Loop

This loop starts rather alarmingly with a long, hard climb up onto the North Downs. Once that is over you are rewarded by a long freewheel down the other side of the Downs, from which you can see distant tall chimneys of Thameside industry, followed by moderately easy riding along the Shoreham valley with its many hop fields.

There is a ford at **Eynsford** beside the ancient bridge, but check the water level before cycling through it. The village has some half-timbered buildings, but you will know that this is chalk country from the flints in the bridge, the church, and the massive walls of the ruined twelfth-century castle (DoE, open). Nearby Lullingstone Villa (DoE, open) is one of the best preserved in Britain. It has told us much about the way of life in Roman times, and you can see murals and mosaics depicting ancient legends.

Lullingstone Castle (open) is both Tudor and eighteenth century, its chapel possessing a Tudor rood screen. You can find food and drink in both **Eynsford** and **Shoreham**, where the King's Arms has the added interest of an ostler's box. Shoreham church has a porch hewn from a massive timber, a good screen and a window by Edward Burne-Jones. Another early nineteenth-century artist, the visionary Samuel Palmer, did some of his best work while living in Water House. From Shoreham's centre, look up to the western valley-side to see an unusual war memorial, a white cross made by cutting away the turf to expose the chalk beneath.

THE HEVER ROUTE

This is a delightful, lazy route taking you past bluebell woods, and fields of corn or grazing sheep and cattle. Many farms have their own small ponds, and at **Haxted**, water drives the mill wheels as it has done since the fourteenth century. Inside the white weatherboarded mill is a museum with displays of milling and also the early iron industry on which the Weald thrived.

Kent's other renowned source of wealth is hops for use in brewing. The hops were slowly dried in oast houses, many of which have now been converted into homes. Just before **Hever** you can see a lovely group whose white caps still turn with the wind. At Hever, too, is the castle (open), home of the ill-fated Anne Boleyn, Henry VIII's second wife. Magnificent gardens with a maze and chessmen of yews surround a fifteenth-century crenellated manor house, restored by a wealthy American early this century. **Edenbridge** has several attractive buildings, and a choice of cafés and pubs serving food.

The Chiddingstone Loop

The cycling here is still mainly easy, and this loop takes you past small fields whose irregular shapes suggest that they were only gradually reclaimed from the huge Wealden woods. **Hoath House** is easily missed, so keep a look out for this rambling half-timbered house commanding a lovely view. **Penshurst** and **Chiddingstone** are both pretty villages, many of their houses built with wealth from the Wealden iron industry. Penshurst Place (open), built originally for a fourteenth-century Lord Mayor of London, has a Barons' Hall, reputedly the finest domestic hall in England. The village has some tempting tea shops. Chiddingstone is a National Trust village, and a fine group of oast houses nearby has been converted to modern use with inspired care. There are good carvings in the church, and look for the footpath to the Chiding Stone, a great boulder where nagging persons were punished by being nagged and chided by the entire village. The castle (open) is mock gothic, and contains collections of Stuart furnishings and ancient Egyptian and Japanese objects.

The Royal Tunbridge Wells Loop

As Tunbridge Wells stands on the High Weald, an area of sandstone hills, this loop has some delightful swoops down into the valleys of the river Medway and its tributaries, and some correspondingly long hauls up. The Medway traditionally divides the country, the 'Men of Kent' being to the east, and the 'Kentish Men' on the west. The sandstone crops out in places and is easily weathered and worn into interesting shapes. At **High Rocks** you can pay to see some of the best, although there are others on the commons at Tunbridge Wells. The sandstone is popular with climbers, and at **Groombridge** there is even a Mountain Rescue Post which sometimes doubles as a café. There are other eating places at Groombridge, including the sixteenth-century Crown Inn by the picturesque village green. A footpath above the church leads over parkland to the Christopher Wren-style Groombridge Place. Its gardens were designed by John Evelyn, the Jacobean diarist.

Royal Tunbridge Wells came into being in 1606, when chalybeate springs were found in a wild, uninhabited area. At first royal and other visitors had to camp, but later the elegant spa town developed. Beau Nash lorded over the town for years, and he doubtless often strolled the shady Pantiles walk, as you can do today. There is a local museum and information centre in the Town Hall. On your return journey look out for the black and white **House of 1593**, the number written in its timbering. Just beyond it are some enormous hawthorn hedges, which have been encouraged to grow high to protect the hops from wind.

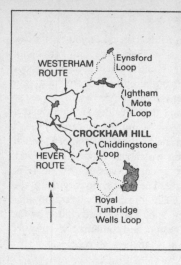

WESTERHAM
ROUTE

Eynsford
Loop

Ightham
Mote
Loop

CROCKHAM HILL

HEVER
ROUTE

Chiddingstone
Loop

N

Royal
Tunbridge
Wells Loop

THE WESTERHAM ROUTE
15 miles (24 km)
anticlockwise

CROCKHAM HILL. Leave (B269, Limpsfield). R (Westerham, B2026, Chartwell). R (Chartwell). Pass **Chartwell**. L (Toys Hill ¾). Cont at the next junction. L (Brasted, Sundridge). R (Ide Hill). Reach

a **Emmetts**. *Join the Ightham Mote Loop, or cont.* Leave

a (Sundridge, Brasted). R (Sundridge, Riverhead). Cont at the next junction. Enter Sundridge. Cont (Chevening). Reach

d. The Ightham Mote Loop rejoins the Westerham Route. Leave

d (Knockholt). L on a 6′ 6″ width restriction road. Cont (Westerham 2½, Oxted 6¼). Cont (Westerham). Cont at the next junction. Cont crossing the A233, onto the Pilgrims Way. L (Westerham, Edenbridge). Enter

Westerham R (Godstone, Reigate, A25) *otherwise detour L to explore* **Westerham** Centre. L (Crockham Hill, Edenbridge). Pass **Squerryes Court**. L (Edenbridge B2026).

Ightham Mote Loop
adds 18 miles (29 km)
anticlockwise

Leave

a (Ide Hill). Cont at the next junction. Enter

Ide Hill. L (Sevenoaks 5, Edenbridge 6). L (Riverhead, Sevenoaks). R (Sevenoaks, Tonbridge). Cont (Sevenoaks 3). R at the junction just past Everlands entrance where there is no sign at the junction. R (Sevenoaks Weald 2). Cont (Weald 1, Tonbridge 6). L (Weald). Enter

Sevenoaks Weald. Cont through the village, passing the green and the Windmill pub. Cont (Hildenborough 3, Tonbridge 5½). Roundabout exit (Tonbridge North, B245, Hildenborough). L (Underriver). R (Hildenborough 2½, Tonbridge 4¾). L (Shipbourne 2¼). R (Shipbourne). Cont (Shipbourne). L (Ivyhatch). Pass **Ightham Mote**. L (Ightham 1½, Seal 3). L at the next junction. Pass The Plough, Ivy Hatch. L.(Stone Street). Cont at the next junction. Cont (Seal). R opposite the village hall and the Stone Street village name sign. Cont (Styants Bottom, Heaverham). Cont at the next junction. L at the T junction. R (Heaverham 1½, Kemsing 2¼). Cont (Heaverham ¾, Kingsdown 3¾). Enter

Heaverham. Cont (Kemsing, Otford). R (East Hill, Wrotham). Reach

b. Join the Eynsford Loop, or cont. Leave

b (Otford 2½). Follow the Otford signs to a main road. L (Sevenoaks, A225). Enter

Otford. Roundabout exit (A21, Bromley). Cont at the next junction. Cont to go under a 14′ 9″ height limit bridge. Reach

c. The Eynsford Loop rejoins the Ightham Mote Loop. Leave

c (Dunton Green, Sevenoaks, London). Reach the A21, dismount, cross the road, and walk a short way to the left.

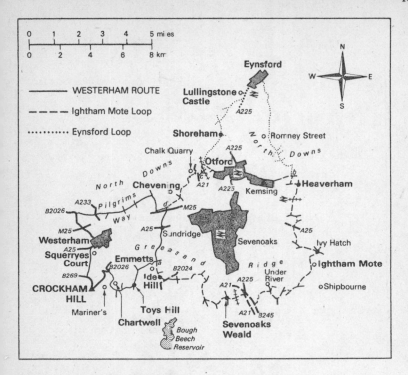

Go through a wooden gate, up a public path, then L to go between bollards onto an old road. Pass the Chalk Quarry. L at the T junction. R (Sundridge 2½, Brasted 3¼). Pass the signposted turn-off to

Chevening. Cont (Sundridge, Brasted, Westerham). Reach

d. Rejoin the Westerham Route.

The Eynsford Loop
adds 5 miles (8 km)
anticlockwise

Leave

b (East Hill 2¾, Eynsford 4¾). Cont (East Hill, Romney Street, Eynsford). Keep L by the small pond. Cont where a no through road is signposted to the R. Cont at the next two junctions. Enter

Eynsford. L by the war memorial. Pass the entrance to **Lullingstone Castle**. R

(Lullingstone Park). L (Shoreham, Halstead). Cont (Shoreham, Halstead). L (Shoreham, Otford). Cont on Filston Lane *otherwise detour 200 yards (metres) L on Church Street for* **Shoreham** centre. Cont (Dunton Green ¼, Sevenoaks 3¾). Cont at the next junction. Reach

c. Rejoin the Ightham Mote Loop.

HEVER ROUTE
14 miles (23 km)
anticlockwise

CROCKHAM HILL. Leave (Edenbridge B2026). R (Itchingwood Common). R (Limpsfield, Oxted). L at the T junction. Cont (Lingfield, Edenbridge). Cont (Crowhurst, Lingfield). R (Oxted, Lingfield). L (Lingfield, East Grinstead). L (Edenbridge) *otherwise detour 100 yards (metres)*. R (Lingfield, East Grinstead),

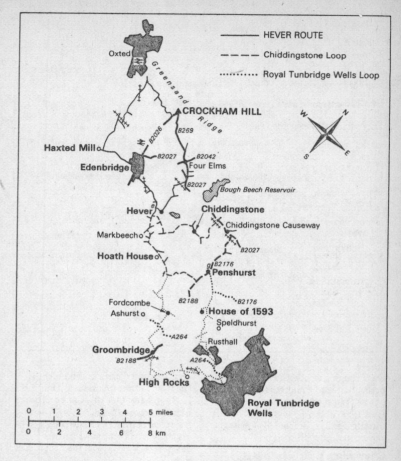

HEVER ROUTE
- - - - Chiddingstone Loop
.... Royal Tunbridge Wells Loop

for **Haxted Mill**. Enter

Edenbridge, passing Pound Green. R
(B2026, Hartfield). L (Hever 2¼,
Chiddingstone 5). Cont (Hever 1¼,
Mark Beech 2¼). Cont (Hever ½,
Tonbridge 10). Reach

e. Join the Chiddingstone Loop, or cont.
Leave

e (Hever ¼, Tonbridge 10). Pass
through

Hever. L (Four Elms, Westerham). L
(Four Elms, Westerham). Cont (Four
Elms ¾, Westerham 5). Enter Four
Elms. Follow signs for Crockham Hill.

Chiddingstone Loop
adds 12 miles (19 km)
anticlockwise

Leave

e (Markbeech 1½, Tunbridge Wells
11). Cont (Marks Beech, Cowden).
Cont (Mark Beech 1, Cowden 3,
Penshurst 4½). Cont (Markbeech,
Cowden). L (Chiddingstone 3). R
(Mark Beech ¾, Cowden 2¾). Cont
(Penshurst 3½, Fordcombe 4¼, Tun
Wells 8¼). Keep L at the next junction.
Keep R at the next junction, to go into a
sunken lane. Pass **Hoath House** on

your R. R (Penshurst 2½, Forccombe 3, Tunbridge Wells 7). Reach

f. Join the Royal Tunbridge Wells Loop, or cont. Leave

f (Penshurst 2). L (Penshurst, Leigh, B2188). Reach

g **Penshurst**. *The Royal Tunbridge Wells Loop rejoins the Chiddingstone Loop.* Leave

g On the road opposite Quaintways Teas. L (B2176. Edenbridge). L (Edenbridge, B2027). Cont at the next two junctions. L (Chiddingstone, Cowden). R (Chiddingstone, Edenbridge). Pass through

Chiddingstone. Cont (Mark Beech 2½, Hever 3, Cowden 4¼). R (Hever 1½, Edenbridge 3). R (Hever, Edenbridge). R (Hever, Edenbridge). Reach

e. Rejoin the Hever Route

Royal Tunbridge Wells Loop
Adds 12 miles (19 km)
anticlockwise

Leave

f (Fordcombe 2½, Tun Wells 6½). Cont (Blackham 1½, East Grinstead 9). L (Fordcombe, Penshurst). R (Fordcombe, Tunbridge Wells). R (Ashurst). L (Langton Green 1½). Next R, at a Speldhurst signpost with no finger pointing along your road. Enter

Groombridge. Pass the green. R on the main road. L (Eridge 2¼, St Thomas Church). L (Tun Wells 4½, Frant 3¾). Cont (Frant, Tun Wells). L (High Rocks). Cont (High Rocks). Pass **High Rocks**. Cont at the next junction. Cont (To Tunbridge Wells). Cont on Fir Tree Road. L (To Rusthall, Happy Valley & Toad Rock *otherwise detour ½ mile (1 km), R on (Mount Ephraim), R (Town Centre) for centre of* **Royal Tunbridge Wells**. R (Rusthall, Toad Rock). Follow the road to leave Rusthall on Nellington Road. Where the road bends L, cont to go through the signs indicating the end of a speed limit zone. R (Speldhurst). R then L onto Bullingstone Lane. Keep L at the end of Bullingstone Lane. Reach the **House of 1593**. R (Penshurst 1½, Leigh 4). L (Penshurst ¾). Reach

g **Penshurst**. *Rejoin the Chiddingstone Loop.*

Finchingfield

EAST ANGLIA

This gentle countryside is so peaceful that its proximity to London is difficult to believe. The main roads are busy, yet on one of the lanes, I passed an old knife-grinder pedalling along, his tools clanking against his ancient bicycle.

Grain ripens under long hours of sunshine on this drier, eastern side of England. In early summer, when the corn is still young and green, the low hills are patterned with the bold yellow of rape fields, and the drifts of white flowers that border the lanes. Few livestock are kept and so most of the fields are not enclosed—giving you good views over large areas; the few hedges and trees emphasizing the clean curves of the land. The cycling is easy, even the stiffest climbs taking their time to rise 200 ft (60 m), and there are some long, gentle freewheels along the valley bottoms.

Chalk lies beneath the fields, and within it are flints which were collected to build the enduring churches and houses. The cottages of the common folk however, were built with plaster walls, many of them patterned by the distinctively East Anglian technique of pargetting. Today these cottages, thickly thatched and painted in white or colour wash, make this one of England's most picturesque regions.

Easy cycling. Very quiet with a few busy miles.

SAFFRON WALDEN

Location: 14 miles (23 km) south-east of Cambridge.

Trains: Audley End Station, 2 miles (3 km) south-west of Saffron Walden, is on the main London to Cambridge line. London: 1 hour 15 mins.

Coach: A coach runs from London through Saffron Walden to Haverhill.

Tourist Information Bureau: Corn Exchange, Market Square, Saffron Walden, Essex, tel: (0799) 23178 (accommodation service).

Accommodation: Hotel and bed and breakfast accommodation is available in Saffron Walden. There are YHs in Saffron Walden, and in Castle Hedingham on the Castle Hedingham Loop. There are no camp sites. Advance booking is recommended.

Cycle hire: F. C. Moore Ltd, 94 High Street, Saffron Walden, tel: (0799) 22311. There are also several in Cambridge.

Cycle shop: F. C. Moore Ltd as above.

Maps: OS 1:50 000 (nos 154, 155, 167, 168); Bartholomew's 1:100 000 (nos 16, 20); OS 1:250 000 (no. 9).

Saffron Walden

The fine buildings in **Saffron Walden** were built from the wealth earned from the cloth trade, and the growing of saffron for medicines and dyes. The oldest house in the town, excepting the scant ruins of the twelfth-century castle, is a half-timbered Tudor building now used as a youth hostel. The floors are charmingly uneven and it has some valuable old tapestries.

The church of St Mary the Virgin is a marvellous example of the Perpendicular style, being lofty and light. Its possessions include a rank of silver trumpets belonging to the organ's trompeta stop, and brasses which you can rub for a fee. But the most famous building is the former Sun Inn, now an antique shop, which has plasterwork gables pargetted with striking pictures and designs, and set amidst mellow limed-oak timbers. An explanation of the skill of pargetting is amongst the displays in the local museum.

On Saturdays you can join the market by the half-timbered market hall. The town common is large and has an ancient turf maze (now strengthened with bricks) whose unravelled length is a mile.

THE AUDLEY END ROUTE

This route gives you a portrait of the region in miniature. There are wide views over gently rolling countryside, a tiny ford in the valley which rises to Duddenhoe End, and a shady chestnut avenue on the approach to **Audley End**. There are a few slopes, but they are moderate and, except for short stretches near Wendens Ambo and Audley End, the lanes are very quiet.

Arkesden is a village made for picnics, where comfortable thatched houses and a pub face the green complete with its old pump and seats. Indeed, the wealth of pleasantly sited benches is a welcome feature of the entire area. The King's Head at **Elmdon** serves food.

A row of pretty thatched houses leads to **Wendens Ambo** church, within which a cycle of medieval wall-paintings depicts the life of St Margaret.

The highlight of the ride is **Audley End** (DoE, open), a great Jacobean mansion built on a dissolved abbey site. You will enjoy a good view of its intricate facade and copper turret-tops where your road crosses the stone bridge over the river Cam. The grounds, landscaped by Capability Brown, boast a temple and an ice-house lodge, and there is a restaurant too. Nearby is the College of St Mark, a street of clean, white pargetted terraces built as almshouses in Elizabethan times.

The Pelhams Loop

Peruse a map of East Anglia and you will find many groups of villages bearing versions of one name, like the three Pelhams on this loop. 'Brent'—meaning 'burnt'—appears often too, a clue that Essex was once covered with thick forest where small pockets of farmland were cleared by fire. Today, the landscape is open, its smooth lines broken in May with fields of yellow rape whose oil-rich seeds are fed to livestock.

Peaceful lanes follow the slow rise and fall of the land, and there are lazy freewheels from both Arkesden and Rickling. Sometimes trees line the unfenced roads, and it is a pleasure to see new leaves on the ancient elms again.

Furneux Pelham is an attractive village. Over the church clock is written the motto: 'Time flies, mind your business'. A friendly local warned me against the common mistake of reading an 'own' into it, for it changes the meaning entirely. Ask to see the tomb with superb brass figures kept in the vestry. The Brewery Tap serves food, as does the Bull at Lower Green.

Brent Pelham has a tempting seat on the green by the flint church, and if you look out you may see 'Albert', a bus converted into living quarters.

The Barley Loop

This loop explores the edge of these East Anglian hills where they overlook a flat plain, the site of Duxford Airfield. It was a Battle of Britain fighter station, but now its World War I hangars house a national museum of military aircraft, and a Concorde can sometimes be visited too. The windmill near **Great Chishill**, built on an exposed ridge above the plain, is complete with sails and a smaller fantail at the back which keeps the sails turned to the wind. In the village itself is a house delightfully painted with roses, and the Pheasant serves food.

Opposite the church in **Barley** is an unusual Tudor town house. Its ground floor was originally used as almshouses, and there are two sets of roofed outside stairs, their wooden treads worn with centuries of use. Food can be bought at the Fox and Hounds.

Beyond Barley your route descends to the plain on the B1368, which bears occasional bursts of busy traffic, but has interesting **milestones** beside it. Their old-fashioned painted hands point out the directions and show that this was a turnpike road, maintained with tolls levied from its users. The B road near Duxford can also be moderately busy, but otherwise the roads are quiet, and the gradual 200-ft (60-m) rise back into the hills beyond Ickleton is the hardest climb you have to tackle.

THE CHURCH END ROUTE

This route is flatter than the Audley End Route but not so picturesque. The housing around Wimbish and **Radwinter** is a little dull, but there are a few pargetted houses, one with a scarecrow in the garden politely saluting passers-by. At **Church End** the little village school of 1833 was built to last in local flints and red brick. Near **Pamphillions** you ride past a succession of attractive buildings including a lovely old farm by a stream, and a white thatched house with unusually shaped wooden window-frames.

A few small orchards bring variety to this route, but as grain is grown on most of the land, you will doubtless see many seed-eating birds such as the yellow-hammer which has become quite bold on these undisturbed lanes.

At Ashdon there is a tea-room, and the Rose and Crown sells food, as does the Plough near **Radwinter**.

The Thaxted Loop

There are few places in Britain where picturesque villages crowd so thickly together, as they do on this loop. The pretty thatch at Great Sampford is only a foretaste of **Finchingfield**, where the houses, the green and village pond complete with ducks, could have been laid out with artists and photographers expressly in mind. Pass through the old half-timbered almshouses to reach the church, where grotesque beasts are carved in the wooden screen.

Great Bardfield has been dubbed the 'Chelsea of Essex', and no doubt its wealthy inhabitants provide custom for the Rolls-Royce and Bentley specialists there. Spacious streets are flanked by charming buildings, one of them unusually roofed in a mixture of thatch and tile.

Thaxted prospered not only from the cloth trade, but before that also from cutlery-making—a nearby hamlet still being called Cutlers Green. Summer music festivals are held in the church which has a lofty carved roof and a strikingly painted eagle lectern. There are elegant Georgian houses, but the half-timbered Guildhall was built long ago by the cutlers. Its three overhanging storeys contain a small museum which includes a display of photographs of Thaxted at the turn of the century. Nearby is Dick Turpin's Cottage, but even the present owner has his doubts as to whether that notorious 'Gentleman of the Road' ever lived there.

Finchingfield, Great Bardfield and Thaxted all have tea-rooms and pubs where food is available, and each has its own windmill too. The one at Great Bardfield is pretty and painted in white while that at Finchingfield is a post mill, the whole mill rather than just the sail-bearing cap having to be turned to face the wind. The mill at Thaxted (open) contains its old machinery and gives a good view over the town.

The B roads on this loop are reasonably quiet and offer easy cycling through tranquil countryside. On the B1053 to Finchingfield is a house sundial with the optimistic legend '*No shadow without sun*'.

The Castle Hedingham Loop

As you cycle further from Saffron Walden the countryside broadens out, to 'Constable' country where clumps of trees stand in wide expanses of cornfields beneath dramatic skies. Parklands and big country mansions such as Dynes Hall add a touch of elegance, and in **Gosfield** Hall park, two statues of deer watch you ride by. The lake below the hall's great white facade, is popular with weekend leisure-seekers. In Gosfield itself the King's Head serves snacks, and beside it stands a brightly painted gypsy caravan.

Only near Sible Hedingham will you find any ugly twentieth century development, but it is soon passed on the way to **Castle Hedingham**, a gem of a village. Graceful Georgian houses and older half-timbered buildings harmonise below the monumental castle keep, built on a strategic hill by the Normans. Their workmanship can also be seen in the church, which has a beautiful carved double hammerbeam roof. Nearby is the Trading Post, an old indoor market of antiques and local crafts, and at the Handloom Weavers you can watch fabrics being woven on nineteenth-century machines. Needless to say, a village with so many attractions has plenty of pubs serving food.

AUDLEY END ROUTE
16 miles (26 km)
clockwise

SAFFRON WALDEN. Leave from the cross at the top of the High Street (Bishops Stortford, B1052, B1383). R (Audley End). L (Wendon, Royston). L (Newport, Bps Stortford, B1383). R (Royston 11, B1039). Enter

Wendens Ambo. Bear R in the village, although only the road ahead is signposted. L (Arkesden 1½, Wicken Bonhunt 3¼, Clavering 3). Cont at the next junction. Reach

a **Arkesden**. *Join the Pelhams Loop, or cont.* Leave

a (Duddenhoe End). L (Duddenhoe End). Reach

b. The Pelhams Loop rejoins the Audley End Route. Leave

b (Elmdon, Wenden). L directly after a little ford which might be dry. R to pass Cogmore house. R at the T junction. L (Elmdon 1, Crishall Grange 4, Ickleton 4¾). Reach

c **Elmdon**. *Join the Barley Loop, or cont.* Leave.

c (Ickleton 3½, Chesterford 4½, Cambridge 14). Reach

d. The Barley Loop rejoins the Audley End Route. Leave

d (Littlebury 3, Saffron Walden 4). R (Strethall ½, Catmere End ¾). Cont on a Single Track Road. L (Littlebury 2, Saffron Walden 3¾). Cont at the next junction. Cont (Audley End). L (Cambridge, Gt Chesterford, B1383). R (Audley End House, Ancient Monument). Pass **Audley End**. Cont (Saffron Walden).

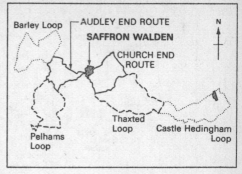

Barley Loop — AUDLEY END ROUTE · N · SAFFRON WALDEN · CHURCH END ROUTE · Thaxted Loop · Castle Hedingham Loop · Pelhams Loop

Newport). L (Wicken 1½, Rickling 2¼, Newport 3¼). L (Newport 2, B1038, A11). R (Rickling 1). R (Clavering, Berden). L (Manuden, Bps Stortford). Cont (Manuden, Bps Stortford). Cont at the next junction. R (Furneux Pelham). Cont at the next junction. L (Albury, Little Hadham). R (Furneux Pelham). Cont (Furneux Pelham, Braughing). R (Furneux Pelham, Great Hormead). Enter

Furneux Pelham. R (Stocking Pelham 2, Berden 3, Manuden 4½). Cont by the Brewery Tap. L (Stocking Pelham, Berden). L (Brent Pelham, Meesden). Cont at the next junction. L (Brent Pelham, Buntingford, B1038). Cont at the next junction. Enter

Brent Pelham. Cont (Meesden, Anstey). R (Meesden). R (Langley). L (Langley). L (Langley Upper Green ½, Little Chishall 2½, Royston 7). Reach The Bull. R (Langley Upper Green, Elmdon, Saffron Walden). L (Duddenhoe End 1½, Arkesden 4¼). R by the Duddenhoe End village name sign. Reach

b Rejoin the Audley End Route.

The Pelhams Loop
adds 15 miles (24 km)
clockwise

Leave

a Arkesdon. (Clavering, Wicken

The Barley Loop
adds 17 miles (27 km)
clockwise

Leave

c. The signpost for this road was broken

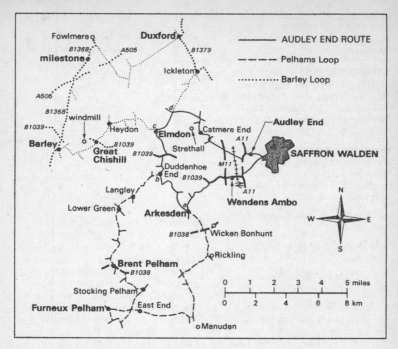

when the routes where checked, but leave to pass the Kings Head. L (Crishall, Heydon, Royston). R (Heydon). R (Heydon, Royston). L (Gt Chishill 1, Royston 6). Enter

Great Chishill. Cont (Saffron Walden 9, Barley 2, Royston 5). Cont on May Street. Cont (Barley 1, Barkway 2, Royston 4). R (Barley ½, Royston 4). Enter

Barley. L at the T junction. R (Flint Cross, Fowlmere, B1368). Cont at the next junction. Cont (Flint Cross, Fowlmere, B1368). Cont (Fowlmere 2½, Melbourne 2½, Cambridge 11, B1368). R (Newmarket, A505). L (Cambridge 11, B1368). Pass the **milestone** on your L. R (Crishall). Cont (Crishall 4). L (Thriplow 3, Duxford 3). R (Duxford 2). Enter

Duxford. R (Gt Chesterford 3½, B1379) *otherwise detour 1 mile (1½ km) following RAC signs to Duxford Airfield.* R (Elmdon 3, Chrishall 5). L (Elmdon).

Reach

d. Rejoin the Audley End Route.

CHURCH END ROUTE
15 miles (24 km)
clockwise

SAFFRON WALDEN. Leave from the north-east corner of the town common. (Ashdon, Haverhill). L (Ashdon, Haverhill). Pass through

Church End. R (Radwinter 3¾, Gt. Sampford 6). Cont at the next two junctions. Cont (Radwinter, Gt. Sampford). Reach

e The Plough. *Join the Thaxted Loop, or cont.* Leave

e. (Saffron Walden 5, B1053, Radwinter). Pass through

Radwinter. Cont (Saffron Walden 5, B1053). L (Wimbish 1). R (Saffron Walden 4¼, Thaxted 4¼). Cont at the next junction. R (Saffron Walden 4). L

(Debden 2, Newport 4). Reach

h. The Thaxted Loop rejoins the Church End Route. Leave

h (Saffron Walden, Newmarket, Norwich avoiding low bridge). Pass **Pamphillions**.

Thaxted Loop
adds 12½ miles (20 km)
clockwise

Leave

e The Plough. (S. Bumpstead 5, Haverhill 8, B1054, Hempstead 1). Cont at the next junction. R (Sampford, Finchingfield). L (The Sampfords 2, Finchingfield 4. B1053). Enter Great Sampford. Cont at the next junction. L (Finchingfield 3, Gt Bardfield 5, B1053, B1057, Lt Sampford 1). Cont (Lt Sampford, Finchingfield 3, B1053). Cont (Finchingfield, Braintree,

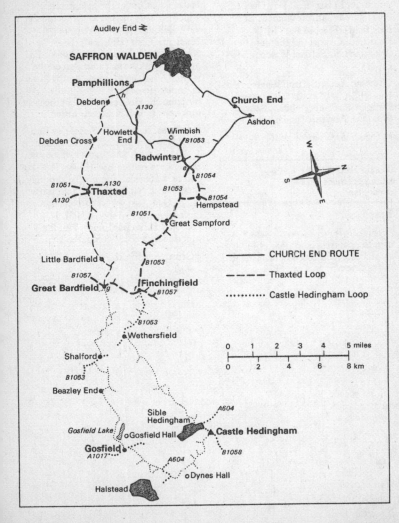

43

B1053). Reach

f **Finchingfield** *Join the Castle Hedingham Loop, or cont.* Leave

f From the signpost near the pond (Great Bardfield, Dunmow). Cont at the next junction. Reach

g **Great Bardfield.** *The Castle Hedingham Loop rejoins the Thaxted Loop.* Leave

g. From a small green with a cross, leave uphill. R (Lt Bardfield 1½, Thaxted 4). L (Thaxted, Saffron Walden, Lt Bardfield). Pass through Little Bardfield. Cont at the next junction. L (Thaxted). R (Saffron Walden, B184). Enter

Thaxted. Cont (Saffron Walden, B184, Haverhill, B1057). L (Cutlers Gn 1, Debden 4). Cont (Debden, Saffron Walden). Pass through Debden. Reach.

h. Rejoin the Church End Route.

Castle Hedingham Loop
adds 19½ miles (31 km)
clockwise

Leave

f **Finchingfield.** From the signpost near the pond (Wethersfield, Braintree). Cont at the next two junctions. Cont (S Hedingham 5). Cont (The Hedinghams). Cont (The Hedinghams). Cont at the next junction. Cont (Sible Hedingham). Cont at the next junction. R (Hedinghams, Halstead, Haverhill, Sudbury). Enter Sible Hedingham. L (Halstead, A604). L (Cambridge, A604, Gt Yeldham 2). R (Castle Hedingham, B1058, Sudbury, A131). R (Halstead) *otherwise cont for 200 yards (metres) for centre of* **Castle Hedingham.** L (Maplestead, Halstead). Cont at the next junction which is easily missed as the turn-off is very oblique. Cont (Gt Maplestead, Halfield). Cont (Halstead). R (Halstead). R (Cambridge, A604). L just before a cow warning sign on the main road, to go up a lane beside a line of poplar trees. Cont uphill at the next junction. R (Gosfield). Cont at the next junction. L on The Street. Enter

Gosfield. R (The Lake, Beazley End 3). R (Blackmore End, Wethersfield). L (Rotten End, Shalford). L opposite the drive to Rotten End House. R at the end of Water Hall Lane. Pass through Shalford. L (Gt Bardfield, light traffic only). Cont past several private roads, including one to Ashwell Hall. L (Bardfield). L (Bardfield). R at the T junction by a small green. Reach

g **Great Bardfield.** *Rejoin the Thaxted Loop.*

The Thames towpath near Henley

THE CHILTERNS

Cornfields, pastures and beautiful woodlands chequer the friendly Chiltern hills, whose smooth folds conceal many single farms and clustered villages of warm red brick and tile. 'Up market' twentieth-century housing suggests a wealthy area as do the many elegant mansions.

Brakspears, the Henley brewers, own picturesque country pubs where you can refresh yourself during these moderately strenuous rides. Rarely rising above 800 ft (250 m), the Chilterns' convoluted ridges and valleys run more or less north-west to south-east, and though many of your roads go easily with the grain, there are steep slopes where you cross it.

The hills either fall steeply to the north-western Oxford Plain in a rampart of turf and woods, or roll more gently down to the Thames' valley of pastures and pottering pleasure boats, but either descent leaves you with a 400-ft (125-m) return climb. Just a few short stretches of main roads are unavoidable, but there is such a maze of lanes twisting with the valleys or following the ridges that few motorists other than locals use them.

Moderate cycling. Quiet though busy in places. Two easy river valley paths.

HENLEY-ON-THAMES

Location: 6 miles (10 km) north east of Reading, and 35 miles (56 km) west of central London.

Trains: Henley-on-Thames station is on a branch line from Twyford, itself on the main line from London to Reading. London 1 hour 15 mins (change at Reading); Bristol: 1 hour 30 mins (change at Reading); Cardiff: 2 hours 15 mins (change at Reading); Birmingham: 2 hours 45 mins (change at Reading).

Tourist Information Bureaux: West Hill House, 4 West Street, Henley-on-Thames, Oxfordshire, tel; (049 12) 2626: Stone Hall, High Street, Wallingford, Oxfordshire, tel: (0491) 36969; Civic Offices, Civic Centre, Reading, Berkshire, tel: (0734) 55911 (accommodation service).

Accommodation: Hotel and bed and breakfast accommodation is available in Henley. These are YHs at Henley, and Streatley on the Wallingford Loop. You can camp at Swiss Farm, Henley, Oxfordshire, tel; (049 12) 3205, or at Wallingford. Henley is popular with tourists, so prior booking is recommended, especially during the Regatta in July.

Cycle-hire: None.

Cycle-shop: Brocks in Friday Street sells spares but does no repairs. Havants is not a specialist cycle-shop, but will do some repairs.

Maps: OS 1:50 000 (nos 165, 175); Bartholomew's 1:100 000 (nos 8, and 14 or 15); OS 1:250 000 (no. 9).

Henley-on-Thames

Henley's Royal Regatta, held in the first week of July, started as an inter-university boat race in 1829, but has since grown into an exciting, fashionable event. The faces of Father Thames and the goddess Isis are carved on the bridge which stands next to the attractive Angel pub. The cellars flood if the tide runs high, but terraces overlooking the river are an ideal place to drink on balmy summer evenings.

Henley has many pleasant and sometimes bow-windowed buildings. Brakspear's brewery has an unusual big bow-door, and its solid brick buildings, white-capped towers and worn brass plaques breathe an atmosphere of tradition and prosperity. The town has a wealth of enticing pubs (some serving food), a few restaurants and a fish and chip shop.

St Mary's flint tower looks down on a street of pleasingly simple almshouses. The nearby little Thames Gallery deals in pottery and paintings, and can be found by the riverside, next to the boathouses.

THE HAMBLEDEN ROUTE

Temple Island is a starting point for Regatta races, and its white 'temple', half-hidden in a clump of trees, is but one of many elegant Thameside buildings. The occasional awkwardness of the towpath is more than repaid by the beauty of the riverside meadows, and the bustling, pretty scenes at **Mill End**. Boats wait their turn to go through the lock, and fishermen stand in the surging water of the many-tiered weir, said to have first been built in the fifteenth century. Roads were then so poor that rivers were vital for cargo transport, and weirs were built at turbulent places to take the greater flow of water away from the parallel channels which boats could use more safely.

Rivers were an important source of energy too, and Mill End's lovely white weatherboarded watermill stands on a site where the Domesday survey of 1086 recorded an earlier mill. Much more grain could be milled here by use of the Thames' constant, powerful flow, than in the windmill near Turville even though the latter is built on an open ridge to make the most of the fickle wind.

St Mary the Virgin by **Hambleden's** peaceful little green has a boldly decorated chancel roof, and a richly carved wooden altar front which is said to have been Cardinal Wolsey's bed-head. It bears the arms of that powerful advisor to Henry VIII who fell into disfavour on failing to win papal approval for the king's divorce of his first wife, Catharine of Aragon. The austere church of St Bartholomew at **Fingest** boasts one of the country's finest Norman towers, with walls nearly 4 ft thick. You might well see a Saturday wedding there, when the churchyard gates are locked, forcing the groom to lift his bride over; an old custom supposed to bring the couple good luck. The nearby wooden enclosure is the village pound for straying or confiscated livestock. The King's Arms serves food.

From Mill End the road climbs nearly all the way to Turville Heath, at first rising slowly through the pretty village of Hambleden, but later snaking quite steeply through a valley just wide enough to shelter a single brick and flint farmhouse. From there you swoop quickly down to Stonor past shady woods, into a gentle, ever-widening valley. The B480 is reasonably quiet and certainly scenic, but the A423 is busy, although the gradient helps you to cycle it quickly.

Just north of the junction at *d* on the map, a signposted footpath crosses a wooded deerpark overlooking ancient **Stonor** House (open), one of the country's longest established family seats, being inhabited by the Stonors for over 800 years. Stonor was a centre of Catholic resistance during their Elizabethan repression, and you can see the room where a secret printing press was run and where Catholic rebels were arrested before being imprisoned in the tower.

The Ewelme Loop

The Stonor family's influence can be seen to have extended to **Watlington** where a plaque states that they built the arched and turretted town hall. Though a little drab, the town has some pleasing buildings in the High Street, and there are a couple of restaurants and a teashop. It prospered thanks to its position on the Icknield Way, a route vital to prehistoric Britons as it linked East Anglia's cornlands to their cultural centre around Salisbury Plain and Stonehenge. The Way continued to be important down the centuries, and today the long distance Ridgeway footpath follows it in part.

The Icknield Way originally followed the Chilterns' edge because it was relatively easy to find and to keep to, when tangled woods still covered most of the land. This loop explores the hills' scarp, which is made of chalk, as you can see in the M40's huge cutting. Beeches grow well on chalk, and your exhilarating freewheel to Kingston Blount passes woods carpeted with russet leaves in autumn, and with bluebells in May.

Nearly flat and occasionally busy, the B4009 runs below the Chilterns. These slopes are sometimes too steep to be farmed but you can explore the **Nature Reserve**, where display boards describe the area's natural history.

Amongst **Ewelme's** many mellowed red-brick buildings is a fifteenth-century school, one of the oldest state schools still in use. A peaceful almshouse cloister abuts the church, where the age of an ornate font-cover, so huge that it has to be lifted with pulleys, is given away by its wooden Tudor Rose counterweight. Jerome K. Jerome, writer of the hilarious tale of boating on the Thames, *Three Men in a Boat*, is buried in the churchyard.

From Ewelme a 400-ft (125-m) climb up a smooth-curved lonely vale takes you back into the Chilterns, where tranquil lanes wind down from Russell's Water to Stonor, through farmlands and beautiful woods.

The Chalgrove Loop

This is an easy, short loop, where quiet roads pass between shelterbelts of oaks and tangled shrubs, or enjoy wide views across the Oxford Plain. Big, regular fields pattern gently undulating land, although the area near **Chalgrove** is sufficently flat to have been used as a battlefield in the Civil War and as an airfield today.

Chalgrove village has some picturesque cottages of whitewash and thatch which are reached by little footbridges across the roadside stream. The Crown serves food, and if the church is open, the ancient frescoes are worth seeing.

Pyrton hamlet has some pleasing brick buildings both old and new, and Brightwell Baldwin is small but pretty. Both have a pub. Ducks paddle in Cuxham's clear stream, which flows by houses of stone and thatch or brick and tile; the Half Moon sells snacks.

THE STOKE ROW ROUTE

On the whole this is a pleasant, quiet route, but it can be marred by traffic around the sprawling houses at Stoke Row and Sonning Common; better ridden on a Sunday perhaps. Curiously enough, each place has an interesting well: that in **Sonning Common** is still fitted with its cogged winding wheels, whilst east of the Cherry Tree in **Stoke Row**, you can see the domed Maharajah's Well and discover the story behind its name.

It takes ten minutes to raise a bucket of water at the deep Maharajah's Well, for Stoke Row stands 450 ft (140 m) above the water table and can therefore only be reached after a steep climb from Henley-on-Thames. **Greys Court** (NT, open) still has a Tudor donkey wheel for raising well water. The stables contain a collection of miniature rooms and the sixteenth-century house stands by older ruins amidst spacious grounds. A twisting lane takes you down the valley to **Harpsden** where there is a barn opposite the church whose gables are of beautiful, cunningly textured wooden diamonds.

Sunlight filters through trees onto narrow lanes leading to both High-moor Cross and Gallowstree Common. There are no places serving food so make sure you take provisions with you.

The Wallingford Loop

Six lazy miles (10 km) take you down 500 ft (150 m) from Stoke Row to Wallingford, passing a tea-garden near Ipsden, where the landscape widens out into open slopes curving down to the Thames.

Wallingford grew up beside a fording place on the Thames, and was once guarded by a massive castle—the Civil War's last Royalist stronghold to surrender to the Parliamentarians who razed it to the ground. Now Wallingford is shabby in parts, but the market place with its town hall, flint church, and ornate canopied drinking fountain is pleasant. There are several restaurants, and pubs serving food.

Streatley and Goring grew where the ancient Icknield Way crossed the Thames, whose valley here separates the folded Chilterns from the indulating Berkshire Downs. Wooded hills form a backdrop for Streatley's substantial and charming Georgian houses. There is plenty of interest to see at the river where there are houseboats, a weir, a lock, and a reedy island.

The quiet B4009 crosses rolling cornfields, to South Stoke, whose church rises prettily against the distant Berkshire Downs to your right. New housing occasionally lines the ride from Streatley to Stoke Row, but your first 350-ft (100-m) ascent is up a deserted lane to a little, shady valley.

The Mapledurham Loop

This loop repeats the pattern of the Wallingford Loop, with a 350-ft

(100-m) descent into the Thames valley, a level ride along it, and a final climb back up, although this last is steep for its first half mile only. The A4074 can be busy in parts, but beyond Cane End where The Fox serves food, peaceful lanes rise gradually through woods of beech and oak, where attractive red-brick and flint houses stand in farmland clearings.

Jerome K. Jerome's 'three men in a boat' tarried awhile in **Pangbourne,** and Kenneth Graham, author of *The Wind in the Willows*, made this place his home. Now it is busy but it does have a tempting teashop, benches on the riverside green, and a toll-bridge which is free to cyclists.

Mapledurham is a tiny old-world hamlet with simple, lichened almshouses, and a solid pink-brick watermill (open). The Thames once again powers its wooden cog-wheels, producing stone-ground wholewheat flour which is for sale here. Set in lovely Thameside grounds, the Elizabethan Mapledurham House (open) has original moulded ceilings, a great oak staircase, and a teashop serving home-made cakes and cream teas.

Picturesque stables and a cottage nestling below luxuriantly wooded slopes are passed on the Hardwick House bridleway. Later on a stony track forces you to cycle slowly, but gives you time to enjoy the view of buttercup meadows and the willow-fringed Thames.

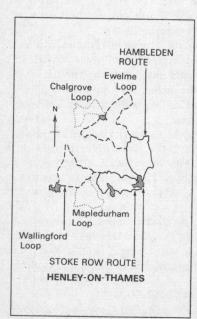

HAMBLEDEN ROUTE
15 miles (24 km)
anticlockwise

HENLEY-ON-THAMES. Read directions as far as Mill End, and if you do not wish to take towpath, go to Mill End on A4155. Leave from Thames bridge (A423, Maidenhead). L (Remenham Church 1). L by church. Cross stile, lifting bike over. R on towpath. The Thames Conservancy currently allows cycles to use towpath, but it is not a right of way for cycles. Parts are able to be cycled and others are bumpy over grass. There is one awkward gate, 2 stiles, and a long narrow bridge which is awkward if there are many other people about. Pass **Temple Island**. Cross lock. Pass in front of lock-keeper's cottage, then L to cross weir bridge. Reach

Mill End. R at T junction with main road. L (Hambleden 1, Skirmett 3,

Fingest 3½). Cont at next junction *or
detour 200 yards (metres), R (Village), for*
Hambleden. Cont (Fingest 3, West
Wycombe 7¾, Stokenchurch 8½).
Cont (Skirmett 2¼, Fingest 2¾). Cont
(Skirmett 1¼, Fingest 2). Cont
(Skirmett ½, Fingest 1½). L (Fingest
¾). Cont (Fingest, Marlow 6½.
Wycombe 7½). Enter

Fingest. L (Turville ½, Turville Heath
2¼, Northend 3¼). Cont (Turville,
North End 3½, Watlington 6). L
(Turville Heath 2, North End 3). Cont
at next junction. Cont (North End 1½,
Stonor 2, Watlington 5). Reach

a. Join the Ewelme Loop, otherwise cont.
Leave

a (Stonor 2, Henley 6). L (Assendon
2½, Henley 4¾, B480). Reach

d **Stonor**. *The Ewelme Loop rejoins the
Hambleden Route.* Leave

d (Assendon 2, Henley 4½, B480).
Follow Henley signs at all junctions.

Ewelme Loop
adds 20½ miles (33 km)
anticlockwise

Leave

a (North End 1, Watlington 5). L
(Christmas Common, Watlington 4). R
(Watlington 1½, Stokenchurch 4). Cont
(Kingston Blount 5, Stokenchurch 5).
Pass **Nature Reserve** on your L. Cont
at next junction. Cross M20 flyover.
Cont at next junction. L (Oxford, A40).
R (Kingston Blount 1½, single track
road). Cross **Icknield Way**, Ridgeway.
L (Lewknor 1¼, Watlington 4¾.
B4001). Follow Watlington signs, until
you reach

b near Watlington name sign. *Join the
Chalgrove Loop, otherwise cont.* Leave

b (Watlington ½, Benson 5¾, B4009).
Reach

c **Watlington**. *The Chalgrove Loop
rejoins the Ewelme Loop.* Leave

c. From town hall, go slightly downhill,

HAMBLEDEN ROUTE
----- Ewelme Loop
.... Chalgrove Loop

towards brick and timber house with 3
chimneys. R (Benson, B4009). Cont
(Britwell 1¼, Benson 5, Wallingford
7½, B4009). Cont (Ewelme 2, Benson
3¼, B4009). Cont at next junction.
Cont (Benson, Wallingford, B4009). L
(Ewelme 1). Enter

Ewelme. L (Swyncombe 3, Cookley

51

3½). L (Swyncombe, Cookley). L (Swyncombe 2, Cookley Green 3). L by war memorial on B481, which is not signposted in your direction. R (Russells Water ¾, Maidensgrove 2). Cont at next junction. Reach

d **Stonor**. *Rejoin the Hambleden Route.*

Chalgrove Loop
adds 13 miles (21 km)
anticlockwise

Leave

b (Pyrton ½, Stoke Talmage 3). Cont at next junction. L (Cuxham 2, Brightwell 2¾). Cont at next junction. R (Chalgrove 2, Stadhampton 4¼, Oxford 12¼, B480). Cont (Oxford 11, B480). At end of village, by black and white posts, walk L through black gate. L opposite The Lamb on old B480 to Watlington. Enter

Chalgrove. R (Berrick Salome 2½, Benson 4¼). Cont (Berrick Salome 2, Benson 3¾). L (Ewelme). Cont at next junction. L at cross-roads with a Give Way sign. L (Brightwell Baldwin 1¼, Cuxham 2¼). L (Brightwell Baldwin ½, Cuxham 1). Bear R by gateposts with stone birds. R (Watlington 1¾, Nettlebed 7, Henley 12, B480). Cont at next junction. L on Brook Street. Reach

c **Watlington**. *Rejoin the Ewelme Loop.*

STOKE ROW ROUTE
15 miles (24 km)
anticlockwise

HENLEY. Leave from Market Place, passing to L of town hall. Ignore all turn-offs within Henley. Cont at next junction. Pass entrance and lodge to **Greys Court** to your R. R in valley bottom, by chevrons on main road. R at T junction to pass Highmoor village name sign. L (Witheridge Hill ¼, Stoke Row 1½, Checkendon 3). Cont at next junction. L (Stoke Row ¾, Checkendon 2½, Nuffield 3½). Cont (Nuffield 3, Ipsden 3½). Reach

e **Stoke Row**, Cherry Tree pub. *Join the Wallingford Loop, otherwise cont.* Leave

e (Industrial Site), on Busgrove Lane. Cont at next junction. Cont (Cane End 1½, Kidmore End 1¾). L (Peppard 1½, Henley 6¼). Cont (Peppard 1, Henley 6). Enter

Sonning Common. R (Sonning Common 1, Reading 6). Cont (Binfield Heath 2½, Shiplake 4). Cont (Binfield Heath 2, Harpsden 4). 1st L, to pass drive to Crosscroft house in 400 yards on your L. Keep L by 4/24 hydrant. Cont (Henley, Binfield Heath). Cont past school sign. Enter

Harpsden. Cont past church, then soon bear L. L by Three Horseshoes pub.

Wallingford Loop
adds 20 miles (32 km), including detours to Wallingford and Streatley.
anticlockwise

Leave

e. (Checkendon 1¾, Woodcote 3, A4074). Cont at all junctions through village. Cont (Nuffield 2¼, Nettlebed 4¼). L (Ipsden 2¾, North Stoke 4, Crowmarsh 4¾). Cont (Ipsden 2½, Crowmarsh 4½). Cont (Well Place 1, North Stoke 3½, Crowmarsh 4¼). L (North Stoke 2¾, Crowmarsh 3½). R (Hailey ½, Crowmarsh 2¾). Cont at next junction. Cont *not* R on 3 ton limit road. L (Oxford 14, A423). Cont at next junction. L (Goring 6) *otherwise detour 1 mile (1½ km), cont (Wallingford Bridge ½). for*
Wallingford. R (Goring 5, B4009). Cont (South Stoke 2, Goring 3¾, B4009). Cont at next 2 junctions. Cont (Goring). Cont (Goring 1¾, Reading 10¾, B4009). L (Woodcote 3½, Ipsden 3) *otherwise detour 1 mile (1½ km), following Streatley signs, for* **Streatley**. Cont at next junction. Reach

f. *Join the Mapledurham Loop, otherwise cont.* Leave

f (Shervells Hill). L at end of Potkiln Lane. R onto road called Greenmore, sign on wall may be overgrown. Skirt

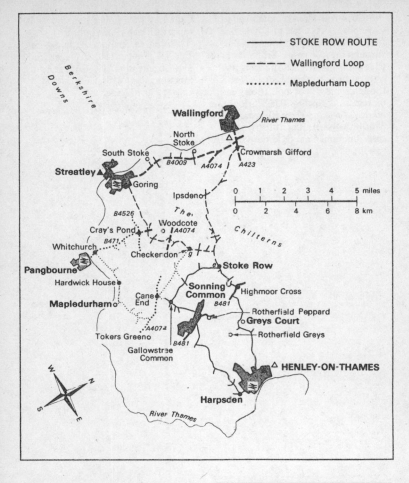

new estates. R at end of Greenmore. R then L over A4074 (Exlade Street ½, Checkendon ¾). Cont (Checkendon ¾). Reach

g Four Horseshoes pub. *The Mapledurham Loop rejoins the Wallingford Loop.* Leave

g (Stoke Row 1¾, Nuffield 3¼). Cont at next junction. Cont (Stoke Row 1¼, Nuffield 2¾). Cont at next junction. R (Stoke Row ¾, Peppard 3). Reach

e **Stoke Row**, Cherry Tree pub. *Rejoin the Stoke Row Route.*

Mapledurham Loop
adds 7½ miles (12 km) anticlockwise

Leave

f (Goring, Whitchurch, B471). Cont (Whitchurch 2, Pangbourne 2, B471). Cont (Whitchurch 1½, Pangbourne 2¼, B471). Cont at next junction. Cont (Whitchurch ¾, Pangbourne 1¼, B471). Reach top edge of Whitchurch. L onto Hardwick Road *otherwise detour ¾ mile (1 km), continuing downhill to*

53

Pangbourne. Cont (Bridle Road to Caversham). At triple fork, take one furthest L (to Mapledurham). Cont through big iron gates. Bridleway here changes from tarmac to a nearly level, bumpy stone surface. Usually firm, though some risk of mud at very end. L on regaining road by The White House *otherwise detour 300 yards (metres) R for* **Mapledurham**. R at little triangular road junction. Cont (Kidmore End 1½, Cane End 1¾). L at T junction *not* R towards Black Horse pub. R (Gallowstree Common ½, Kidmore End 1½, Peppard ²/₃). L (Hook End 1¼, Checkendon 2¼). Cont at next junction. Cont with white lines at Lower Farm. Reach

g Four Horseshoes pub. *Rejoin the Wallingford Loop.*

Ancient beeches in Savernake Forest

THE WESSEX DOWNS

The laziest freewheels in Britain follow chalk downland valleys, where the descents are so long and so gradual that you need never pedal or brake. Of course you must sometimes climb too, but the rolling hillsides rarely rise through more than 400 ft (120 m), and so ascents are either slow, or hard work, but over fairly quickly.

The landscape can have an exhilaratingly open aspect, and yet the snakey 'bottoms' hide lots of secret places: you will even pass a drive to 'North Hidden Farm'. The valley rivers flow swiftly through willowed pastures and often harbour trout in their clear water. There are riverside and hilltop villages, some with pretty thatched cottages, and substantial red brick farms and country mansions too.

Quite often in this region, you will find that as you travel towards a village, the mileage still to go, grows bigger at each signpost. Don't be disheartened: the fault lies with the signmakers. It is best to take a picnic with you, as on several of the rides it is difficult to buy meals.

Quite easy cycling though fairly strenuous at times. Very quiet. Two tracks, both easy but needing some wheeling.

HUNGERFORD

Location: 25 miles (40 km) west of Reading.

Trains: Hungerford Station is on the main line from London to the south-west, and on a direct line from Reading. London 1 hour 30 mins; Bristol: 1 hour 30 mins (change at Westbury or Reading); Cardiff: 3 hours (change at Westbury or Reading); Birmingham: 3 hours (change at Reading).

Coaches: A coach runs from Bristol through Hungerford to Brighton, and another runs from London through Hungerford to Wells.

Tourist Information Bureau: St Peter's Church, High Street, Marlborough, Wiltshire, tel: (0672) 53989 (summer service only, accommodation service).

Accommodation: There is some hotel and bed and breakfast accommodation in Hungerford. The only YH in the area is at Overton, 6 miles (10 km) from the Watership Down Loop near Litchfield. There is a Forestry Commission camp site near the Marlborough Loop, in Savernake Forest.

Cycle-hire: Hungerford Cycle Shop, Bridge Street, Hungerford, Berkshire, tel: (048 86) 3618.

Cycle-shop: As above.

Maps: OS 1:50 000 (nos 174, 185 and 173 just for the Marlborough Loop); Bartholomew's 1:100 000 (no. 8); OS 1:250 000 (no. 9).

Hungerford

Hungerford has offered hospitality to many a traveller in its past. The Romans built a road to Bath through here, and nearly 2000 years later navvies dug the Kennet and Avon Canal to link the Bristol Channel to the Thames. The Old Bear Hotel has an interesting history having belonged to Anne of Cleves and Katharine Howard; two of the six wives of Henry VIII.

Canal towpath walks lead past the church to several locks, and there is a trout farm beside the river Kennet. The town is proud of its fishing rights which were granted in the fourteenth century by John of Gaunt, Duke of Lancaster, and the tradition of presenting a red rose of Lancaster to any passing Monarch is upheld to this day.

Pleasant Georgian buildings and pollarded trees line the sloping high street, where several antique shops, restaurants, pubs and a fish and chip shop do brisk trade.

Just above the town to the east is Hungerford Common, and should you fancy an outing out of the saddle, the interesting market town of Marlborough can be visited by bus.

THE FROXFIELD ROUTE

Neither strenuous nor lazy, this loop has four gradual climbs of about 150 ft (50 m). The first looks down to **Froxfield** and the big red and white building of Somerset Hospital. Set around a square with its own chapel and arched gateway, it was endowed as a hospice for clergy and widows by a seventeenth-century Duchess of Somerset.

The canal-side lane to **Little Bedwyn** passes several locks, and small bridges, numbered so that travellers by boat can keep an easy check on where they are. Little Bedwyn is charming, with a neat row of red houses overlooking the canal.

You can see excavations of the Roman villa beside **Littlecote** House (open), which is a Tudor mansion with a fine collection of Cromwellian armour in the great hall. There is also a 'Wild West Town' in the grounds.

Beyond Chilton Foliat is **Leverton**, its five identical thatched cottages built in warm yellow brick. Even this tiny hamlet must have had its wrongdoers, for the stocks still stand by the crossroads.

After passing a farm with a lovely half-timbered granary, you can freewheel along a typical downland vale to Hungerford Newtown.

The Marlborough Loop

The Kennet and Avon Canal and the river Kennet valley are divided by a broad, wooded ridge. **Savernake** was already a mature forest when the Normans conquered England, and splendid beech avenues were added in the eighteenth century. Your road follows the Grand Avenue and is straight but roller-coasts as it goes past dense conifers and tranquil glades.

Marlborough is reached on the A4. Built to accommodate many market stalls, its main street is wide, but much older than it looks since many of the old houses were burnt down over the years and it now has the Georgian aspect typical of towns on the old coaching roads. The famous public school is grandiose in the nineteenth century style, but it was schoolboys of an earlier generation who cut the White Horse in the hillside turf. Popular with tourists, Marlborough has lots of antique shops and places serving food.

Swans and geese idle in willowy meadows by the Kennet, whose smooth-sided valley shelters many pretty buildings. A mill just past **Mildenhall** still has its hoist-wheel, and a pear tree is trained against the warm red wall. Nearby a lantern tower tops an octagonal Gothic building. The riding is fairly easy, although the road climbs 150 ft (50 m) around Ramsbury Manor. Ramsbury village has several attractive buildings, and the Crown and Anchor serves food.

The 2-mile (3-km) bridleway to Littlecote takes you right away from the traffic, at the cost of a little bumpy riding here and there. The picturesque farm beside it incorporates an old round oasthouse. Later you travel along a gracious tree-lined drive past the Tudor **Littlecote** House.

The Lambourn Loop

This loop rises up into Wiltshire' expansive downlands, where **Baydon**, the county's highest village, is built on a Roman road. The M4 sweeps across the hills, but your ride is quiet and leisurely.

At **Aldbourne**, the grey tower of St Michael's church stands among thatched houses. It contains a clear-glass etching of his struggle with Lucifer, as well as cheerfully painted monuments and an old fighting helmet. Big and bustling, the attractive village offers pub food and fish and chips.

Lambourn's village stocks are kept in the church, which is also adorned with memorial brasses. Famous for its racehorses, the village has a number of stables and saddlers amongst its pleasant red-brick and flint buildings. The Lamb serves food and there is a fish and chip shop.

Lambourn shares its name with its river, which flows below little footbridges in Eastbury. Eastbury has a pleasing range of buildings including a black weatherboard barn, thatched cottages and a gabled red-brick mansion.

THE INKPEN ROUTE

Low and broad, the Kennet valley south and east of Hungerford is a gently swelling country of fertile fields and trees. There are big country houses, although in some cases their splendour is fading; near **Kintbury**, tall gateposts support crowned lions, arrogant still, though ivy soon will hide them. Within dull outskirts, Kintbury's old centre has a few red and blue patterned buildings. Both the Prince of Wales and the Blue Ball serve food.

To the south, the valley is hemmed in by a 400-ft (120-m) scarp, which is so steep that you will probably have to dismount and walk. In prehistoric times, when lower grounds was impenetrably wooded or swampy, a route along a scarp edge would be easier to find, to clear and to follow. The ancient trackway along these hills is still in use today, and crosses Walbury Hill, a prehistoric camp some 80 acres. Its superbly defensive site commands panoramic views, but life on that windswept hill far from any water, must have been very harsh indeed.

Stone Age man buried his dead in a long barrow by the **Combe Gibbet**, which is still kept in repair as the duty of a local tenant farmer. High on the hills' very edge, the gibbet looks macabre, standing above the slope where at times brightly-coloured hang-gliders wheel and dip.

Curiously named **Inkpen** was once 'the stockade of Inga', but now it is a village with some pretty thatch cottages, and a rectory with gardens laid out by Le Nôtre, who also worked at Versailles. The churchyard is entered through a true lych-gate: *lych* comes from the Germanic word for corpse, and coffin-bearers can rest their load on the central wooden shelf before entering the church. Within is a great rood screen carved from oaks grown in the rectory grounds. Nineteenth-century wall paintings in the pre-Raphaelite style brighten the church, and the old north windows are built in chalk or 'clunch'.

The Combe Loop

From Walbury Hill this loop descends a long, sinuous chalkland valley, sometimes broad with open fields, and sometimes narrow between slopes of turf or soft trees. **Combe** manor nestling by the ancient church was reputedly a haunt of Charles II and his mistress Nell Gwynn.

A huge thatched barn stands in the gracious hamlet of Netherton. Bladon Gallery (open) in **Hurstbourne Tarrant**, contains work of the Guild of Hampshire and Berkshire Craftsmen. Although faded, the fourteenth-century wall paintings in the church can still be seen. Amongst Parsonage Farm's substantial thatched outhouses is a delightful half-timbered granary perched on mushroom-shaped staddle stones so that vermin cannot reach the stored grain.

The riding continues to be easy on a quiet B road, alongside the willow-lined Bourne Rivulet to Stoke. 'Stoke' occurs often in English place names because it means 'church', but here the word survives without the building.

Dairy farms are dotted along the lane to Ashmansworth, which climbs relentlessly and sometimes steeply over 3 miles (5 km). Ashmansworth stands near the hills' scarp, above a freewheel back to the Kennet valley.

The Watership Down Loop

An isolated little church and farm can be seen on the open downs at Woodcott, before the lane swoops down to a comfortable valley farm. In the quiet of the tree-shaded avenue beyond, I had to swerve around two fighting cock-pheasants; these colourful seed-eating birds are often seen in country where corn is grown.

Another peaceful lane twists slowly up a valley to Watership Down, passing through a gated farmyard where free-range chickens scratch and strut. Water for livestock in this country of few streams (the underlying chalk being porous to water) is a problem, so shallow little dewponds have been dug to collect dew water on the hills. You pass one on your left, just before the exhilarating freewheel down the hills' scarp, alongside the Watership Down of Richard Adams' famous book of the same name.

As you ride through Sydmonton, look up to Ladle Hill, where a lumpy skyline betrays the work of prehistoric man. He never finished these earthworks, but made an inspiring job of Beacon Hill. This iron-age hill-fort crowns the end of a rough grass-land spur and overlooks Highclere Castle, once the home of Lord Carnarvon who excavated Tutenkamen's tomb.

Burghclere Chapel (NT, open) is a First World War memorial. Wall paintings, painted by Sir Stanley Spencer depict the everyday life of the soldiers. In the following 3 miles (5 km) you meet a few very short but sharp gradients, but once past East End the riding becomes easy again.

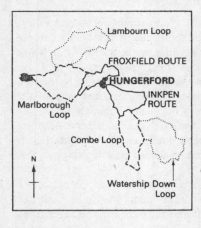

d **Littlecote** *drive gateway. The Marlborough Loop rejoins the Froxfield Route.* Leave

d as if you were turning L on the lane on emerging from Littlecote drive. L (Cirencester, A419). R (Leverton ¾). Reach

Leverton. L (Old Hayward 1). R (Newtown 1, Avington 3½). Cont (Newtown 1, Avington 3). Cont (Newton 1, Avington 3). Cont (North Denford ½, Avington 2½). R (Upper Denford ½, Hungerford 2). Cont (Leverton 1½, Hungerford 1). Cont (Leverton 1½, Hungerford 1). L (Hungerford ¾, A338). Follow Hungerford signs.

FROXFIELD ROUTE
15 miles (24 km)
clockwise

HUNGERFORD. Leave the High Street on a road signposted 'Toilets, Free Car Park'. Cont, passing RHM Mills on your R. Cont (Stype 3, Oak Hill 3). Where a lesser road goes straight ahead, go R to descend along the R edge of some woods. L (Little Bedwyn 1, Great Bedwyn 2). Enter Little Bedwyn. Cont (Great Bedwyn 1). Reach

a. Join the Marlborough Loop, or cont. Leave

a (Froxfield 1, Hungerford 4). R (Froxfield 1, Hungerford 4). Enter **Froxfield**. R (Hungerford, A4). L (Littlecote House 2, Chilton Foliat 2). Reach

Marlborough Loop
adds 13½ miles (22 km)
clockwise

Leave

a (Great Bedwyn 1, Marlborough 8). Cont (Great Bedwyn 1, Marlborough 8). Cont (Great Bedwyn 1, Marlborough 8). R (Bedwyn Common, Marlborough 7). Cont past the Bewley Farm turn-off. Cont at next junction. L (Savernake 1, Burbage 3, Durley 1). Cont at next junction. R opposite a pair of brick ball-mounted gateposts with large iron gates. You now enter Savernake Forest, on a road which is tarmac for nearly all its length, but which has been made rough for a couple of hundred yards (metres) at each of its ends to discourage motor-touring. The

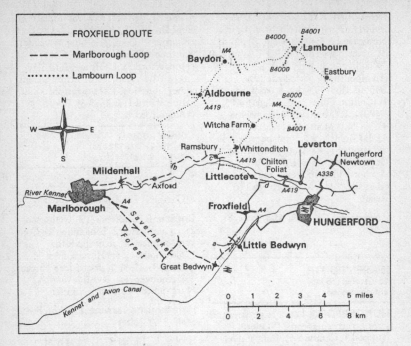

FROXFIELD ROUTE
- - - - Marlborough Loop
.... Lambourn Loop

public are warned that they use the road at their own risk. Leave through a gateway. L on main road. Follow (Town Centre) signs. Enter

Marlborough. Leave Marlborough High Street (Swindon, A345). R (Ramsbury 6, Aldbourne 8). Cont (Ramsbury 6, Aldbourne 8). Enter

Mildenhall. Cont (Ramsbury 5). Cont at next two junctions. Reach

b. Join the Lambourn Loop, or cont. Leave

b (Ramsbury 2). Reach

c Ramsbury. The Lambourn Loop rejoins the Marlborough Loop. Leave

c from The Bell pub on Scholard's Lane to 'Hungerford'. R (Froxfield 3). Cross the river bridge, then L before the hill following a 'Bridleway and footpath' sign. A firm gravel track leads to a farm, where you cont through a gate beside a cattle grid and near the summer-house.

A clear but often bumpy grass track keeps to the L edge of the fields. Emerge onto a pale stone track, and cont to pass to the R of **Littlecote** House. Reach

d **Littlecote** *drive gateway. Rejoin the Froxfield Route.*

Lambourn Loop
adds 15½ miles (25 km)
clockwise

Leave

b (Aldbourne 4). Cont at next junction. R (Aldbourne 2, Baydon). Enter

Aldbourne. Follow (Baydon, Lambourn) signs through the village. Enter

Baydon. R (Lambourn 3, Newbury 15). Cont on Ermine Street. Cont at next junction. L (Lambourn 2). Cont (Ashbury 6, Shrivenham 9½, B4000). Enter

Lambourn. R (Childrey 6¼, B4000, B4001). Cont (Great Shefford 4, Newbury 12, B4000). Cont (Shefford 3½, Newbury 11½). Enter Eastbury. R (Woodlands St Mary 2¼). R (Lambourn 4½, Cricklade 19¼, B4000). Cont (Baydon 4, Cricklade 18). L (Chilton Foliat 3¼, Hungerford 5, B4001). R (Membury 2, Ramsbury 4½). Cont (Membury 1½, Ramsbury 4). L (Membury 1, Ramsbury 3½). R (Membury 1, Ramsbury 3½). Cont (Ramsbury 1). Reach the Crown and Anchor, Whittonditch. Cont (Ramsbury 1¼, Marlborough 7¼). Reach

c Ramsbury. Rejoin the Marlborough Loop.

INKPEN ROUTE
15½ miles (25 km)
anticlockwise

HUNGERFORD. Leave High Street on Park Street, singposted (Station). R (Inkpen 3, Combe 5½). Cont at next junction. L (Inkpen 2, Combe 5). Cont (Inkpen 1½, Combe 4). Cont (Combe 3, Inkpen 1). Enter

Inkpen. R (Combe 3, Ham 2). Cont (Ham 2, Shalbourne 3½). L (Upper Inkpen 1, Combe 3). R (Combe Gibbet 1, Combe 2½). Cont (Combe Gibbet 1, Combe 2). Reach

e **Walbury Hill**. *(Track along hills' edge westwards for 500 yards (metres) for* **Combe Gibbet***). Join the Combe Loop, or cont.* Leave

e (Kintbury 4, Newbury 8½). L (Kintbury 3, Newbury 8). R (West Woodhay 1). Cont (West Woodhay Church, East Woodhay 2, Newbury 8). Reach

h (200 yards (metres) east of spired West Woodhay church). The Combe Loop rejoins the Inkpen Route. Leave

h (Newbury 7). Cont (Newbury 7). L (Holtwood ½, Kintbury 2½). R (Holtwood ½). L (Hamstead Marshall

¾, Marsh Benham 3). Cont (Marsh Benham 2½). L (Kintbury 2). Cont (Kintbury). Cont (Kintbury ½). Enter Kintbury. R on Holt Road. Cont (Hungerford 3). L (Hungerford 3½, Inkpen 2½). Cont (Hungerford). Cont at next junction. R (Hungerford 3). L (Hungerford 1, Inkpen 3). Cont (Hungerford ½).

Combe Loop
adds 13½ miles (22 km)
anticlockwise

Leave

e (Combe 1, Linkenholt 3). Enter

Combe. R (Linkenholt 2, Netherton 2). L (Netherton 2, Linkenholt 2). Cont at next junction (do *not* go R to Linkenholt). Cont (Hurstbourne Tarrant 3). Cont (Hurstbourne Tarrant 1¾, Andover 7½). R (Andover 6, A343, Hurstbourne Tarrant ½). Enter

Hurstbourne Tarrant. L (Church ½, Stoke 1½). Enter

Stoke. L (Binley 2). Cont at next junction. L (Newbury 10½). R (Newbury 9, A343). L (Ashmansworth 1¼). R (Newbury 7). Reach

f The Plough. Join the Watership Down Loop, or cont. Leave

f (Newbury 7). L (West Woodhay 2). Reach

g. The Watership Down Loop rejoins the Combe Loop. Leave

g (West Woodhay 1¾). L (West Woodhay 1¾). Cont (West Woodhay 1¼, Kintbury 4¼). Cont (West Woodhay ¾, Kintbury 3¾). Reach

h (200 yards (metres) east of spired West Woodhay church). Rejoin the Inkpen Route.

Watership Down Loop
adds 14 miles (23 km)
anticlockwise

Leave

f on Cross Lane. L (Newbury 7, A343,

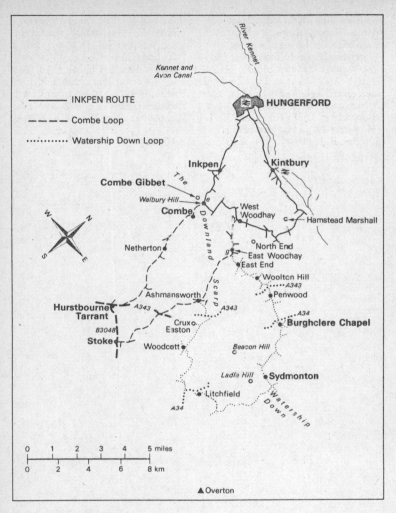

INKPEN ROUTE

Combe Loop

Watership Down Loop

River Kennet

Kennet and Avon Canal

HUNGERFORD

Inkpen

Kintbury

Combe Gibbet

Walbury Hill

Combe

West Woodhay

Hamstead Marshall

The Downland Scarp

Netherton

North End

East Woodhay

East End

Woolton Hill

A343

Penwood

Ashmansworth

A343

A34

Burghclere Chapel

Hurstbourne Tarrant

A343

B3048

Crux Easton

Stoke

Woodcott

Beacon Hill

Ladle Hill

Sydmonton

Watership Down

Litchfield

A34

| 0 | 1 | 2 | 3 | 4 | 5 miles |

| 0 | 2 | 4 | 6 | 8 km |

▲ Overton

Highclere 2). R (Crux Easton 1, Woodcott 1¾, Egbury 3¼). Cont (Woodcott 1, Egbury 2½, Whitchurch 6½). L (Dunley 2, Whitchurch 5½). Cont (Litchfield 1, Whitchurch 4, Newbury 9). L (Winchester, A34, Southampton, A33, Litchfield). R (Litchfield). In the village take the first turning R past the telephone box, soon passing a sign requesting 15 mph only. At the summit, cont on the gravel track.

At the cross-tracks, where the R track goes to a farm, the Right of Way goes straight on. Although used a little by vehicles, it can get quite overgrown in the summer, and ruts make it generally uncyclable. The alternative to using the Right of Way is to go L at the cross-tracks on the gravelled farm drive, which is not a Right of Way, asking permission if possible. Whether you use the Right of Way or the farm drive, turn

L on reaching a lane. Pass through Ashley Warren farmyard. Reach the hills' edge, then descend passing Watership Down. L (Burghclere 1½). Pass through **Sydmonton**. R (Burghclere 2) *otherwise detour 2 miles (3 km), cont (Burghclere Stn ¼). L on A34. R on footpath, for Beacon Hill.* L (Burghclere 1½). L (Highclere 2¾). L (Highclere 2¼). Pass **Burghclere Chapel**. R (Newbury, A34). L

(Penwood 1, Highclere 1¾, Woolton Hill 2¼). Cont at next two junctions. Cont (Woolton Hill 1, Kintbury 5¼). L (Woolton Hill ½, Kintbury 5). Cont (Woolton Hill ½, Kintbury 5). L (East End 1). Cont at next junction. R (East End ¾, Heath End 1¼). Enter East End. Cont (Heath End ½). Cont (East Woodhay ½, West Woodhay 2). Reach

g. Rejoin the Combe Loop.

New Forest ponies

THE NEW FOREST

Sunlight dappling a ferny glade amidst ancient oaks and beeches; wide heaths of springy turf, purple heather and splashes of golden gorse; the silhouette of a mare and her foal beneath a lonely tree; these are the timeless scenes of the New Forest. Its unique character of lowland wilderness owes much to William the Conqueror, who declared it his new Forest *circa* 1078—Forest here meaning a Royal deer-hunting reserve. The Forest Laws forbade fences and walls so that the Royal deer could have freedom to roam. Consequently the Commoners' animals had the run of the Forest too, as they still do today.

The animals' wandering are controlled today though by the many cattle grids in the roads. The technique for crossing them is to not slow down, and to let the pedals and handlebars rather than the saddle take your weight. Generally the cycling is easy, the few gradients being short or gentle.

The New Forest is a popular tourist area with few roads, so very quiet cycle routes are impossible to find. To enjoy your visit in reasonable peace, avoid peak holiday seasons and bank holidays.

Easy cycling, moderate traffic and two easy gravel roads.

BROCKENHURST

Location: 10 miles (16 km) south-west of Southampton.

Trains: Brockenhurst Station is on the main line from London through Southampton to Bournemouth. London 1 hour 45 mins; Bristol: 2 hours

15 mins (change at Southampton); Cardiff: 3 hours 15 mins (change at Southampton); Birmingham: 3 hours 15 mins (changes at Reading and Southampton).

Tourist Information Bureaux: John Montagu Building, Beaulieu, Hampshire, tel: (0590) 612345, and Main Car Park, Lyndhurst, Hampshire, tel: (042 128) 2269 (summer service only, accommodation service).

Accommodation: Hotel and bed and breakfast accommodation is available at Brockenhurst. There is a YH at Burley, on the Rhinefield route, and another at Norleywood, 5 miles (8 km) south-east of Brockenhurst. Camping is allowed at both. The Forestry Commission runs many camp-sites in the New Forest. Hollands Wood site is at Brockenhurst itself, and 2 miles (3 km) to the east is Roundhill site, with a lightweight area where those without motor transport pay considerably lower fees.

Cycle-hire: The nearest are: The Cycle Shop, Bridge Road, Park Gate, Southampton, tel: (048 95) 3249; Renham Cycles, 3 St Denys Road, Portswood, Southampton, tel: (0703) 556470; Chesil Cycle Depot, 3 Chesil Street, Winchester, tel: (0962) 63703; Cy-Sales, 644 Wimbourne Road, Winton, Bournemouth, tel: (0202) 515880; Harveys, 59 Poole Road, Westbourne, Bournemouth, tel: (0202) 761550.

Cycle-shop: Orchards, 51 Brookley Road, Brockenhurst is a small shop. Renham Cycles and Chesil Cycle Depot (see above), are bigger shops with greater ranges of spares.

Maps: OS 1:500 000 (nos 184, 195, 196) or alternatively the OS 1″: 1 mile Tourist Map of the New Forest covers all the routes; Bartholomew's 1:000 000 (no. 5); OS 1:250 000 (no. 9).

Brockenhurst

The same Forest Laws which have given the New Forest its charms of open country and roaming livestock have for centuries hampered the growth of a farming population, so this is an area of pleasing landscapes rather than pretty buildings.

Brockenhurst is a large village, with plenty of food shops, a couple of restaurants and a fish and chip shop. At one end of its main street is a wide ford called the Watersplash, and at the other is a busy level crossing.

You can walk on the heaths west of Brockenhurst, or along gravel tracks in the Forestry Commission's conifer plantations to the east. It is amongst the pinewood that you are likeliest to spot deer, but don't venture deep into the forest without a 1:50 000 or 1 inch:1 mile map and compass.

You can sunbathe on the banks or paddle in the river at Balmer Lawn, or even enjoy a waggon ride in the summer months.

Within a few miles and accessible by bus are Lyndhurst, the New

Forest 'capital' where the Commoners' rights are protected in the Verderers' Court, and Lymington which is a popular Solent yachting port.

THE RHINEFIELD ROUTE

This easy route is pure 'New Forest', passing almost entirely through varied woods and heaths. The **Ornamental Drive** is rather special, with many kinds of foreign trees including some massive redwoods. A Walkers' trail has been laid out, leaflets being available at Black Water car park beside the road.

Towards Burley are some more typical plantations, but the New Forest has wild trees too. The Commoners do not allow many to survive on the heaths though, since they reduce grazing for the animals. At Hinchelsea Moor are a number of wild holly trees, and some fine Scots pines with their distinctive salmon pink upper trunks. Gorse covers a lot of the heathland; the ponies that eat it are supposed to grow wipsy beards.

Rhinefield House in Burley, is one of the area's few big stone-built houses. **Burley** itself is a touristy village with tea-shops and a pub serving food. Just as you leave the village up a short hill, notice on the left the unusual Rest and be Thankful milestone, one of several on the Ringwood road inscribed to mark an historic event; I leave you to discover which one.

The **Old Station** now serves as a teashop, but still has the distinctive shape of a railway station. The straight stretch of road beyond it was converted from the disused railway.

The Linwood Loop

North of the A35 the **Ornamental Drive** passes through woods of magnificent old trees, and lots of dead timber deliberately left to harbour the plants and little animals that thrive on and in it.

In the seventeenth century pollarding was a frequent practice. The top would be lopped off a tree some 25 ft (7½ m) above ground to encourage young shoots which would then be gathered as winter fodder for Royal deer. At **Knightwood Oak** you can see centuries-old beech and oak pollards, and some experimental trees pollarded in the 1970s by the Forestry Commission in their effort to rediscover this old skill. Walkers' trails are laid out near the car park at the north end of the drive.

The Ornamental Drive is a long, fairly hard haul, but later you descend a delightfully snaking lane along a typical New Forest shallow valley or 'bottom'. The views from **Picket Post**, extending to Dorset, have marshy bottoms in the foreground, but a firmer one can be found by the river in Linford Bottom which is a favourite for picnics and paddling.

Several flat heaths were made into airfields in World War II. The simple wooden **Canadian Cross** is where men of the Canadian air force held services until they took part in the D-day invasion. Dame Alicia Lisle of **Moyles Court**, one of the infamous Judge Jeffreys' first victims, was beheaded despite her age of about seventy, for harbouring rebels after the battle of Sedgemoor. Her name is remembered in an inn which serves food a little further along the route.

The Breamore Loop

This loop explores the fields and buttercup meadows of the Avon valley. There are more thatched cottages here, as you might expect in an area with reeds closer to hand. The valley lanes are flat, but you must climb about 100 ft (30 m) to **Castle Hill**, an excellent viewpoint overlooking a great curve of the river. From the bridge beside picturesque Breamore Mill you can see how swift and clear the river is, the water-weeds harbouring food for swans, ducks and geese.

Breamore Mill stands on the site of an earlier mill which was used by the monks of Breamore Priory. The Priory disappeared in Henry VIII's Dissolution, but Saxon **Breamore Church** which they served, remains. It contains many heraldic plaques, and the workings of the wooden bell tower can be seen. Next door is **Breamore House** (open), an Elizabethan Manor House with a carriage museum and teashop. A track from the house leads about a mile (1½ km) up to a well-kept turf maze in a clump of trees. No-one is quite sure what it was for, but crawling its length may have been a penance. It may look small, but if you walk it, you will appreciate its unravelled length! In the nearby village of **Upper Street**, notice the old granary, perched on mushroom-shaped staddle stones to prevent vermin from eating the grain.

After a stretch of undulating terrain you reach **Rockbourne Roman Villa** and its interesting little museum.

THE BOLDRE ROUTE

Over the centuries, the land beside Lymington River was gradually 'stolen' from the Forest to be farmed, and the pastoral scenes around Boldre contrast with the open heaths towards Hatchet Pond. The hardest climb is only about 100 ft (30 m), so your greatest annoyance will probably be from bursts of traffic on the B roads.

St Nicholas Church, one of the two New Forest churches listed in the Normans' Domesday survey of properties in conquered England, even incorporates some Roman masonry. Beside it stands a thousand year-old yew, and in the churchyard is the grave of 'Brusher' Mills, an eccentric snake-catcher whose gravestone depicts his lifestyle.

Near **Boldre** the route passes Spinners (open), a garden featuring unusual plants including blue poppies. There are many theories as to where the name 'Boldre' came from. I like to think that it came from 'boulder' meaning 'bulrush', for downstream and further along the ride Lymington

River widens between great fringes of reeds and rushes. This is a nature reserve, and you may see bundles of reeds awaiting use in thatching.

Lymington was a trading station in 1000 B.C. and rivalled Southampton and Portsmouth under the Norman Barons, but today it is a charming yachting port. Cobbled Quay Hill and the wide main street have attractive Georgian buildings, many now being craft shops, tea shops and restaurants, and good fish and chips can be found.

The heathland B roads afford wide views, with the Isle of Wight hills in the distance. Hatchet Pond, a pleasant spot to stop and relax, has developed from marl-pits dug long ago by farmers hoping to improve their poor soils by the addition of marl. **Beaulieu** is not far from Hatchet Pond and is signposted from it.

The Keyhaven Loop

This loop ventures toward an area of seaside resorts, so it is not really a rural ride (although there are occasionally some pretty scenes), but it has some unusual points of interest. The route-finding is rather fiddly in parts too, so have patience.

Just after you leave the main road out of Lymington, you can see a long, low, tree-covered slope in a field to your right. It is one face of **Buckland Rings**, a seven acre prehistoric camp.

Sway Tower was built by an avid supporter of Portland cement. His intention was to show critics that the material was both strong and attractive, and the strange, slender tower does indeed have pleasing detail. In the area several buildings bear versions of the name Arnewood, home of Captain Maryatt's *Children of the New Forest*.

Beyond Lymore a pleasant lane with views of the Isle of Wight hills, leads to tiny **Keyhaven** village. You can sit outside the Gun Inn, which serves snacks, and gaze at the yachts in the little harbour, or you can take the ferry to the end of Hurst Spit and **Hurst Castle**. Alternatively cycle ½ mile south west, and walk along the Spit, where the open sea on one side contrasts with the stillness of marshy Solent waters on the other side. At the end, stark Napoleonic defences surround a Tudor fortress (DoE, open) where Charles I was imprisoned. Especially impressive is the utter pitch-darkness of the munitions cellar.

The track back to Lymington skirts a marshy area, now rather overgrown, but previously used to make salt by the evaporation of sea-water. These Salterns were an important source of wealth to Lymington until competition from the Cheshire salt mines grew.

The Bucklers Hard Loop

East of Lymington peaceful lanes wander through a flat and prosperous farming area. Before the Dissolution, the Cistercian monks of Beaulieu

Abbey were powerful landowners. Sowley Pond, with its softly wooded banks was formed by the damming of two streams to serve as their fish-pond. The area is dotted with rambling red-brick farms. **Bergerie**, a typical example, derives its name from the french 'Berger' for 'shepherd', since it was once a sheep-farm belonging to the French Cistercian order. At **St Leonards** the massive stone gable-ends remain to show us just how huge their tithe barn was.

Beaulieu itself is a pretty village of tile-hung, gabled houses. The church was the abbey refectory, and you can still see the stone pulpit where one of the brothers would read out religious texts during meals. The Abbey (open) has been the home of the present Duke of Montague's ancestors since they bought it for £1350 6s 8d at the Dissolution. It now incorporates a magnificent motor museum, with exhibits ranging from old cycles to land-speed record-breaking cars.

Bucklers Hard (open) was planned by the Second Duke of Montague to be a sugar-refining port, using New Forest timber for fuel and sugar shipped from his property on the islands of St Vincent and St Lucia. Only the port's spacious main street had been built when England lost the islands through a treaty, leaving Bucklers Hard as one of the country's oddest villages. Later it was famed for ship-building, again using New Forest timber, and there is now a maritime museum here. Refreshments are available, and cruises run on Beaulieu River.

Beyond Beaulieu the ride continues to be flat, first across a great heathland expanse, and then on a track through beech and oak woods, and past conifer plantations where you might well spot a deer or two. If you don't feel like using the track, cut from Beaulieu to the Boldre Route at Hatchet Pond by following signs for Brockenhurst. Six times a year the **Beaulieu Road Station** Sales are held, when New Forest ponies are rounded up and auctioned.

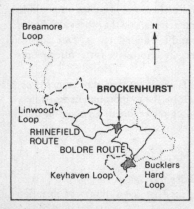

RHINEFIELD ROUTE
15½ miles (25 km)
anticlockwise

BROCKENHURST. Leave from the Watersplash on Rhinefield Road. Cont past the Forest Park Hotel. Follow the **Ornamental Drive**. Reach

a. Join the Linwood Loop, or cont. Leave

a (Ringwood, Bournemouth). R (Burley 4¾, Ringwood 9½). Cont (Ringwood). Reach

c. The Linwood Loop rejoins the

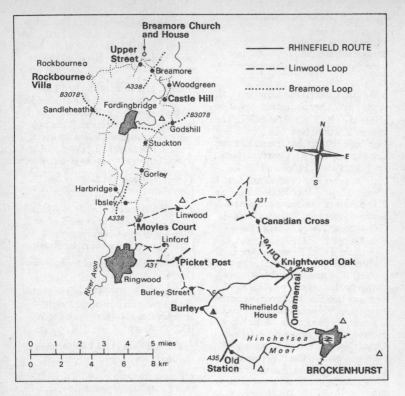

Rhinefield Route. Leave

c. (Burley, Christchurch). Cont (Burley ½). Cont at next junction. Enter

Burley. L (Lymington, Brockenhurst). Cont at the next junction. Cont (Brockenhurst 6¾, Lyndhurst 8, Lymington 8½). Cont (Brockenhurst 5¼) (many other destinations are given too). Pass the **Old Station**. Cont (Sway 3¾, Brockenhurst 5¼, Lymington 7½). Cont (Sway 2½, Brockenhurst 3¾, Lymington 6¼). Cont (Brockenhurst 3¼). Cont (Brockenhurst 3¼). Pass through Hinchelsea Moor. Cont at all junctions.

Linwood Loop
adds 13 miles (21 km)
anticlockwise

Leave

a (Bolderwood Arboretum, Ornamental Drive). Pass **Knightwood Oak.** L at T junction. Pass the **Canadian Cross.** Go through an underpass. Cont (Linwood 2½, Moyles Court 4). Reach

b **Moyles Court.** *Join the Breamore Loop, or cont.* Leave

b. (Rockford ½, Poulner 1½). Cont (Rockford ½, Poulner 1½). Cont (Ringwood 2½). Cont (Ringwood). Cont (Ringwood). L (Linford 1¼, Shobley 1¾). L (Linford ½, Shobley 1). L on dual carriageway. R (Burley 2½) at **Picket Post.** L (Burley 1¼, Brockenhurst 7½). L (Lyndhurst via Ford 7¼). Reach

c. Rejoin the Rhinefield Route.

Breamore Loop
adds 18 miles (29 km)
anticlockwise

Leave

b **Moyles Court**. (Mockbeggar ½, N. Gorley 2½). Cont at next junction. Cont (North Gorley 1½, Stuckton 2¾). Cont at next junction. Cont (To Fordingbridge). Cont at next junction. Cont (Stuckton 1¾). Cont (Stuckton 1¾). R (Hyde 1, Frogham 1¾). L (Stuckton ¾). Cont at next junction. L (Fordingbridge 1¼). R (Godshill 1½). R at next junction onto the main road, *not* hard right onto Blissford Road. L (Woodgreen 1¾). L (Castle Hill ½). Pass **Castle Hill**. L (Woodgreen). L (Breamore 1). R (Downton 2¼). L (Whitsbury 3½). Where the road bends L, bear R to pass to the R of a house with 4 central chimney stacks. L opposite the 'Saxon Church' sign *otherwise detour 300 yards (metres), R (Saxon Church), for* **Breamore Church and House**. Cont at next junction. Enter **Upper Street**. Cont (Whitsbury). R (Whitsbury 1½). Cont (Rockbourne 2, Damerham 3). Cont (Rockbourne 2½). L (Sandleheath 1½, Fordingbridge 3) *otherwise detour 100 yards (metres) R to* **Rockbourne Villa**. L (Fordingbridge 2, B3078). Cont (Fordingbridge 1½). R (Cottage Hospital). Cont (Somerley 4). L (Harbridge 1½, Ibsley 2). Cont at next junction. L (Ibsley ½, Ringwood 4). R (Ringwood, A338). L (Mockbeggar ¾, South Gorley 1¼). R (Moyles Court ½, Linwood 2¼). Reach *b* **Moyles Court**. *Rejoin the Linwood Loop.*

BOLDRE ROUTE
17 miles (27 km)
anticlockwise

BROCKENHURST. Leave from the level crossing (Lymington 4, A337). L (St Nicholas Parish Ch). Pass **St Nicholas**. Cont across the main road onto a 6' 6'' width restriction road. Cross a cattle grid and turn R at the T junction. Cont (New Milton 6, B3055,

Sway 1¾). L (Boldre 2½. Lymington 4). R (Lymington 3, A337). First L on Lower Sandy Down. Cont at the next three junctions. At the end of Lower Sandy Down, R at the T junction. Enter

Boldre. L in front of the Red Lion. Cont at the next junction. R (Vicars Hill ½, Portmore 1¼, S. Baddesley 2¼). Cont at the next junction. R at a junction by a small green with an oak tree. R at the T junction. R (Lymington 1 and several other destinations given). Reach

d. Join the Keyhaven Loop, or cont.
Leave

d. Follow signs for the Isle of Wight Ferry *otherwise detour ½ mile (1 km) following (Town Centre) signs for* **Lymington**. Cross the river. Reach.

e. Join the Bucklers Hard Loop, or cont.
Leave

e. (Beaulieu 6, B3054). Cont following the B3054 at all junctions. Reach Hatchet Pond. L (Brockenhurst 5, B3055). Reach

f. The Bucklers Hard Loop rejoins the Boldre Route. Leave

f. Follow the tarmac road (the B3055) so that Roundhill campsite is to the L of the road. L (Brockenhurst 1).

Keyhaven Loop
adds 11 miles (18 km)
anticlockwise

Leave

d (Lyndhurst 8¾, Southampton 18, Bournemouth 17½). L (Lyndhurst, B'mouth, A337, So'ton, A35). Cont along East Hill. R (Lyndhurst 8, A337, Southampton 17, A35). L (Sway 2¾, Hordle 3½). Pass **Buckland Rings**. Cont (Hordle 3, New Milton 4½). Cont (Hordle 2¼, New Milton 4). R (Sway 1½). L to cross a white-railed bridge. Reach **Sway Tower**. L on Barrows Lane. R (New Milton, Christchurch). L on Woodcock Lane. L (Everton 1M, Lymington 4M). L on Frys Lane. R by Everton Post Office. Cont (Milton on Sea 1½). R at the T junction. L (Hurst

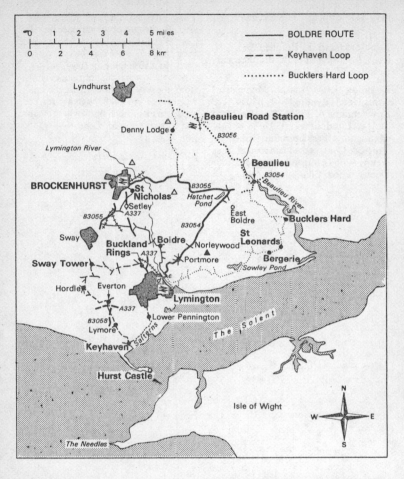

Castle, Ancient Monument). Cont at the next three junctions. L on School Lane. L (Keyhaven). Enter

Keyhaven. Ferry or walk to **Hurst Castle**. L on a 6' 6'' restriction road. Cont past an 'Unsuitable for Motor Vehicles' sign. Skirt the Salterns where the tarmac lane becomes an earth track. At the corporation dump, cont on the tarmac lane. Cont on Lower Pennington Lane. R (Lymington 1, Lyndhurst 9, Southampton 18, A337). Follow the (Town Centre) signs. Reach

d **Lymington**. *Rejoin the Boldre Route.*

Bucklers Hard Loop
adds 9½ miles (15 km)
anticlockwise

Leave

e (IOW Ferry ½ and several other destinations given). Cont past the ferry terminal. Cont at the next five junctions. Cont on South Baddesley Road. R (Sowley 1¼, Bucklers Hard 5). L (Sowley 1, Bucklers Hard 4½). Pass Sowley Pond. R (Bucklers Hard 2¾, Beaulieu 4¾). Cont (Bucklers Hard 2¾, Beaulieu 4¾). Pass **Bergerie**. Cont to

73

pass **St Leonards**. R (Bucklers Hard ¾). Reach

Bucklers Hard. L (Beaulieu 2½). Cont, following signs for Beaulieu and Beaulieu Village. Reach.

Beaulieu. Leave from the Montagu Arms Hotel (Lymington 7, B3054, Brockenhurst 6, B3055, Bucklers Hard 2½). R (Lyndhurst 7, B3056). Cont at all junctions. Pass **Beaulieu Road Station**. Cont on the main road as far as Denny Wood campsite entrance. L into Denny Wood. Cont past the 'No Through Road, Denny Lodge only' sign. At the end of the tarmac, fork L. Cont through a gate into 'Denny Lodge Inclosure'. You are now on a forestry track on which the Forestry Commission allow walking but not cycling. Cont at every junction. Cross the railway bridge and go through a gate. You are again on a gravel track where cycling and cars are allowed. Cont at every junction. Reach

f. Rejoin the Boldre Route.

The Lock-up at Castle Cary

SOMERSET

Associated with the legendary kings Arthur and Alfred, these landscapes of Somerset (and parts of Devon) have a haunting quality. Though pretty with little orchards and Ham stone buildings, the farmlands gain a timeless atmosphere from the lonely turf-clad hills. Glastonbury Tor is the most famous of these and is easily visible across the miles of flat Somerset Levels which man has drained from the marshes to form rich pastures. Empty but for the willows beside these drainage channels or 'rhines', the Somerset Levels merge to the south with rolling fertile hills, whilst the Mendip ridge rises 1000 ft (300 m) high to the north. Exploring all three areas, the routes cross terrains ranging from a steep 600-ft (200-m) ascent, to mile after mile on the flat.

Short stretches of busy roads take you to some outstandingly interesting places, but on the whole you ride on peaceful lanes. The network hereabouts is exceptionally complex, and some junctions are not signposted, so do take time over your route-finding.

Homely rather than picturesque, the loose-knit villages rarely offer food, as the region is not often explored by tourists. Lush pastures make this excellent dairying country, a fact highlighted by a warning notice which reads 'Caution, cattle crossing, slippery road'!

Easy to moderately strenuous cycling. Very quiet but with a few stretches of busy roads.

CASTLE CARY

Location: 25 miles (40 km) south of Bristol.

Trains: Castle Cary Station is on the main line from London through Reading to Exeter and Penzance. London: 2 hours 15 mins; Bristol: 1 hour 15 mins; Cardiff: 2 hours 30 mins.

Tourist Information Bureaux: Town Hall, Market Place, Wells, Somerset, tel: (0749) 72552 (summer service only, accommodation service) and Taunton Area Library, Corporation Street, Taunton, Somerset, tel: (0823) 84077 (accommodation service).

Accommodation: Hotel and bed and breakfast accommodation is available in Castle Cary. The nearest YH, is at Street, 3 miles (5 km) from Glastonbury. There are campsites at Wookey Hole, Priddy, Glastonbury and Sparkford.

Cycle-hire: The nearest are at Taunton Holiday Cycle Hire, 10 Queens Down, Creech St Michael, Taunton, Somerset, tel: (0823) 442728 and Quantock Rent-a-Bike, Rowford Cottage, Cheddon Fitzpaine, Taunton, tel: (082 345) 248. Both the above are about 3 miles (5 km) from Taunton, which is on a direct train link with Castle Cary.

Cycle-shop: Berni Hockey, on the Bath road in Castle Cary.

Maps: OS 1:50 000 (nos 182, 183); Bartholomew's 1:100 000 (nos 4, 7); OS 1:250 000 (no. 8).

Castle Cary

Castle Cary prospered as a wool spinning and weaving town before the innovations of the Industrial Revolution gave northern towns the advantage. Many pleasing houses survive from that time. Most are built in the glowing brown stone typical of the area, which is quarried from the nearby Ham Hills. The sixteenth-century George Inn stands near the arcaded market and town hall, which is now used as the local museum. A single tiny window lights an old lock-up whose diameter is a mere 7 ft (2 m).

It is pleasant to stroll through the old streets, but take care at the kerbs, as some of the pavements (called 'batches') are built unusually high. Look out too, for the swans that sit on the pavement by the old horse-pond and war memorial. There are several antique shops, a couple of pubs which serve meals, and a fish and chip shop.

Earlier this century, schoolchildren made a delightful mosaic of Christ and two angels in the church, which also has a richly carved pulpit.

Hadspen House lies 2 miles (3 km) south-east of Castle Cary on the A371, and its gardens (open) specialise in trees with interesting bark or foliage.

THE GLASTONBURY ROUTE

Elm tree skeletons look gaunt in the otherwise soft lowlands around Castle Cary where sheep and cows graze contentedly in the orchards and fields. There is a vineyard at **Wraxall** where the Queen's Arms serves food.

This cosy landscape gradually gives way to the Somerset Levels' lush emptiness near **Baltonsborough**, where a shell makes an unusual war memorial, and a mellow stone gatehouse is prettily roofed with thatch. Thereafter your route is haunted by Glastonbury Tor, rising beyond willows and the flowery pastures which stretch unbroken for miles. The lanes which are deserted and flat (although flanked by a gentle sweep of parkland near Butleigh Wootton), twist alongside the River Brue on the way to West Bradley. There you begin climbing the low hills, before tackling the route's hardest climb of 200 ft (60 m).

The fifteenth-century **Court Barn** (NT) has buttresses of pale stone, and an interesting roof construction which you can see by asking the tenant of the nearby house to let you in. **Ditcheat** church is unusually weather-conscious, being equipped with both a weathercock and a tall sundial cross. An ancient cross at **Alford** surmounts a four-tiered plinth.

Glastonbury is the ancient Avalon where, according to legend, King Arthur and Queen Guinevere were reburied in the abbey (open). Amidst its ruins stands a delightful eight-sided stone building which was the abbot's kitchen. Legend also says that Joseph of Arimathea buried the Holy Grail (the chalice used at the Last Supper), below a spring on the Tor, and that when he stuck his staff in the ground it grew once again as the winter-flowering Glastonbury Thorn. Pilgrims to the hallowed place often stayed at the fifteenth-century George Inn, which together with several restaurants and cafés, cater for the many tourists who visit the town today. In the High Street an old drinking fountain is carved with the sign 'Police Notice. Commit no Nuisance', and the old Tribunal (DoE, open) houses finds from prehistoric lake villages of the Somerset Levels. Centred on the fourteenth-century abbey barn, the Somerset Rural Life Museum includes cider-making equipment amongst its displays.

The Wells Loop

Before the draining of the Somerset Levels, the ground was a marshy waste, where prehistoric man sought protection from sudden attack by living in villages built on stilts. Slight mounds and a couple of plinths in a field to your right, are the only hints of the **Lake Village** south of Godney. Godney itself was built on a ridge which although only a few yards high still offers protection from floods.

Low hills rise from the Levels near Launcherley and Fenny Castle. Their austerely natural lines remain uncluttered by man, save for defensive motte and bailey earthworks topping the knoll to the right of the road near **Fenny Castle**.

The pale limestone of the Mendip Hills can be seen in the many dry-stone walls which pattern the Mendip plateau, and also in a large but pleasingly simple mill at **Wookey Hole**, where high-grade paper has been made since 1610. There, too, is the entrance to a huge cave system (open), where Iron Age implements have been found amongst the rock formations. Many tourists come here, and a pub serves food.

An old road sign in Wookey Hole warns that the road climbing 600 ft (200 m) onto the Mendip ridge is unsuitable for charabancs. It is hard work for cyclists too, but the views over the Levels to Glastonbury Tor and the Quantock Hills in the south west, and Wales in the north west, make it worthwhile. Nature trail leaflets for the **Ebbor Gorge** nature reserve are available at the car park, but you need a good hour to explore its wooded limestone wilderness.

Although so short of water, the Mendip plateau standing safe above the marshes with easily defensible sites, was favoured by prehistoric man, and burial barrows can be seen as mounds on the skyline near **Priddy**. The Queen Victoria offers food there.

Though less imbued with legend than Glastonbury, **Wells** is a more gracious city. Its fine twelfth-century cathedral has a medieval clock where knights joust on the hour, and the precinct's lawns are entered through Penniless Porch where the needy used to beg for alms. Slender octagonal chimneys adorn the fiteenth-century terrace in Vicars Close, whilst the Bishop's Palace (open) is surrounded by shady gardens and a moat, where swans ring a bell for food. The local museum has a display of rocks and fossils of the Mendips, and there is a brass-rubbing centre.

This loop is forced to use busy A roads for a couple of miles around Wells and Glastonbury, but otherwise it keeps to quiet lanes.

THE CADBURY CASTLE ROUTE

Undulating, wooded farmlands lie south and east of Castle Cary, and can be explored by both these rides on peaceful lanes which rise and fall over 300-ft (100-m) hills. Food cannot be bought on this route, so take provisions with you.

A narrow lane to North Cadbury passes through orchards beside a stream, where an old cottage still has a mill wheel. **North Cadbury** Court is Elizabethan, and remains in view above your valley road to Compton Pauncefoot. Home Farm at North Cadbury has a quaintly warped roof, whilst that of a chapel by the A359 is of thatch. A charming lane descends from North Cadbury with views ahead to tree-fringed Cadbury Castle hill.

The church of South Cadbury nestles beside it, and is dedicated to Saint Thomas à Becket who was murdered in Canterbury Cathedral.

Cadbury Castle is believed by some to have been King Arthur's court of Camelot and remains from the Stone and Iron Ages, and the Roman and Anglo-Saxon eras have been unearthed here. Climb a steep footpath signposted near the church, and you will pass magnificent earthworks to the flat summit, where cows graze oblivious to the far-ranging views.

Linger awhile in **Bruton** to seek out the roofless dovecote (NT) and the tiny pack-horse bridge hidden amidst a jumble of houses and the stone buildings of a seventeenth-century hospital. The church has a lacey stonework tower, and there are flood-level marks on the churchyard wall.

From Bruton, your road is narrow with steep, flowery banks on either side. Enjoy the views of rambling Gants Mill, but do not ride too fast, as you will have to stop and struggle past any car you should happen to meet. As you ride up a sheltered little valley at **Honeywick**, notice the vineyards on a south-facing slope to your right.

The Stourhead Loop

This loop continues through gentle farming country, although empty turf-clad hills sweep upwards both at White Sheet Hill, and near Corton Denham where a climb rewards you with a lovely view past Cadbury Castle, across the Levels, to Glastonbury Tor.

As far as Bourton your ride crosses a succession of broad valleys and ridges. Cucklington commands wide views from the ridge's 300-ft (100-m) edge, whilst white-turretted **Shank's House** shelters below. Curious catches on its gates are designed so that a horse-rider can work them without dismounting. **Horsington's** Ham stone market cross is said to date from the thirteenth century, and the church is worth a visit too.

After Zeals (where a pub serves food), you must pick you way through a maze of lanes overlooking a richly-wooded valley and many lakes. A stone arch spanning your road and a temple standing beside it are but forerunners of the splendid Stourhead mansion (NT, open). Its romantic lakes, temples, statues and colourful gardens, are a magnificent setting for this fine Palladian house. **Stourton** village churchyard has a mausoleum to the Hoare family of Stourhead, and their double-headed eagle is carved even on the buildings now serving as a restaurant and craft shop.

The B3092 is quiet, and the lane beyond is lined with lovely beech trees. In the gentle valley to your left, look out for a grotto which stands over the **Stour Head**; fount of the waters which fill Stourhead's beautiful lakes.

In 878 King Alfred raised his standard to gather an army against the invading Danes. His choice of Kingsettle Hill was a good one: the spot is visible for miles and is now marked by the triangular **King Alfred's Tower**.

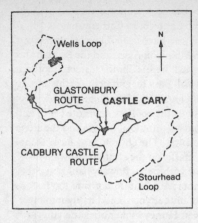

GLASTONBURY ROUTE
25½ miles (41 km)
clockwise

CASTLE CARY. Leave from pond and war memorial (Shepton Mallet 8, Bath 26, Bristol 28). L (A371, Bath, Bristol). L (North Barrow 3, Lovington 3½, Somerton 10). R (Alford 1¾, Somerton 10). L (Alford 1¼, Somerton 9½). Cont through Alford *or turn R opposite pillar box to detour 400 yards (metres) to* **Alford** *church*. R (Hornblotton 1½). L (Hornblotton 1¼). Cont at next junction. Cont (Lottisham 1, Baltonsborough 3½, Glastonbury 5). L (Southwood 1, and other directions overgrown by the hedge). R (Southwood 1, Baltonsborough 2½). R (Baltonsborough 1, West Pennard 3¾). L (Baltonsborough 1, Butleigh 3). Cont at next junction. Enter

Baltonsborough. L (Butleigh 2, Street 4¾). L (Butleigh 1½, Street 4½). R (Glastonbury 3½, Street 3¾). R (Street 2½, Glastonbury 3). R (Glastonbury 1¼). L (Glastonbury ¼, Wells 6¼). Cont (Town Centre and Abbey Ruins). Cont (A39, Wells). Reach

a **Glastonbury** market cross. *Join the Wells Loop, otherwise cont.* Leave

a. Leave Glastonbury from the market cross by the Crown Hotel (Wells,

Bristol, A39). R (A361, Shepton Mallet). L (Shepton Mallet 9). R on Cinnamon Lane, which is easy to miss, but is just beyond a L turn signposted 'To the Tor'. R at next junction to head towards a column in a distant tree-gap. L at T junction by pillar box. R (West Bradley 1¼, West Pennard 1½). R (East Pennard 4¼, West Bradley 1) *otherwise L to detour 500 yards (metres) to* **Court Barn**. R (Baltonsborough 1). L (Farbrook 1, East Pennard 3¼). Cont (East Pennard 2½, Ditcheat 4¼). Cont (East Pennard 2½, Ditcheat 4¼). Cont (East Pennard 2, Shepton Mallet 7½). Cont (Ditcheat 3, Castle Cary 6¼). Cont (Ditcheat 2, Castle Cary 5¼). Cont at next junction. Enter

Wraxall. Cont (Ditcheat 1½, Castle Cary 4¾). Enter

Ditcheat. R (Alhampton 1¼, Castle Cary 3½). R (Alhampton 1, Castle Cary 3¼). Cont at next junction. L (Castle Cary 2¼). R (Castle Cary 2). Cont (Castle Cary 1½). R at T junction. Sharp L (Castle Cary). R (Castle Cary, B3152).

WELLS LOOP
adds 22 miles (35 km)
clockwise

Leave

a **Glastonbury** market cross (B3151, Meare, Godney). R (Godney). Cont at next junction. Reach the

Lake Village. Cont to cross bridge with white railings. Cont (Panborough 2½, Wedmore 5¼). R (Fenny Castle 1¼, Wookey 3, Wells 4½). R (Fenny Castle ¾, Wookey 2½, Wells 4). Cont at next junction. Pass **Fenny Castle** on your R. Cont (Wookey 1½, Wells 3½). Cont at next junction. R at a triangular road junction with a house in it. R at T junction. Cont (Wells 2¼, B3139). L (Wookey), by Burcott Inn. Enter Wookey. R (Haybridge 1, Wookey Hole 2¼). Cont on road with 'Unsuitable for heavy vehicles' sign. L (Easton 1¼, Cheddar 6¼) *otherwise turn R at end of Titlands Lane to detour 300 yards*

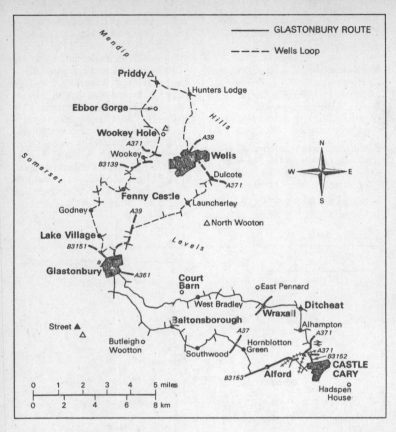

GLASTONBURY ROUTE

Wells Loop

(*metres*) *to* **Wookey Hole**. R on a 'Single Track road with passing places'. Pass car parks for **Ebbor Gorge**. Enter

Priddy. R (Wells 6). R by Hunters Lodge on a road 'Unsuitable for heavy goods vehicles'. L at T junction. R on New Street. Cont (Glastonbury, A39). Enter the centre of

Wells. Leave Wells from St Andrews St at single tower end of cathedral (A371, Shepton Mallet). R (North Wootton 2¼, Coxley 2¾). Cont (Coxley 2¾). Go under railway bridge then turn L. L at T junction to go uphill. Cont at cross roads to pass Launcherley Farm. First R, crossing white lines. Cont at next junction. L at T junction with main

road. R (A39, Glastonbury). R (Town Centre, Abbey Ruins). Reach

a **Glastonbury**. *Rejoin the Glastonbury Route.*

CADBURY CASTLE ROUTE
**19 miles (31 km)
anticlockwise**

CASTLE CARY. Leave from pond and war memorial. (Shepton Mallet 8, Bath 26, Bristol 28). L (A371, Bath, Bristol). L (North Barrow 3, Lovington 3½, Somerton 10). Cont (North Barrow 2¾, Babcary 6). Cont at next junction. Cont to cross railway bridge, then turn L. L at T junction to cross railway bridge. Cont (Yarlington 1¾). Cont past March

81

Lane. First R. Cont at next junction (*not* L to cross stream). L (South Cadbury 1¼, Woolston 1½). Enter

North Cadbury. Cont (South Cadbury 1) *otherwise detour 300 yards (metres)*, *L (Woolston 1¼). R To the church, for North Cadbury manor house.* Cont (South Cadbury ½, Sutton Montis 1½, Compton Pauncefoot ¼). Reach

b Red Lion, South Cadbury. *Walk up a signposted track beyond the church for* **Cadbury Castle.** *Join the Stourhead Loop, otherwise cont.* Leave

b (Compton Pauncefoot 1). Cont at next junction. Bear L into village. Cont at

next 2 junctions. L (Wincanton 5). R (Andover, London, Honiton, Exeter, A303). Cont (Bruton, A359). L (Bruton, A359). R (Bruton, A359). L (Yarlington 2). Cont (Yarlington 1½, Bruton 5). Cont (Wincanton 3½, Castle Cary 3¼, Bruton 4¼). Cont at next junction. Cont (Shepton Montague 1½, Bruton 3). Cont (Shepton Montague ¾, Bruton 3¾). Cont (Bruton 2½, Frome 13½). Pass views ahead to **Alfred's Tower**. Cont at next junction. Enter Shepton Montague. Cont at next junction. R (Redlynch 2¼, South Brewham 4¾). L (Redlynch 2¼, South Brewham 4¼). R at T junction by Chequers House. Reach

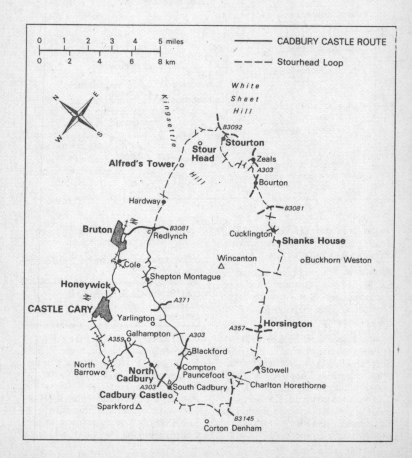

c. The Stourhead Loop rejoins the Cadbury Castle Route. Leave

c (Bruton 1½, Frome 12, B3081). Cont at next junction. Enter

Bruton. Cont on Silver Street. Cont (Yeovil, Frome, A359, Shepton Mallet, A371, Sparkford, A303). L (Sparkford, A303). R on Gants Mill Lane, which is easy to miss. R at T junction to go under railway bridge. Cont at next junction. R (Castle Cary 1, Ansford 1¼). Pass **Honeywick.** Cont (Castle Cary ¼). Cont Town Centre.

Stourhead Loop
adds 17 miles (27 km)
anticlockwise

Leave

b Red Lion, South Cadbury. Leave uphill to pass the church. Cont at next junction. L (Corton Denham 1¾, Sherborne 7). L (Corton Denham 1¼, Sherborne 5½). Pass drive to Witcombe Farm, then turn next L. R at T junction. L at next junction (*not* ahead to pass along L edge of woods). L (B3145, Charlton Horethorne 1¼, Wincanton 6). First R, crossing white lines. L at T junction. Cont towards hills (*neither* L to church *nor* R to terrace of houses). Cont (Horsington 2¼, Templecombe 3½). Keep L near

railway bridge. Pass church and Plessey research unit. Cont at next junction. L on 6' 6'' width restriction road. L at T junction. R (Horsington). Enter

Horsington. Cont at next 2 junctons. R (Buckhorn Weston 2). L (Cucklington 2). Pass **Shanks House.** R at T junction by Red Gables. Cont at next junction. Enter Cucklington. L at summit *not* sharp L to descend. Fork R *not* ahead to Wincanton and the church. Cont (Bourton 1½). Cont (West Bourton, Bourton 1). Enter Bourton. R (Zeals 1¼). L at slope bottom, into lane with stream behind wall on R. Cont past small factory. L at summit T junction. R at T junction. L and L again to pass church. R at next junction *not* ahead to descend into wooded valley. R at next junction. L (Stourton 1½). R (Stourton, Stourhead). Cont (Stourhead, Stourton). Cont (Stourton 1). Enter

Stourton. Cont (Mere, Frome). L (Maiden Bradley 4, Longleat). L (Alfred Tower, Bruton, Kilmington Common). L (Alfred Tower). Cont at next junction. Pass view L to **Stour Head.** Pass **Alfred's Tower** amidst trees to your L. L (Redlynch 1½, Shepton Montague 3½). Cont to pass Bull Inn. Reach

c. Rejoin the Cadbury Castle Route.

Burford

THE COTSWOLDS

The Cotswold villages were founded on the wealth of medieval wool-merchants whose masons built the local mellow stone houses and churches that make them so famous today. The names and even portraits of the wool merchants are often etched on brasses within the churches they endowed. The drystone walls built to enclose their sheep are crumbling now, and have been replaced by hawthorn hedges which today are more frequently seen surrounding cornfields than animals.

When you bowl along the open ridges or wind along the valleys you will find the going easy, but you will meet hard gradients when you cross the grain of the land, especially in the west where the hills are higher.

The countryside seen from the ridge-tops is fertile yet scarcely populated for farmhouses are rare, and most of the villages are tucked away in sheltered valleys. The lanes are tranquil, particularly those which bear 'Single track only' and 'Unsuitable for Motors' signs. Provided that you are wary of the occasional pot-holes, cycling on them is idyllic.

Moderate cycling. Very quiet but with tourist traffic at times.

BOURTON-ON-THE-WATER

Location: 20 miles (32 km) east of Gloucester.

Trains: The nearest stations are at Moreton-in-Marsh and Kingham, both about 8 miles (13 km) away. London: 1 hour 30 mins; Birmingham: 2 hours (change at Worcester); Bristol: 3 hours 30 mins (change at Hereford).

Coach: A coach connects Cheltenham, Bourton-on-the-Water, Bedford, Cambridge and Norwich.

Tourist Information Bureaux: The Burford Welsh Shop, High Street, Burford, Oxon, tel: (099 382) 2168 (accommodation service), and Council Offices, Moreton-in-Marsh, Gloucestershire, tel: (0608) 50881.

Accommodation: Hotel and bed and breakfast accommodation is available in Bourton-on-the-Water; there is also a Holiday Fellowship house there. The nearest YH is at Stow-on-the-Wold, with others at Cleeve Hill and Charlbury. You can camp at The New Inn, Nether Westcote, Kingham, Oxon, tel: (0993) 830827, 4 miles (7 km) from Bourton-on-the-Water. Prior booking is recommended and if full try Stow-on-the-Wold, 4 miles (7 km) away.

Cycle-hire: Teagues, Sherborne Street, Bourton-on-the-Water, Glos tel: (0451) 20248; Hire-a-Bike, Badger's End, Fosseway, Stow-on-the-Wold, tel: (0451) 31103, and Manor House Antiques, The Square, Stow-on-the-Wold, Glos, tel: (0451) 30379.

Cycle-shop: Teagues, as above.

Maps: OS 1:50 000 (nos 150, 163, and 151 for the Chipping Campden Loop); Bartholomew's 1:100 000 (no. 14); OS 1:250 000 (no. 7 or no. 9).

Bourton-on-the-Water

Like many other Cotswold villages, Bourton-on-the-Water is built on the two banks of a river — the Windrush which placidly flows beneath low stone bridges. Dubbed the 'Blackpool of the Cotswolds', the village is popular with tourists in the daytime, but is more peaceful in the evening.

Nevertheless, the tourist attractions are there for a rainy day. There is a perfumery, and a motor museum in the old mill. Exotic and ornamental birds can be seen in Birdland, where the adjacent gallery displays wildlife pictures by David Shepherd, Sir Peter Scott and other artists, but the most famous attraction is the complete model village behind the Old New Inn. The church has fine twentieth-century oak screens and roof.

Stow-on-the-Wold, a pleasing Cotswold market town with many attractions, is only 4 miles away and accessible by bus.

THE SLAUGHTERS ROUTE

This route follows the ridge overlooking the River Windrush, and returns along its secluded valley. The riding is therefore easy apart from a couple of 300-ft (100-m) rises onto the ridge, and a few steep but short slopes.

Start your ride at a reasonably early hour, and you might see **Lower Slaughter** devoid of tourists (not counting yourselves, of course). Rose-covered cottages with dormer windows overlook little footbridges that cross the river. The mill which used to be driven by the river is an unusual Cotswold building since it was built of red brick and not the local stone.

The lane to **Upper Slaughter** passes buttercup meadows, and the lovely stone manor house. A delicate brass with colour inlay lies in the darkness of the church: small wonder that a plaque records the 'installation of electric light to the glory of God'.

The Rare Breeds Survival Trust runs the **Cotswold Farm Park**, where you can see descendants of the Stone Age Soay sheep, and watch seasonal tasks such as sheep-shearing and harvesting, and heavy-horse work. Farm-cart rides are run, and there is a restaurant.

Temple Guiting is an odd name (Guiting rhymes with lighting) and 'Temple' recalls the founding of the church by the Knights Templars *circa* AD 1170. Inside is an impressive plasterwork Royal Arms, and an old belfry wheel with a note explaining its complex construction in oak, elm and ash.

Recent houses built in Cotswold stone at Kineton look harsh now, but it is pleasing to think of them mellowing in years to come and thereby continuing a tradition. The Halfway House serves food, as does the Black Horse in **Naunton**, a pleasing village of little cottages and stone-walled gardens tucked into the steep-sided valley.

The Chipping Campden Loop

The Cotswold hills climb slowly but inexorably higher towards the north and west, until they drop away abruptly in a scarp. Battlemented **Broadway Tower**, built on the hills' very edge in the Gothic revival style, overlooks Broadway town in the Vale of Evesham, 700-ft (200-m) below. Today scenic footpaths are laid out in the Country Park around it.

This loop continues on the Slaughters Route ridge, crossing lonely country where skylarks can be heard, until a sudden vista reveals **Chipping Campden** spread in the fertile valley below. A superb freewheel takes you to this ancient wool-town of spectacular beauty. Stand on the huge, irregular cobbles of the first Lord Campden's market hall, and you will look under stone arcades along the spacious tree-lined street where every house is a delight. The fourteenth-century Woolstaplers' Hall contains a museum of folk and country tools and bygones, and there are plenty of opportunities for buying food, including fish and chips.

Although there is a little thatch, most of Chipping Campden's walls and roofs are of the golden Cotswold stone. The stone can be seen at the **quarry** nearby but being newly cut it is harsher in colour.

After a long climb out of Chipping Campden passing Broadway Tower, easy lanes lead to **Snowshill**. Here a steep valley cuts back into the scarp, the village nestling in its head and yet commanding impressive views. The church and pub (which serves food) face each other across a green, and Tudor Snowshill Manor (NT, open), with its terraced gardens, and unusual collection of musical instruments, toys and clocks is worth visiting. From Snowshill the ride gradually descends into the valley of the Windrush, which is here, just a young and narrow stream.

The Winchcombe Loop

This is a strenuous loop with several steep climbs, an especially long one rising 400 ft (120 m) back into the hills from Winchcombe at their foot. The first climb on an 'Unsuitable for Motors' lane takes you over a rise to a valley where cars seldom venture, and where peace is assured.

The mixture of Cotswold stone buildings and black and white houses typical of the Vale of Evesham belie **Winchcombe's** position at the meeting of hills and plain. To the right of the T junction where you enter the town, the stocks stand in front of the local museum. The church is well-known for its gargoyles, and inside, three locks secure an ancient almsbox, which can be opened only when three keepers are present. A mouldering yet finely-worked altar cloth embroidered by Katharine of Aragon has her pomegranate emblem.

Katharine Parr, Henry VIII's last wife, once lived at **Sudeley Castle** (open). Pale and battlemented, it is an elegant landmark on the long freewheel down to Winchcombe. It was a Royalist fortress in the Civil War, and today has displays of royal relics, and a William Shakespeare costume collection; the Elizabethan gardens are lovely too. There are tea rooms and a restaurant.

Belas Knap is named from the Old English *bel* meaning beacon and *cnaepp* meaning hill-top. Prehistoric man shifted massive quantities of earth to build this 178-ft (54-m) long burial barrow, and despite his simple tools, the fineness of the dry-stone walling is without rival. The clearly-marked footpath to it climbs steeply so allow yourself at least three-quarters of an hour for the walk.

The green at Guiting Power has a shady chestnut tree and a bench, and there are pubs serving food.

THE WINDRUSH ROUTE

Towards the south and east, the Cotswolds become lower and more expansive, so that this set of rides is easier than the Slaughters set. Even so, this route has two gradual 300-ft (100-m) climbs through Great Rissington and up to Clapton, on the ridges either side of the Windrush valley. Natural features of the land were often chosen as parish boundaries, and here one of the most convoluted in Britain follows the meandering river.

The views from the ridges extend over open cornfields, though they are sometimes blocked by tall bramble hedges. Great Barrington, Windrush and Sherborne are all prettily secluded in the valley and Sherborne House itself serves cream teas.

The Burford Loop

Beyond rambling Taynton village the ride climbs 300 ft (100 m) over 2 miles (3 km). On the broad uplands the crops are protected from damaging winds by long shelter-belts of trees.

A narrow valley winds down to **Swinbrook**, where a weathervane witch sits astride her broom, and the church has interesting storied tombs. Pastures and pollarded willows by the Windrush make charming settings for the stone bridges at Asthall and Swinbrook, and the tiny **Chapel** which stands alone in a field. There is a restaurant in the Maytime Inn at Asthall, and all sorts of facilities for buying food in **Burford.** The town's gracious main street climbs the valley-side, where several of the fifteenth-century and Georgian buildings are now used as book or craft shops. The twin-gabled Tolsey, where fifteenth-century wool-merchants used to meet and confer, now houses the local museum.

An Earl of Warwick built the neat row of almshouses by the church-yard, where distinctive barrel-shaped tombs are adorned with skulls and cross-bones. The church was previously much smaller, and it now shelters a rare Pagan slab (*circa* A.D. 100). Carved with a Celtic goddess, it was placed on what was then the outside wall, perhaps symbolising the exclusion of the old gods from a Christian building.

Northleach Loop

This strenuous loop climbs out of the valley, towards the steeper hills in the west. A deep, winding vale hides the Roman **Chedworth Villa** (NT, open), whose mosaics are amongst Britain's finest. Coln St Dennis and Eastington both nestle in cosy valleys.

Near **Yanworth** the lanes climb and fall through wooded countryside, and take you past Stowell mansion set in a tree-studded park. Faint but distinct, a painted skeleton dances on the wall of Yanworth's simple Norman church. The mechanically minded can wonder at the ancient, iron

'Robin Hood Junior', a stove bristling with gauges including, apparently, an altimeter!

Northleach church is the 'cathedral of the Cotswolds', having the good fortune to have been richly endowed by medieval merchants. Brasses depict their feet resting on wool-sacks, the source of their wealth, and a worn carving of a cat fiddling to three mice is in the south porch, whose Perpendicular splendour is unsurpassed in England, and much appreciated by nesting martins. Northleach has a café and pubs serving food. Although the busy A40 spoils the town, there are some attractive houses both in black and white half-timbering and Cotswold stone.

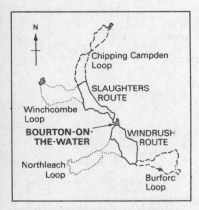

SLAUGHTERS ROUTE
16½ miles (27 km)
anticlockwise

BOURTON-ON-THE-WATER. From the war memorial take the road passing a telephone box and the Butterfly Exhibition. R (Stow, A429). L (Cotswold Farm Park). R (Lower Slaughter 1, Upper Slaughter 1½). R (Lower Slaughter ¼). Enter

Lower Slaughter. L at the T junction. R (Upper Slaughter ¼, Cheltenham 15½). Cont (Upper Slaughter ¼), Cheltenham 15½). L (Cheltenham 15) *otherwise R to detour a few hundred yards (metres) into* **Upper Slaughter**). L (Cheltenham, B4068). R (Cotswold Farm Park). Cont (Snowshill 6, Tewkesbury 18½). Cont (Snowshill 5,

Tewkesbury 17½). Pass the drive to the **Cotswold Farm Park**. Cont (Snowshill 4, Tewkesbury 16½). Reach

a. Join the Chipping Campden Loop, or cont. Leave

a (Tewkesbury 15, B4077). L (Temple Guiting ½). Reach

b **Temple Guiting** *school. The Chipping Campden Loop rejoins the Slaughters Route.* Leave

b (Kineton ¾, Guiting Power 2¾). Reach

c An 'Unsuitable for Motors' turn-off only 100 yards (metres) from b. Join the Winchcombe Loop, or cont. Leave

c Cont on the road away from *b*. Cont (Kineton, Guiting Power 2). Reach

d Lodge gates to Guiting Grange. The Winchcombe Loop rejoins the Slaughters Route. Leave

d (Naunton 1¾, Andoversford 6¼). Cont (Andoversford 6, Cheltenham 12). L (Naunton 1¼, Stow-on-the-Wold 6¼). L (Stow, B4068). L (Naunton ½). Enter

Naunton. Bear R to go through the village. Cont at the next junction. Cont at the next junction (*not* R along the 'Lower Harford Farm only' road). R (The Slaughters, Bourton-on-the-Water 2). Cont (Bourton-on-the-Water 2, The Rissingtons). Cont (Bourton-on-the-Water 1, The Rissingtons). R

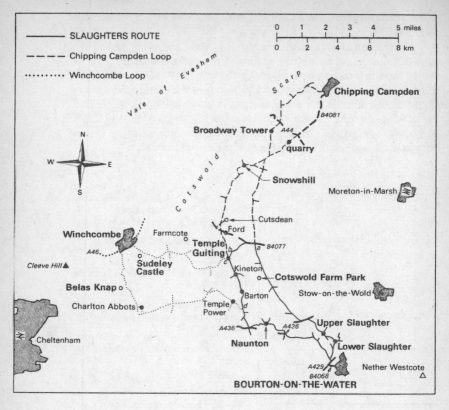

SLAUGHTERS ROUTE
Chipping Campden Loop
Winchcombe Loop

Vale of Evesham
Scarp
Chipping Campden
B4081
Broadway Tower • A44
quarry
Cotswold
Snowshill
Moreton-in-Marsh
o ← Cutsdean
Ford
Farmcote
Winchcombe
Temple Guiting
a B4077
A46
Cleeve Hill ▲
Sudeley Castle
Kineton
o Cotswold Farm Park
Belas Knap o
Stow-on-the-Wold
Charlton Abbots •
Temple Power
Barton
d
Cheltenham
A436
Upper Slaughter
A436
Naunton
Lower Slaughter
A429
Nether Westcote
B4068
△
BOURTON-ON-THE-WATER

(Cirencester, A429). L by the river bridge.

The Chipping Campden Loop
adds 17 miles (27 km) anticlockwise

Leave

a (Snowshill 3½, Broadway 6). Cont (Snowshill 2, Broadway 4). Cont (Snowshill 1½, Broadway 4¼). R (Bourton on the Hill 4½, Moreton in Marsh 6¾). Cont (Broadway Tower 1¾, Chipping Campden 4½). R (Broadway Tower 1¼, Chipping Campden 4). R (Campden). Pass the **Quarry**. Cont (Chipping Campden 2½, B4081). Cont at all junctions. Enter

Chipping Campden. Leave from the Red Lion (Weston-sub-Edge 2). R (Dovers Hill 1, Weston-sub-Edge 1¾, Broadway). L (Willersey 2½, Broadway 3¼). L (Broadway 2¾, Snowshill 4¼). L (Broadway 2¼, Snowshill 2½). Cont (Broadway Tower Country Park). Pass **Broadway Tower**. R (Snowshill). Cont (Snowshill 1, Broadway 3½). R (Snowshill ½, Broadway 3). Cont (Snowshill, Ford 3). Enter

Snowshill. L at the T junction by the church. R (Ford 2½, Stanway 4). Bear L with the white lines on the road at the next junction. Cont (Ford 1½, Stow-on-the-Wold 8½). Cont (Ford ½, Stow-on-the-Wold 7½). Cont (Temple Guiting 1¼, Guiting Power 4). Reach *b* **Temple Guiting** *school. Rejoin the Slaughters Route.*

Winchcombe Loop
adds 10½ miles (17 km)
anticlockwise

Leave

c uphill on a road marked 'Unsuitable for Motors'. After crossing a stream bridge, turn R. L (Winchcombe 2½, Andoversford 7½). Cont (Winchcombe 1¾, Cheltenham 8). Cont at the next junction. R (Winchcombe 1¼, Cheltenham 8¼). Pass views of **Sudely Castle**. Cont at the next 2 junctions. Enter

Winchcombe. L at the T junction. L (Brockhampton 4, Andoversford 6). L (Charlton Abbotts 1¾, Andoversford 4¾). Pass the signposted footpath to **Belas Knap.** L (Charlton Abbots ¼). L (Guiting Power 4, Naunton 6). Cont (Guiting Power 2¾, Naunton 4¾). R (Guiting Power 1¼, Naunton 3¼). Enter Guiting Power. Cont at the next junction. Reach

d Lodge gates to Guiting Grange. Rejoin the Slaughters Route

WINDRUSH ROUTE
13½ miles (22 km)
clockwise

BOURTON-ON-THE-WATER. Leave from the post office (The Rissingtons, The Barringtons, Burford 8). R (Gt Rissington 2, The Barringtons). Cont at the next junction. Enter Great Rissington. Follow signs for (The Barringtons) and (Burford) until you reach Great Barrington. Reach

e Great Barrington. Join the Burford Loop, or cont. Leave

e (Little Barrington ¾, Windrush 1¼). Reach

f. The Burford Loop rejoins the Windrush Route. Leave

f (Windrush ¾, Sherborne 2¼). R

(Sherborne 1¼, Bourton-on-the-Water 6¼). Cont (Sherborne ¼, Bourton-on-the-Water 5¼). Enter Sherborne. Reach

g. Join the Northleach Loop, or cont. Leave

g (Clapton, Bourton-on-the-Water). L (Bourton-on-the-Water). R (Bourton-on-the-Water 2¼, Stow-on-the-Wold 6¼). Reach

h. The Northleach Loop rejoins the Windrush Route. Leave

h (Bourton-on-the-Water 2, Stow-on-the-Wold 6). R (Bourton-on-the-Water 1).

Burford Loop
adds 15 miles (24 km)
clockwise

Leave

e (Taynton 1¾, Burford 3¼). L (Shipton-u-Wychwood 4¼, Stow-on-the-Wold 9½). Cont on a single track road with passing places. L (Milton-u-Wychwood, Shipton). R on a single track road with passing places. Cont (Charlbury 7, B4437, Ascott-u-Wychwood 4). R (Swinbrook 2½). Cont (Swinbrook 2¼). R (Burford). Cont at the next junction. Enter

Swinbrook. Bear R by the telephone box. Next L opposite hydrant 3/SV/7. R at the T junction. R (Asthall). Cont (Asthall, Witney). R to pass the Maytime Inn. R at the T junction at the top of a short slope. Cont (Burford, Fulbrook). Pass view R to the **chapel.** R (Burford 1¼). Enter

Burford. L (Lechlade, Swindon). R just below the Tolsey Museum. Cont past The Lamb. R on a road bearing an 'Except for access and buses' sign. Enter Little Barrington. R at the T junction to pass the telephone box. Reach

f. Rejoin the Windrush Route.

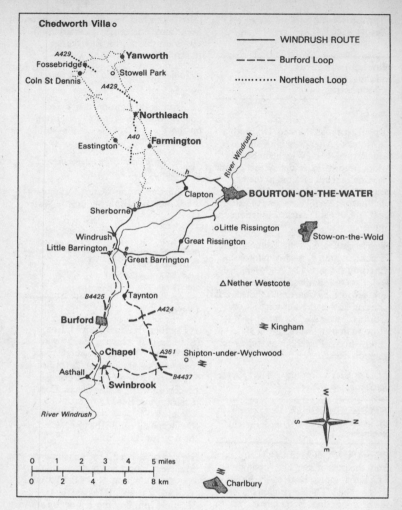

Chedworth Villa ○

A429 ● **Yanworth**
Fossebridge ●
Coln St Dennis · ○ Stowell Park
A429

● **Northleach**

A40
Eastington · ● **Farmington**

River Windrush

h
Clapton
BOURTON-ON-THE-WATER
Sherborne *g*

○ Little Rissington
Windrush
Little Barrington *f* ● Great Rissington
e
Great Barrington
Stow-on-the-Wold

△ Nether Westcote

B4425 ● Taynton
A424

Burford
≋ Kingham

○ **Chapel** *A361*
Shipton-under-Wychwood ○ ≋
Asthall *B4437*
Swinbrook

River Windrush

——— WINDRUSH ROUTE
– – – Burford Loop
··········· Northleach Loop

0	1	2	3	4	5 miles
0	2	4	6	8 km	

≋ Charlbury

Northleach Loop
adds 13½ miles (22 km) clockwise

Leave

g (Farmington 3, Northleach 4¾). Cont by Sherborne war memorial. Cont (Farmington, Turkdean). L (Northleach 2¾, Burford 7¾). R (Cheltenham, A40). L (Eastington 1).

Enter Eastington. Cont at the next 2 junctions. Cont (Fossebridge 3½). R (Northleach 2, Fossebridge 2). L (Coln St Dennis 1, Fossebridge 1½). R (Coln St Dennis, Fossebridge ½). R (Fossebridge ½). Cont (Chedworth 3, Roman Villa 3½, Cirencester 7). L (Roman Villa 3½). Pass Fossebridge. R (Yanworth 1¾, Roman Villa 3½). Cont (Roman Villa, Stowell 1, Yanworth 1). Cont (Yanworth 1¾, Withington 4½).

R (Northleach 3¼) *otherwise on strenuous detour 1½ miles (2½ km) to* **Chedworth Villa**. R at the T junction in Yanworth hamlet. Cont at next junction *otherwise detour 300 yards (metres), L (Church Farm and Church) for* **Yanworth** *church*. Cont (Northleach 2, Stow-on-the-Wold 10). Cont (Northleach 1, Stow-on-the-Wold 9). Cont (Mill End ½). L (Northleach). Enter

Northleach. Leave from the main road (Farmington 1½). R (Farmington ¼, Bourton-on-the-Water 4¼). Enter Farmington. L (Bourton-on-the-Water 4, Stow-on-the-Wold 8). Bear R past a L turning bearing a Gates sign. Reach

h. Rejoin the Windrush Route.

The Almonry in Evesham

THE VALE OF EVESHAM

Sheltered and fertile, the Vale of Evesham makes excellent fruit-growing country. The many orchards are a sea of white blossom in maytime, or rosy with fruit in the autumn. On the other hand there are dreary cabbage fields, glasshouses and some shabby farm buildings; more than any other area in this book, the Vale of Evesham has its faults. These are not routes for those looking for uninterrupted peace and loveliness, but the sight of the picturesque and the historic amidst a working twentieth century landscape gives them a charm nevertheless.

The rich soil has brought prosperity to the Vale of Evesham for centuries, as is evident in the old black and white wattle-and-daub buildings. Thriving farms and market towns mean busy main roads, but most of the lanes are still very quiet. They wander over low, flat or softly rolling farmlands, with occasional views of the Welsh borderland hills to the west. The richly-wooded Cotswolds' edge rises steeply to the south-east, and your only long, hard climb occurs where the Snowshill Loop explores this range.

Easy cycling in parts, moderate in others. Quiet but with a few busy roads.

EVESHAM

Location: 25 miles (40 km) south of Birmingham.

Trains: Evesham Station is on the Worcester to Reading line. Worcester connects with trains to Birmingham, Bristol and South Wales. Reading connects with trains to London and southern England. Birmingham: 1 hour 30 mins (change at Worcester); Cardiff: 2 hours 45 mins (change at Hereford); Bristol: 3 hours (change at Hereford).

Tourist Information Bureau: The nearest is Judith Shakespeare's House, 1 High Street, Stratford-upon-Avon, Warwickshire, tel: (0789) 293127 (accommodation service).

Accommodation: There is hotel and bed and breakfast accommodation in Evesham. The only YH near the routes is the Stratford-upon-Avon hostel, 2 miles (3 km) from the town centre. There is a camp site for caravans but not tents in Evesham. There is a camp site at Broadway on the Dumbleton Route, and two sites near Stratford-upon-Avon.

Cycle-hire: The nearest is at 39 High Street, Broadway, Worcs, tel: (038 681) 2458 on the Dumbleton Route. Cycles are hired to YHA members staying at the Stratford YH and by the following commercial concerns in Stratford: Clopton Bridge, Stratford-upon-Avon, Warwickshire, tel: (0789) 69669; Knotts, Greenhill Street, Stratford; Bancroft Service Station, Guild Street, Stratford, tel: (0789) 69323.

Cycle-shop: Halfords in Evesham. Hodgetts near Workman Bridge in Evesham although not specifically a cycle-shop deals in many spares.

Maps: OS 1:50 000 (no. 150 and no. 151 for the Stratford-upon-Avon Loop); Bartholomew's 1:100 000 (nos 13, 14, 19); OS 1:250 000 (no. 7 or 9).

Evesham

For centuries Evesham has been the major market town for the Vale. The greatest part of the town is rather dull and busy, but pass under the Norman gateway and you enter a different world. Two churches face each other over a smooth lawn, sharing the one massive bell tower which stands alone, a superb example of the English Perpendicular style. An archway through it leads to lawns and the river where boat trips are run.

Scant remains of Evesham Abbey stand in the riverside park. The abbey almoner's duty was to distribute alms to the needy, and the black and white almoner's house is now the local history museum which includes old farm implements amongst its displays. Booth Hall is curiously nicknamed the 'Round House', although its three overhanging half-timbered stories are rectangular. There are several other fine half-timbered buildings, including a 'new' medieval part built over the abbey gateway's Norman foundations.

Evesham has plenty of shops and there are several restaurants, cafés and a cinema.

THE DUMBLETON ROUTE

Although this route keeps to easy lowland roads, it skirts the isolated hills of Bredon and Dumbleton, and the Cotswold range. The lanes are peaceful and the A46 is surprisingly quiet, but you will start out in busy traffic on the A44.

Bredon Hill rises ahead of the orchard-lined road to **Elmley Castle**. The Vale of Evesham boasts a diversity of pleasing building materials, having for centuries used not only the mellow red brick, and bold black and white wattle-and-daub typical of soft-soiled and wooded lowlands, but also honey-hued stone from the Cotswolds. A pretty row of three houses beside Elmley Castle's Queen Elizabeth pub has one example of each.

The Old Manor Farm at **Aston-under-Hill** repeats that harmony and its granary is raised on tall pillars to prevent mice and rats from climbing in. Bredon Springs Gardens (open), have a near-wild profusion of hardy plants.

Dumbleton, too, has varied and lovely buildings, with a thatched bird spreading its fan-tail on one of the roofs. Some thatchers use a bird or animal in this way to 'sign' their work, each thatcher having his own particular creature.

Beyond Dumbleton you bowl along a laburnum avenue, aglow with its 'golden showers' in May. Look up to the Cotswold Hills' horizon, and you will see embattlemented **Broadway Tower** which was built as an eighteenth-century gazebo to command views of several counties.

Broadway itself lies close beneath the hills, and has a wealth of beautiful Cotswold stone buildings. The Lygon Arms housed both Oliver Cromwell and Charles I, the king he overthrew in the Civil War. There are various places serving food in this popular tourist town.

Beyond Willersey's spacious greens, you are cycling through country-side, but from Wickhamford, rather dreary market gardening scenes repeat those near the A44 at the start of the ride.

The Bredon Loop

Bredon Hill was once a part of the Cotswolds, but the erosion of millions of years has worn away at the Cotswolds' edge, isolating the enduring rocky masses of the Bredon and Dumbleton Hills in the lowland plain. Such lonely hills made excellent defensive sites, and you can see the flat-capped earthworks of an Iron-age camp high above Great Comberton. The skeletons of more than fifty brutally murdered people have been discovered in excavations.

This loop skirts Bredon Hill and passes the many currant crops which grow on its lower fields. Gipsies work the fruit harvests, and some camp here all year long. Apart from a series of short, sharp gradients near Great Comberton, the riding on this loop is easy and pleasant, although the B4080 is somewhat dull.

Nash's Farm at **Little Comberton** has a circular medieval dovecote, used today by martins in the summer and apparently by a roosting kestrel in winter. Great Comberton has pretty black and white cottages roofed with thatch; Beckford has a gracious and large Georgian rectory, and at Kemerton, a large message on a wall says: 'Landaus, Waggonettes & Hunters for Hire'.

Approached by spacious parklands, **Overbury** is a charming estate village of stone houses. A vine is trained over one of the trim cottages, and the church's unusual lych-gate shelters a flat-topped tomb-chest, serving both as a war memorial and as a support for coffins.

Pershore is a sleepy but prosperous town of Georgian houses; its wealth based largely upon its plum harvests. Meals can be bought, or you can picnic in the peaceful park beside the abbey church. A cats-cradle for the bell-ringers hangs high inside the splendid fourteenth-century tower, and the lovely Norman font was rediscovered after years of use as a cattle-trough. The medieval Avon bridge was repaired with 'new' differently coloured stonework after its destruction by Charles I's army during the Civil War.

Amongst **Bredon's** attractive buildings is a fine medieval tithe barn (NT, open). Rare old heraldic tiles cover the church's altar steps, and a Crusader's tomb contains the heart of a knight whose body remained in the Holy Land.

The Snowshill Loop

Though short in miles, this loop adds lots of effort to your ride, with a long 600-ft (200-m) climb up the leafy Cotswold scarp. The return freewheel into Broadway is exhilarating, but don't fly along too fast or you will miss **St Eadburgha's** church which contains a balustrade almsbox which can be opened only when the three keepers of the three keys are present at once.

High up on the hills, stone walls pattern the lonely landscape of wide fields and dark woods. The picturesque Cotswold-stone village of **Snowshill** nestles in a dip at the hills' edge, its village green standing between the church and the Snowshill Arms which serves food. A collection of early bicycles is amongst the exhibits in Tudor Snowshill Manor (NT, open).

Stanton is a beautiful village of Cotswold stone houses. From there some easy lanes, through oak-wooded parklands, lead to **Stanway** where a grandiose stone gateway has an oriel window, and some lovely carved wooden doors.

THE ROUS LENCH ROUTE

Do not be dismayed by the busy and rather scruffy start to this ride, for once the A435 is left behind, you climb sharply up 150 ft (50 m) into orchards and hills of great charm.

Amidst **Lenchwick's** new houses are some lovely old buildings. A craft and woollen mill can be visited on the hills near Handgate Farm, from where you can see the whale-backed Malvern ridge in the west.

Tranquil lanes swoop and curve through the farmlands. A castellated tower stands on a crest, the first hint of **Rous Lench** Manor. The rambling, half-timbered house has twisted red chimneys, and gateways which lead to romantic statuary gardens. Rous Lench church has a wonderful Norman carving of Christ, Anglo-Saxon carvings, and *two* Elizabethan oak-wood pulpits. Even the pillar box by the attractive village green has a half-timbered shelter.

Beyond Rous Lench the cycling is easy, first crossing wide, wooded farmlands and then descending through orchards to the Avon valley. Here the B4084 can be busy, although stretches by the placid willow-lined river alternate with the duller parts. Haycombe Farm has an antiques market.

Fladbury church has some fine brasses, which you can rub for a fee. The big red lockside mill stands opposite the landing stage for the old chain ferry. Narrow boats sometimes pass the green, which is a good spot for a picnic; the route passes nowhere selling food.

The Cleeve Prior Loop

This loop passes through a lot of unexciting twentieth-century housing around Broom and Bidford, and from the Middletons back to Evesham. Nevertheless, there are pleasant farmland stretches, and fascinating buildings to be discovered beside the easy roads.

140 ft (45 m) long, the fourteenth-century dry-stone tithe barn (NT, open) at **Middle Littleton** has colossal cruck-built roof timbers. Its echoing hall, still in farm use, stored grain for the Evesham abbots of long ago. Corn is still grown in the Vale of Evesham, and straw has been cunningly worked into a little conical roof in Rous Lench.

The medieval bridge at **Bidford-on-Avon** has massive cutwaters on its upstream side for, though normally placid, the Avon flows fast and is deep after heavy rains. The Romans used to ford the river here.

'Cleeve' is an old word meaning 'cliff', so the names of both Cleeve Prior and Marlcliff reflect the growth of roads and villages on a low but steep-sided ridge, safe above the Avon. There are prosperous stone-built houses at **Cleeve Prior**. The Priors of Worcester were lords of the manor (hence the second part of the name), and the church paid a yearly fee of one peahen to the priory. Marks made by archers sharpening their arrows are clear on the tower's south-west buttress, and to its south a tombstone records Sara Charlett's death at the dubious age of 309! Beyond Cleeve Prior you pass pleasant orchards before returning to Evesham.

Ragley Hall (open), is one of England's most magnificent Palladian mansions. Set in a vast park with a lake and gardens, it is lavishly decorated and furnished, and has a library of great value.

The Stratford-upon-Avon Loop

At first this loop climbs slowly through 200 ft (60 m), past picturesque houses in Ardens Grafton to **Temple Grafton** with its rare, partly half-timbered, church spire. After this the cycling becomes easier passing through gently folded country, where large farm houses and occasional trees can be seen amidst the cornfields.

Beyond Stratford, near-level lanes keep close to the Avon, and take you to **Welford-on-Avon** where a maypole, gaily striped in red, white and blue, stands on the green beside rose-covered, thatched cottages.

Renowned the world over as Shakespeare's birthplace, **Stratford-upon-Avon's** centre is a vigorous blend of quaint black and white houses, Georgian elegance, and functional twentieth-century buildings. A visit to the information bureau will help you choose which of the many historic buildings to see, although the ride virtually passes the cottage of **Anne Hathaway** who was Shakespeare's wife. Food can be easily bought and to escape the incessant bustle of the town you could take it to the park near the theatre, for a quiet picnic.

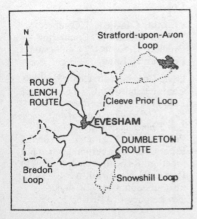

DUMBLETON ROUTE
25 miles (40 km)
anticlockwise

EVESHAM. Leave following the (Worcester, A44 signs). L (Hinton 3). R (Elmley 2, Pershore 6). Cont at next junction. Reach

a **Elmley Castle**. *Join the Bredon Loop, otherwise cont*. Leave

a **Elmley Castle**. (Kersoe, Ashton-U-Hill). L (Kersoe 1, Ashton-Under-Hill 3). L (Ashton-under-Hill 2, Beckford 4). Enter

Ashton-under-Hill. Cont (Grafton 1,

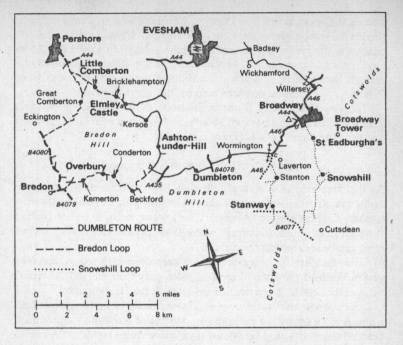

EVESHAM

Pershore

A44

Little
Comberton

Bricklehampton

Great
Comberton

Eckington

Elmley
Castle

Kersoe

Bredon
Hill

B4080

Overbury

Conderton

Ashton-
under-Hill

Wormington

Bredon

Kemerton   Beckford

A435

Dumbleton
Hill

B4079

Badsey

Wickhamford

Willersey

A46

Broadway

A44

A46

Broadway
Tower

St Eadburgha's

Laverton

B4078   A46   Stanton

Dumbleton

Stanway

Snowshill

B4077   Cutsdean

Cotswolds

Cotswolds

—————— DUMBLETON ROUTE

– – – – Bredon Loop

·············· Snowshill Loop

0   1   2   3   4   5 miles

0   2   4   6   8 km

N W E S

Beckford 2). Reach

*b. The Bredon Loop rejoins the Dumbleton
Route. Leave*

b. Leave in the direction opposite to the
road signposted Grafton. R at T junction. L (Dumbleton 1½). Pass through

Dumbleton. Pass views ahead to
Broadway Tower. L (B4078,
Sedgeberrow 2¼, Evesham 5, Broad-
way). R (Wormington ¾, Broadway 5).
L (Aston-Somerville, Broadway). R
(Broadway 4, Stratford on Avon 19).
Reach

*c. Join the Snowshill Loop, otherwise
cont. Leave*

c (Stratford, A46, Broadway 2). Cont on
A46 at all junctions. Reach

d **Broadway**. *The Snowshill Loop
rejoins the Dumbleton Route. Leave*

d following signs for (Stratford, A46).
Enter Willersey. L (Stratford 14, A46).
Cont (Badsey 4). L (Badsey 1½,

Evesham 3½). Cont (Badsey, Evesham
3). L by bus shelter and police station.
L by the Wheatsheaf. R (Evesham).

Bredon Loop
adds 12 miles (19 km)
anticlockwise

Leave

a **Elmley Castle**. (L'' Comberton,
Pershore). Cont (L'' Comberton,
Pershore 4). Cont (L'' Comberton,
Pershore 3). Enter

Little Comberton. Cont (Pershore 2).
Cont (Pershore 2). L (Gt Comberton,
Eckington) *otherwise detour 1 mile (1½
km)*, R (Pershore). Cont at next junction.
L at T junction with main road, for
Pershore. R (Eckington, Bredon).
Enter Great Comberton. Cont at next
junction. R (Eckington 3, Bredon 5).
Pass views L to **Bredon Hill**. Cont at
next junction. Cont (Bredon,
Tewkesbury). L (Bredon 2.

Tewkesbury 6). Cont at next junction. Cont (B4080, Bredon 3, Tewkesbury 7). Cont at next junction. L (Cheltenham 10, B4079) *otherwise detour ½ mile (1 km), R (Tewkesbury 4, B4080). R (To the church and river),* for **Bredon**. Cont (Kemerton 1). Cont (Kemerton, Beckford 4). Cont (Beckford 2½, Evesham 9). Cont at next two junctions. Enter

Overbury. L to pass church. Bear R with road. R at T junction. L at T junction opposite shelter. Cont at next junction. R (Evesham, Beckford). Cont (Alderton 3, Winchcombe 7, Evesham 7). L (Grafton, Ashton-u-Hill). Cont at next junction. Reach

b. Rejoin the Dumbleton Route.

Snowshill Loop
adds 7 miles (11 km)
anticlockwise

Leave

c (Cheltenham, A46, Winchcombe 6). Cont (Cheltenham, A46). L (Stanton ½). Enter

Stanton. R (Stanway). L (Stanway 1¼, Stow on the Wold 11). Enter

Stanway. L (Stow, B4077). L (Snowshill 3, Broadway 5½). R (Snowshill, Broadway). L (Snowshill 1¾, Broadway 4¼). Bear R with white lines at next junction. L (Snowshill ¾, Broadway 3¼). Enter

Snowshill. Cont past Snowshill Arms. Cont (Broadway 2½). Pass **St Eadburgha's.** Cont at next junction. Reach

d **Broadway.** *Rejoin the Dumbleton Route.*

ROUS LENCH ROUTE
17 miles (27 km)
anticlockwise

EVESHAM. Leave following the (Birmingham, A435) signs. L (Lenchwick 1). Enter

Lenchwick. Cont (Norton). L (Church Lench 2). Cont (Church Lench, Rous Lench). R (Rous Lench 2, Inkberrow 4). L (Rous Lench 2, Radford 3). Reach

e **Rous Lench.** *Join the Cleeve Prior Loop, or cont.* Leave

e (Abbots Lench, Bishampton). R (Bishampton, Fladbury). Cont at next junction. L at next junction *not* straight ahead to 'Bishampton 1, Pershore 6'. Cont (Fladbury 1, Evesham 4). L (Evesham 4, B4084) *otherwise detour 1 mile (1½ km), R (Worcester 12, B4084). L (Fladbury ½, Charlton 2, Cropthorne 2),* for **Fladbury.** Cont (Evesham 2). Cont (Evesham 1, B4084). R (Town Centre, Cheltenham, A435).

Cleeve Prior Loop
Evesham to Evesham distance using this loop is 23 miles (37 km), not including the detour to Ragley Hall.
clockwise

Leave

e **Rous lench** (Inkberrow 3). R (Alcester 11). Cont at next two junctions. R (Evesham 8, A441, A435). Cont at next junction. Cont (Dunnington ¼, Broom 1¼, Bidford 3), *otherwise turn L to detour 2 miles (3 km) north on the A435 for* **Ragley Hall.** Cont (Broom 1½, Bidford 2¾). Enter Broom. L (Wixford 1, Bidford 1¼, Alcester 3). R (Wixford 1¼, Alcester 3½). R (Bidford 1, B4085). Cont (Bidford 1, B4085). R (Village Centre). L (Village Centre, Cleeve Prior, Honeybourne). Reach

f **Bidford** bridge. *Join the Stratford-upon-Avon Loop, otherwise cont.* Leave

f. Cont to cross the bridge. Reach

g. The Stratford-upon-Avon Loop rejoins the Cleeve Prior Loop. Leave

g (Marlcliff ½, Cleeve Prior 1¾, Badsey 6¼). Cont (Cleeve Prior 1¼, Badsey 5¾). Enter

Cleeve Prior. Cont at next junction. Cont (B4085, Evesham 5). L (N Littleton, Pebworth 3). Bear R in front

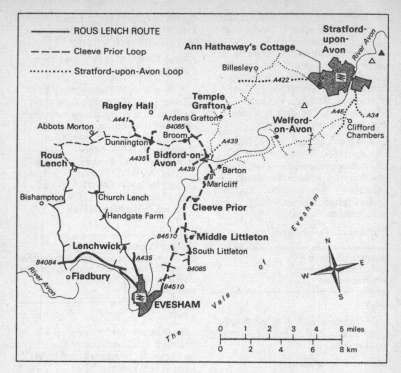

ROUS LENCH ROUTE
Cleeve Prior Loop
Stratford-upon-Avon Loop

Stratford-upon-Avon
Ann Hathaway's Cottage
Billesley
A422
Temple Grafton
Ragley Hall
A441
Ardens Grafton
B4085
Welford-on-Avon
A46
A34
Clifford Chambers
Abbots Morton
Broom
Dunnington
A439
A435
Bidford-on-Avon
A439
Barton
Rous Lench
Maricliff
Bishampton
Church Lench
Cleeve Prior
Handgate Farm
B4510
Middle Littleton
Lenchwick
B4510
A435
South Littleton
B4084
B4085
River Avon
Fladbury
B4510
EVESHAM
Vale of Evesham
The

0 1 2 3 4 5 miles
0 2 4 6 8 km

of the Ivy Inn. R (Middle Littleton). Pass through

Middle Littleton. At top of village, L on Cleeve Road. Cont (Badsey 2, Evesham 4). Cont at next junction. R (Offenham 2, Evesham 3). L on Evesham Road. Cont (B4510, Evesham).

Stratford-upon-Avon Loop
adds 12 miles (19 km)
clockwise

Leave

ƒ **Bidford** bridge (Village Centre). Cont up a no through road, bearing L. Dismount, walk up to the main road, cross and go R in the Stratford direction. L (Ardens Grafton 1½). Cont at the Golden Cross. R (Temple Grafton ½, Binton 2¼). Enter

Temple Grafton. Cont (Binton 1¾, Aston Cantlow 4). Cont (Wilmcote, Aston Cantlow). Cont at next junction. Cont (Billesley ½, Aston Cantlow 3). R (Wilmcote 1¾). R (Stratford 3½). Cont (Stratford). L (Town Centre, Warwick, A422). R (Shottery, Anne Hathaway's Cottage). L opposite Cottage Lane *otherwise detour 200 yards (metres), R on Cottage Lane* for **Anne Hathaway's Cottage.** L into Tavern Lane. Dismount and walk straight on (Public Footpath, Stratford ½). At the fork, cont towards a church spire, then bear L. R on reaching a road. L at end of The Willows. L to follow Town Centre signs. Enter the centre of

Stratford-upon-Avon. Leave the town following signs for (Cheltenham, A46). R (Chipping Campden, Broadway). R (Weston 2½, Welford

3½). Cont at next two junctions. R (Weston ¾, Welford 1¼). Cont (Welford ¾, Long Marston 2½). R (Welford ¼, Bidford 4). Enter

Welford-on-Avon. Cont (Binton 1¼). L just before The Bell. L (To Main Road). R at T junction. Cont (Barton 1¾. Bidford 2¾). Cont (Barton ¾, Bidford 1¾). Reach

g Rejoin the Cleeve Prior Loop.

The view from Grosmont Castle

THE WYE VALLEY AND THE FOREST OF DEAN

Mineral railway lines thread through noble beechwoods in the Forest of Dean, and whilst some sheep graze in the pastures, others are allowed to roam the village streets by the commoners' rights of their owners. The Forest's unique blend of coalmining and iron-working with farming and ancient woodlands has a long history. The Spanish Armada was charged to burn down the trees of Dean to prevent the timber being used for ships, and Dean iron was used to make Crusaders' weapons; there is evidence too that the Romans mined here. Nowadays this blend results in the juxta-position of small industry and workers' houses amidst rural tranquility. Lorries use the B roads, so explore the Clearwell rides on Sunday if possible. Because the villages have many outlying houses it is not easy to mark them accurately on a map or to tell when you have arrived in them; you must bear this in mind as you find your way.

The Wye and its tributary, the Monnow, both mark parts of the English–Welsh border, so it is not surprising that there are many ancient borderland castles. They are built in rock of a dusky red, which is echoed in the few ploughed fields. The hills are big but gentle in outline and dense woods line the slopes of the Wye gorge. A busy A road goes through the scenic gorge, but otherwise the Wye and Monnow rides are on quiet country roads. Both here and in the Forest of Dean you will find the riding strenuous, as the road rises and falls frequently; low gears are a great advantage on long and steep gradients.

Strenuous cycling, moderate traffic.

ST BRIAVELS

Location: Near the B4228, 8 miles (13 km) north of Chepstow, and 20 miles (32 km) north of Bristol.

Trains: Lydney Station is 7 miles (12 km) south-east and Chepstow Station is 8 miles (13 km) south. They are both on the main Birmingham to South Wales line. Cardiff: 45 mins; Birmingham: 1 hour (change at Gloucester); Bristol: 1 hour (change at Newport); London: 2 hours 15 mins (change at Newport).

Tourist Information Bureaux: c/o Nelson Museum, Monmouth, Gwent, tel: (0600) 3899 (summer service only, accommodation service); 20 Broad Street, Ross-on-Wye, Herefordshire, tel: (0989) 2768 (accommodation service).

Accommodation: The George Inn runs a small hotel, and a farm nearby offers bed and breakfast accommodation. There is a YH in St Briavels. Others on or near the rides are at Monmouth, Welsh Bicknor and Mitcheldean. There are campsites near both Monmouth and Ross-on-Wye, and the Forestry Commission runs sites in the Forest of Dean.

Cycle hire: Little and Hall, 48 Broad Street, Ross-on-Wye, Herefordshire, tel: (0989) 2639. Outside the holiday seasons: PGL Holidays, Station Road, Ross-on-Wye, Herefordshire, tel: (0989) 4211.

Cycle shop: Little and Hall, as above.

Maps: OS 1:50 000 (nos 161, 162); Bartholomew's 1:100 000 (no. 13); OS 1:250 000 (no. 7).

St Briavels

'You're not where you think you are' yelled a passing local motorist, as I studied the map just a few hundred yards from the village centre. It wasn't true, but could well have been so, for **St Briavels** is a perplexing maze of lanes and scattered outlying houses flung down a steep hillside. The village

105

has a solid heart, though, from where the twelfth-century castle looks over a vast sweep of the Wye, guarding the once strategic fording-point at **Bigsweir** 600 ft (180 m) below. Later the castle was administrative centre to the Royal Hunting Forest of Dean, and today its stark, slit-windowed walls house a comfortable youth hostel. The broad moat is now a trim little park.

Medieval arrow-heads were made here, and a pile of cinder waste from iron-ore smelting just west of the castle is grassed over and called the Bailey Tump; look out for the name of the road that descends from it.

St Briavels' centre is small and uncommercialized. The George Inn serves food, and there are grocery shops in the village. If you are outside the church after Whitsun evensong you might catch some of the bread and cheese thrown to the crowd—you can discover the story behind this medieval ceremony inside the church.

THE TINTERN ROUTE

Crossing the width of the deep Wye valley twice, this route has two exciting freewheel descents (whose steepness and length demand especially careful checking of brakes beforehand). Of course that means two big ascents as well. One climbs moderately slowly from Chapel Hill to Parkhouse (you can see into an excavation of an eighteenth-century blast furnace and waterwheel pit to the right of your road), but the other is stiffer and you may well have to walk.

Offa ruled the eighth-century English kingdom of Mercia, whose boundary with Wales he marked with a long earthwork called 'Offa's Dyke'. Any Welshman found on the English side would have his right hand cut off. If you have a 1:50 000 map, you may spot faint traces of it.

When you cross the Wye, you enter Wales with its Welsh signs and names. **'Trelech'** means 'three stones', the village being named after the three standing stones which marked its cross-roads. You will pass the big broken shaft of one. The great stone slab in the churchyard is a 'druids' altar' standing beside a preaching cross. Both the Crown and the Lion in Trelech serve food.

This quiet ride does have a couple of level stretches. Trelech's ridge commands vistas of big rounded farmland hills, and later the placid Wye curves between lush pastures. Blue-painted **Bigsweir Bridge** was built by Thomas Telford, and on proving unsuitable for its intended site, was towed here along the river.

Tintern Abbey (DoE, open) which belonged to the Cistercian monks is renowned for the beauty of its twelfth-century ruins, traced against the darkly-wooded hillside. Several places nearby offer food, and though the valley's railway line is now disused, Tintern Station and its exhibition are open to visitors.

The Monmouth Loop

When the Normans conquered England in 1066, they gained a kingdom with a western border harrassed by the Welsh from their mountain strongholds. In order to try to suppress them, the barons built massive new castles. **Skenfrith Castle** (DoE, open) is an ivy-clad ruin which clearly shows the thickness of the thirteenth-century curtain walls. **Pembridge Castle** is still inhabited, its battlemented drum towers commanding views over a wide sweep of lowland. **Monmouth's** position at the confluence of the rivers Wye and Monnow was vitally strategic, and though there are only scant remains of the castle (DoE), the pleasingly proportioned stone gateway on the Monnow Bridge entry to the old town can still be seen. St Thomas' chapel nearby is also Norman, with a simple but lovely font whose carved wooden cover is shaped like a huge dunce's cap.

Henry V was born in Monmouth, and his statue stands by the old Shire Hall in Agincourt Square, which is named after his victory over the French in 1415. Another statue portrays Charles Rolls, co-founder of Rolls-Royce and the first aviator to cross the Channel in both directions without landing. The museum tells the town's history, and has large displays devoted to Horatio Nelson. An added attraction for a hungry cyclist is the baker's shop in Agincourt Square, which is locally renowned for its Chelsea buns; there are cafés and restaurants too.

Pretty though small, the green at **Skenfrith** would make a pleasant picnic spot, and it stands near an unusual two-tiered, half-timbered church tower. Food can be bought at the Bell.

Most of the roads on this loop are quiet though strenuous, as they constantly rise and fall over ample rolling hills. Your first entry into Monmouth is an exhilarating ride down a long hill whilst your second winds through flat pastures beside the red-banked waters of the Monnow shaded by alder trees.

The A466 is perhaps the busiest long stretch of road in this book, although it is used more by cars than lorries. It is recommended because it follows the deep, silent Wye which curves below the majestic wooded hills of its gorge. Try to ride it in the low season, or on a peaceful summer evening, perhaps stopping to eat at Redbrook.

The Grosmont Loop

This peaceful ride continues through country similar to that of the Monmouth Loop, although the roads are a bit easier, and the fields and woods are broken by Garway Hill's grassy summit. Look out for the 'dinosaurs' made of scraps of metal on your right on the B4347 near Skenfrith and for the work of the determined topiarist at Garway Common, whole hedges are as tall as a house.

Grosmont is a picturesque hillside village today, but it was once of much greater importance, being guarded by a castle (DoE, open) which was built in Henry III's reign. The church's size tells of better days too. Today's parishoners use only a partitioned-off section, whilst the rest remains starkly bare of benches. The Angel serves food, as does the Garway Moon in Garway Common.

Garway's church is one of only six English churches built by the Knights Templar, an order founded to protect pilgrims going to the Holy Sepulchre in the Holy Land. Its curious shape and squat, strong tower are both due to its second role as a place of refuge in times of border strife. Instructions inside the church tell you how to visit the ancient 666-holed dovecote in the neighbouring private farmyard.

THE CLEARWELL ROUTE

Whitecroft is the epitome of a Dean Forest settlement. Houses are scattered widely amidst the fields; there is an old-fashioned level crossing on the mineral railway, and the Miners Arms is aptly named in a region proud of its small-scale unnationalised coalmining. Acrid coal-dust can be smelt in the air, and settles on the sheep who rummage over the now grassy spoil heaps.

The 'Scowles' or scars in the land left by Roman mining, are now mostly covered by woodland but despite both these and the open areas of undulating farmland, the unique and vigorous landscape explored by this set of rides is perhaps less picturesque and more busy than those along the Wye. You can avoid lorries serving the industries by riding here on Sunday. Railway enthusiasts can detour to the Norchard Steam Centre near **Lydney** to see the locomotives and rolling stock.

Clearwell is a comfortable red-stone village centred on a stone cross and a fourteenth-century inn. The mock gothic castle (open) has a Regency interior and is set in grounds with formal gardens, a bird park and tea-rooms. Decide there if you want to take the short-cut along the near-level B4231 and B4228 back to St Briavels. For although the route swoops 400 ft (120 m) down a valley, passing a red-stone quarry and with views of the Wye's voluptuous hills widening out ahead, it ascends again to a final 400-ft (120-m) climb up to St Briavels again.

The Speech House Loop

Exploring deeper into the forested hills of Dean, this loop is moderately strenuous, but it takes you past woods and glades, shady combes, and wide verges of bracken with pink foxgloves. You can enjoy the view across the Forest from **New Fancy** viewpoint, wander deeper into its leafy silence on waymarked forest trail footpaths (starting near **Speech House**), or learn about the different trees at the nearby arboretum.

Opposite Speech House stands a pillar marking the Forest centre, and commemmorating the fifty years work of a Verderer. Whilst foresters tend the timber and game in this one-time Royal Hunting Reserve, the Verderers are elected to look after the interests of the commoners, namely the locals with rights in the Forest to graze animals or collect firewood. Discussions between foresters and Verderers used to take place ten times a year in the Foresters' Court in Speech House, now used as an hotel.

The industrial settlements around the Forest's edge includes Cinderford, whose name recalls smelting of long ago, and where iron is still worked in the foundry and manhole cover factory. (There is a fish and chip shop in the village). From Ruardean a 500-ft (150-m) descent brings you quickly down to the Wye valley before rising up again to the Forest proper.

The Ross Loop

Little extra effort is needed for this fairly quiet ride, which descends to the Wye at Ross and then keeps virtually level till it rejoins the Speech House Loop. Working men's houses at Crooked End give way rapidly to folded, richly-wooded farmlands.

Ross-on-Wye is still proud of John Kyrle, the philanthropic seventeenth-century 'Man of Ross' who gave so much to his town including Britain's first public water supply. His black and white house contrasts with the arcaded market hall and the sixteenth-century row of almshouses which are built of soft red stone. The church contains some fine alabaster monuments, and a memorial brass etched with a charming hedgehog, whilst the cross outside commemorates the 315 victims of an epidemic of the plague. Meals can be bought in the town, or at the Spread Eagle in Walford.

Flat lanes pass fields and parkland near Hom Green from where you can see **Goodrich Castle** (DoE, open), rising impressively on a strategic riverside bluff. The great semi-circular tower over the gatehouse was once used as the chapel. From there, your ride continues alongside the meandering Wye in its deep, wooded valley.

TINTERN ROUTE
16 miles (26 km)
clockwise

ST BRIAVELS. Leave from castle (Lower Meend ½). Cont on Lower Road. L at T junction. R (Brockweir, St Briavels Common). Cont at next junction. L (Brockweir, Woodspring, Hilgay). Keep L at next 2 forks. Keep L by a telephone box. Cont (Brockweir).

Cont at next junction. R (Brockweir, Tintern). L (Tintern, Chepstow, A466). Reach Tintern Parva. Cont at next junction. R (Llanishen) *otherwise detour 400 yards (metres) straight on to* **Tintern Abbey**. R (Devauden). R (Raglan). R (Llanishen, Trelech, Usk, Raglan). Cont (Parkhouse 1, Trelech 2½). Cont at next junction. Cont (Trelech 1½, Monmouth 7¼). Cont at next junction. L (Trelech ½,

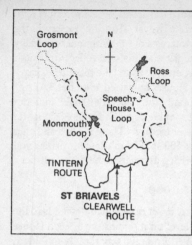

Grosmont
Loop

N

Ross
Loop

Speech
House
Loop

Monmouth
Loop

TINTERN
ROUTE

ST BRIAVELS
CLEARWELL
ROUTE

Monmouth 6). Enter

Trelech. R (Monmouth 5¾). Cont at next junction. Cont (Monmouth). Cont (Monmouth). Reach

a. Join the Monmouth Loop, otherwise cont. Leave

a (Whitebrook 2½). Cont (Whitebrook 1¾). Cont at junction near telephone box. L (Monmouth, A466, Redbrook). Reach

d near **Bigsweir Bridge.** *The Monmouth Loop rejoins the Tintern Route.* Leave

d (St Briavels 1¾, Coleford 5). R (St Briavels 1¼, Hewelsfield 3). L (St Briavels ½, Hewelsfield 2½). Fork R to ascend steeply into village.

Monmouth Loop
adds 22 miles (35 km)
clockwise

Leave

a (Monmouth 4). Cont (Monmouth 4½). Cont at next junction. Cont (Monmouth). R (Monmouth 1½). Cont (Rockfield 2½, Monmouth ½). L (Rockfield 2½). Enter

Monmouth passing near St Thomas and Monnow Bridge; the rest of the

town is better seen on the return journey. Cont (Abergavenny). Cont at next junction. R (Skenfrith 6, B4347). R (Maypole ½, St Maughans 1½). R (St Maughans Green). L (Skenfrith 2½). Reach.

b **Skenfrith.** Join the Grosmont Loop, otherwise cont. Leave

b. Turn R at T junction by bridge to follow the B4521 at all junctions as far as Broad Oak. Reach

c Broad Oak. The Grosmont Loop rejoins the Monmouth Loop. Leave

c (Welsh Newton, Monmouth). Pass **Pembridge Castle** on your L. R (Monmouth 4, A466). Cont at next junction. R (Llanrothel). Cont at next junction but take care on descent with blind corners. L (Trigate). L just before river bridge. Cont at every junction till reaching North Parade, on which turn R. Cont to pass Monmouth Baptist Chapel *otherwise detour, R (Town Centre), to explore centre of* **Monmouth**. L by Pitman's Court. R by war memorial. Dismount at Queen's Head pub and walk down Wyebridge Street. Go under subway. Cross river bridge. Follow (Forest of Dean, Chepstow 16) sign. R (Tintern, Chepstow, A466). Cont at 2 more junctions signposted (Tintern, Chepstow, A466). Reach

d near **Bigsweir Bridge.** *Rejoin the Tintern Loop.*

Grosmont Loop
adds 10 miles (16 km)
clockwise

Leave

b. Turn L at T junction by bridge. R by telephone box. R at T junction to pass 'The Shirmal Herd, British Friesians' sign. Cont at next junction. Enter

Grosmont. Cont at next junction. Cont (Kentchurch 1½, Hereford 13½). R (Garway 4, Monmouth 12). Bear R with white lines to pass church. Cont at next junction *otherwise detour 300 yards (metres) R for* **Garway** church. Cont

(Monmouth). Cont (Broad Oak, Monmouth). Cont at next junction. Cont (Broad Oak, Welsh Newton, Monmouth). Cont at next junction. Reach

c Broad Oak. *Rejoin the Monmouth Loop.*

CLEARWELL ROUTE
14 miles (23 km)
anticlockwise

ST BRIAVELS. Leave on an un-signposted lane, passing a hydrant numbered 75/1, and in the *opposite* direction to a road into the village centre signposted 'St Briavels Castle'. Cont at next junction. L (Bream ¾, Coleford 4). R (Bream). R (Lydney 2½, B4231). Cont at next junction. L (Blackhollands, Whitecroft). Cont at next junction. R (Whitecroft). L (Parkend 1¼, Coleford 4, B4234) *otherwise detour 2 miles (3 km) following 'Steam Centre' signs for* **Lydney**. Cont (Lydbrook 5, B4234). Reach

e. Join the Speech House Loop, otherwise cont. Leave

e (Coleford, B4431). Cont (Coleford 3½, B4431). L (Ellwood, Sling ¾). Cont (Sling, Clearwell 1½). Cont at next 2 junctions. R (Coleford, Ross). First L, opposite a 'Forestry Commission Forest of Dean' sign. Take care on a very steep descent. L at T junction. Enter

Clearwell. L (Bream 2, Lydney). R (Bigsweir 3, Wye Valley, Stow). Bear L by a telephone box. L (St Briavels 1¼, Hewelsfield 3). L (St Briavels ½, Hewelsfield 2½). Fork R to ascend steeply into village.

Speech House Loop
20 miles (32 km)
anticlockwise

Leave

e. (Blakeney 5, B4431, Lydbrook 5, B4234). Cont (Blakeney 5, B4431). L (Speech House 2, Cinderford 5). Pass **New Fancy** on your R. Reach

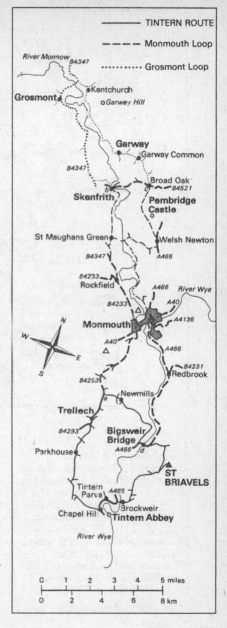

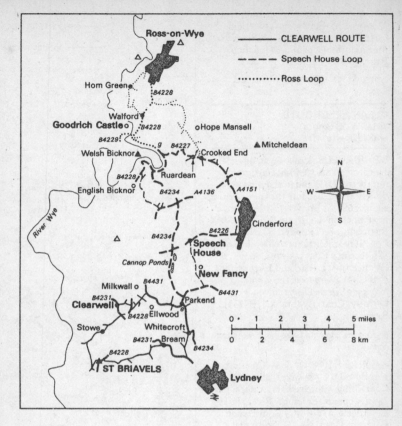

Speech House. R (B4226, Cinderford). L (Cinderford). Follow the road through all its bends as it keeps to the edge of Cinderford, ignoring all turn-offs. L (Drybrook 1½, Ruardean 2½). R (Drybrook ¾, Ruardean 2, Mitcheldean 2½). L (Drybrook ¾, Ruardean 2, B4227). Cont (Ruardean 1¾, Goodrich 5, B4227). Cont (Ruardean 1¼, Goodrich 5, B4227). Cont (Ruardean ¾, Goodrich 4, B4227). Reach

f. Join the Ross Loop, otherwise cont. Leave

f (Ruardean ½, Goodrich 4, B4227). Cont following B4227 signs down to river Wye and B4228 junction. Reach

g. The Ross Loop rejoins the Speech House Loop. Leave

g (Lower Lydbrook 1, English Bicknor 3, Coleford B4228). Cont (English Bicknor 2, Christchurch 4, Coleford B4228). Cont (English Bicknor 1½, Christchurch 3½, Coleford B4228). L (Eastbach 1). Cont at next 2 junctions. L (Gloucester, A4136). Cont (Gloucester, A4136). R (Lydney 8, B4234). Cont (Lydney 6, B4234). R (Parkend ¼, Bream 2, Scenic Drive). Reach

e. Rejoin the Clearwell Loop.

Ross Loop
adds 10 miles (16 km)
anticlockwise

Leave

f (Howle Hill). Cont at next junction. Bear L with white lines at next junction. R at a staggered junction, just beyond a wire-netting enclosure probably containing a little raised reservoir on your R. L at T junction, soon passing The Firs house. Cont (Ross 2). R ⸴Ross

1½, B4228). Enter

Ross-on-Wye. Leave town on road signposted (Coleford 10½, B4228). Fork R in front of the Prince of Wales pub. Cont at next 3 junctions. Enter Walford. R at T junction by war memorial. Pass views to R of **Goodrich Castle**. Cont (Coleford 7½, B4228, Lydbrook 2½) *otherwise detour 1 mile (1½ km) R on B4229 for* **Goodrich Castle**. Cont at next 2 junctions. Reach

g. Rejoin the Speech House Loop.

The Brecon Beacons

THE BRECON BEACONS

The Brecon Beacons lying in south Powys are now designated as a National Park. Barren peaks are divided by great amphitheatre-like valleys, carved out by ice-age glaciers. Their dramatic skyline rises above the farmlands around Brecon, where the occasional ploughed field marks the green hills with patches of red. Tall hedges enclose the fields and often obscure your view from the lanes.

Several clear rivers flow quickly to Brecon, their valleys separated by rounded ridges and hills. The cycling is quite strenuous for even the valley roads are rarely level, but the routes are very peaceful excepting on the trunk roads near Brecon itself.

There are few big villages, but many hamlets and lone farms, their drives often tarmaced and easily confused with public roads. Also many 'true' junctions are not signposted, so be especially meticulous in your route-finding.

Strenuous cycling. Quiet with one optional but challenging and strenuous track through the mountains.

BRECON

Location: 35 miles (55 km) north-north-west of Cardiff.

Trains: There is no station in or near Brecon. The closest stations are Llandovery, Builth Road and Merthyr, about 20 miles (30 km) west, north and south respectively.

Coach: A coach runs from Brecon to Cheltenham, and another to Birmingham, Leicester and Nottingham.

Information Bureau: Market Car Park, Brecon, Powys, tel: (0874) 2485, (summer service only, accommodation service).

Accommodation: Hotel and bed and breakfast accommodation is available in Brecon. The Ty'n-y-Caeau YH is 2 miles (3 km) east of Brecon and on the Llanfrynach Route. Llwyn-y-Celyn is 8 miles (13 km) south-west of Brecon. The nearest camp sites are at Upper Cantref, Llanfrynach, Brecon, tel: (087 476) 223, and at the Royal Oak, Pencelli, Brecon, tel: (087 476) 621, both on the Llanfrynach Route. There are several sites near Llangorse Lake.

Cycle-hire: D. H. Griffiths, Ship Street, Brecon, Powys tel: (0874) 2651.

Cycle-shop: D. H. Griffiths, as above.

Maps: OS 1:50 000 (nos 160, 161); Bartholomew's 1:100 000 (nos 12, 17); OS 1:250 000 (no. 7).

Brecon

Brecon is a busy market town, its shops, swimming pool and cinema serving the several valleys which radiate from it. Dark and roofed with Welsh slate, the houses are unpretentious, but muted purple stone has been beautifully worked both in the sixteenth-century Christ's College and the cathedral. Amongst the cathedral's treasures is a rough stone cresset, a rare example of a medieval form of lighting.

Napoleonic officers were held prisoners of war here, and one of their favourite strolls is still called Captains' Walk. There are paths and small green spaces by the river Usk, where fishermen often stand thigh-deep in surging water. The Usk is one of several rivers converging on Brecon, giving it a strategic position that has been appreciated for thousands of years. Within a couple of miles are the remains of Pen-y-Crug iron-age hill-fort, and a Roman station at Y Gaer.

The Brecknock Museum, housed in a grandly porticoed Victorian building, illustrates the local history of the town and its area, and has a reconstruction of the old Assize Court.

THE MYNYDD ILLTYD ROUTE

Mynydd in Welsh can mean mountain or moorland. A long haul up 500 ft (150 m) brings you to Mynydd Illtyd, too low to be a mountain, but with a broad moorland top of rough grass, bracken and gorse where many people still exert their commoners' rights to graze their animals. Ponies and sheep by the hundred drink from the reedy pools, or roam the open waste. Usually to the left of the road is a re-seeded strip of land, which marks the course of an underground pipeline linking the oil terminal at Milford Haven with Manchester and the Midlands.

The **Mountain Centre** on the common's flank describes the National Park and its life by means of displays and film shows. Its comfortable armchairs look out on inspiring views; a tempting refuge if the weather is bad. There is a café, and even a small kitchen where you can prepare your own picnic. Meals can be bought at the **Sennybridge** fish and chip shop, and at the nearby Lion Inn.

You return from Sennybridge along the Usk's voluptuous valley. The lanes constantly climb up and down the valley's side, but they are so rarely used that grass grows undisturbed down their middles.

Y Gaer (DoE, open), built by the Romans in the first century AD, was a fort at the junction of two of their roads. Now its levelled area is a hayfield and although access is restricted when the hay crop is vulnerable, you can usually visit the site.

The Merthyr Cynog Loop

After an initial 100-ft (30-m) rise, this loop climbs gently by the river, or 'afon' Yscir, past fields, tangled thickets and oaks. **Battle** village, on the opposite valley-side, was the site of a daughter abbey to that at Battle in Sussex.

Pontfaen's white and colour-washed cottages are pretty, nestling below a hillside. There is a public water-tap near the telephone box. Beyond Pontfaen the narrowing valley has steep, gorse-clad slopes.

The Yscir and Honddu valleys are divided by two parallel ridges. You climb steeply over both, rising some 500 ft (150 m) altogether, to views of whitewashed farms, set amongst the surrounding woods and pastures.

Scrubby hillsides flanking the B4520, widen to more pastoral scenes as the road descends to the Honddu valley. The Campden Arms at Lower Chapel serves food.

The Llandefalle Loop

Llandefalle Hill is only some 600 ft (200 m) higher than Llandefaelog church where the loop starts, but because the road to it sometimes drops into valleys before it rises again, the first section of this ride is strenuous.

As you approach Garthbrengy, look back to the isolated, bracken-covered hill about 2 miles (3 km) away. This is Pen-y-Crug, *pen* in Welsh meaning top, and *crug* meaning heap. Its lonely summit commands views in all directions, making it a superb defensive site, and you can still see the earthwork ramparts which guarded an Iron-age hill-fort there.

At the top of Llandefalle Hill unfenced lanes pass through grassy commons. To the right, the hillside slopes gently away, cut by sinuous, wooded valleys, one of which you later freewheel down before completing the ride.

THE LLANFRYNACH ROUTE

This route explores the foothills of the Brecon Beacons, never leaving the sheltered farmland lanes, but with frequent glimpses of barren mountains close by. After a gradual climb through 300 ft (100 m), your road swoops and curves through little folds in the land, whilst others seem to lead to nowhere in particular. Cars are rare, but they can suddenly come around the tight corners, so do keep well to the left. There are few signposts, so take care in finding your way.

Near a steep and wooded stream-gorge, a farm at Cantref offers pony-trekking. **Llanfrynach** (*Llan* meaning church in welsh), has a church with immensely thick tower walls; the White Swan serves food. At **Pencelli** the Royal Oak offers meals too, catering for travellers on the Brecon and Abergavenny Canal and its towpath.

The rest of the ride crosses low farm country, passing the youth hostel at **Ty'n-y-Caeau**, whose very name means the house in the fields.

The Cwm Cynwyn Loop

The sides of the Cwm Cynwyn valley soar upwards in smooth, sweeping curves. A rocky Roman road climbs obliquely up one side, to a pass at 2000 ft (600 m). Carved out by a powerful glacier, Cwm Cynwyn's great walls are grassy except where the red sandstone shows through. To travel the Roman Road with a bicycle is arduous, but it enables you to journey through some grand and lonely country where you might even see some buzzards. Once you are back on the tarmac you have only one 300-ft (100-m) climb left: the rest is level or a freewheel, part of which is very steep and dangerous in slippery conditions. You pass through conifer plantations overlooked by bare ridges, and by a roadside picnic area with a stone-built shelter.

Beyond a spectacular waterfall to your left, you descend Capel Glyn Collwn's medieval foundations to the peaceful Talybont Reservoir.

The Llangorse Loop

Llangorse Lake lies in a shallow bowl amidst rolling hills. The lanes surrounding it climb and fall, never very high, but sufficiently frequently to make the going quite hard. There are views over the lake and its yachts to the Black Mountains in the north-east.

Legend says that a city was swallowed up by Llangorse Lake in an earthquake. Finds suggest that there may have been prehistoric huts here, built on stakes and protected from attack by marshy ground. Today there are just flowery meadows and a common where boats can be hired and fishing licenses bought. There are tea-rooms in **Llangorse** village, and pony-trekking is offered at the Red Lion pub.

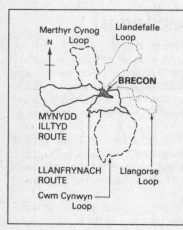

MYNYDD ILLTYD ROUTE
18½ miles (30 km)
clockwise

BRECON. Leave from St Mary's Church, following signs for Llandovery, until you reach a large roundabout. Take the Public Weighbridge exit. Cont at the next two junctions to carry on climbing onto Mynydd Illtyd. Cont at the next junction *otherwise detour ½ mile* (1 km), L *(Mountain Centre) for the* **Mountain Centre**. Cont at next junction. R (Defynnog 2, Sennybridge 4.) Cont at the next junction. Cont (Defynnog 1, Sennybridge 2). R (Sennybridge ½, Brecon 9). Cont at the next junction. L (Sennybridge). Enter

Sennybridge. R by the Usk and Railway pub. L (Pentre'r-felin 1, Llandeilo'r-Fan 4). First R, to follow the left-hand edge of a wood. R (Trallong 1½, Cradoc 4¾). Cont (Trallong 1¼, Cradoc 4½). Cont by

Trallong post office. Cont at the next junction. Cont (Aberyscir 1). Bear R at the next junction i.e. *not* L to Llanfihangel Nant Bran. Cont at a junction by white fencing. Reach

a Pontaryscir. *Join the Merthyr Cynog Loop, or cont.* Leave

a. R (Brecon 2¾). Cont at the next junction *or detour on 1st track to R for 500 yards (metres) to* **Y Gaer**. R at a Give Way junction. R (Brecon 2¼).

MERTHYR CYNOG LOOP
adds 11 miles (18 km)
clockwise

Leave

a Pontaryscir. L to go north, do *not* follow the 'Brecon 2¾' sign. Pass views of **Battle**. L (Merthyr Cynog 2¾). Cont along the valley at all junctions until turning R (Merthyr Cynog ½, Upper Chapel 3). Pass the Merthyr Cynog name sign. Enter Merthyr Cynog. In the village, turn R past a big barn with long slits in its wall. Cont over the first river bridge, then immediately keep R. R at the T junction with the main road. Cont at the next junction. Reach

b Llandefaelog Church. *Join the Llandefalle Loop, or cont.* Leave

b (Brecon 3). Cont (Brecon 2). Cont at the next junction.

Llandefalle Loop
adds 12½ miles (20 km)
clockwise

Leave

b Llandefaelog Church (Garthbrengy 1½). Cont at the next junction to go uphill. Pass views back to Pen-y-Crug.

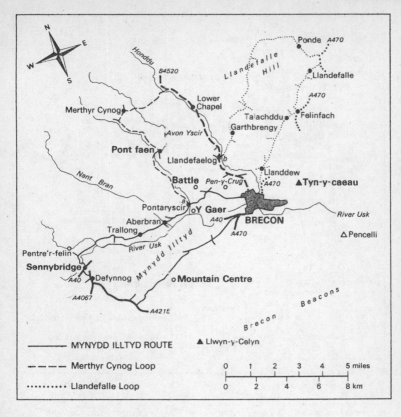

MYNYDD ILLTYD ROUTE
- - - Merthyr Cynog Loop
.... Llandefalle Loop

▲ Llwyn-y-Celyn

```
0    1    2    3    4    5 miles
0    2    4    6    8 km
```

Enter Garthbrengy. Cont to pass L of the church. L at the T junction. Cont (Ponde 4½, Llandefalle 5½). Cross a cattle grid then cont. Cont to pass pillar box, number 426. Cont at all junctions. Pass through Ponde. R at the T junction with the main road. R (Llandefalle). Keep L at all the junctions below a slope to your R, with a church partly hidden by trees. R at the T junction to pass a telephone box. Cont at the next junction. R at the T junction with the main road. R (Talachddu ½). Cont at the next junction. Enter Talachddu. Cont at the junction by the church. Cont at the next two junctions. Cont (Brecon 2, Llanddew ¼). Cont (Brecon 1¾). Cont following signs for **Brecon**.

LLANFRYNACH ROUTE
**14½ miles (23 km)
anticlockwise**

BRECON. Leave following signs for (Llandovery). Cross the river, pass St David's Church, then L on Ffrwdgrech Road. Cross a stream, and at the fork of three roads by a small pillar box, take the middle road. Cont at the next junction. At the next cross-roads, where the 'road' ahead is a track, L to cross a stream in 50 yards (metres). Reach Heol Fanog Farm. R (No Entry to MOD vehicles). At the staggered cross-roads, go L then R to cross a stream. Cont at the next junction. R at the T junction. Reach

119

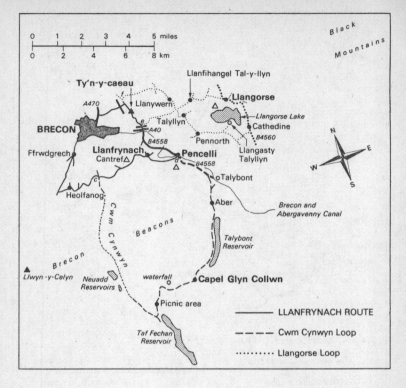

c. Join the Cwm Cynwyn Loop, or cont. Leave

c (Cantref 1¼, Llanfrynach 2½). Keep L near the telephone box. R (Llanfrynach 1½). R (Llanfrynach ½). Enter

Llanfrynach. R at the T junction to pass a School sign. R to pass a telephone box. Cont at all junctions until you pass by a R turn signposted 'Church', then next L on a track crossing a canal bridge. Reach

d **Pencelli** *telephone box. The Cwm Cynwyn Loop rejoins the Llanfrynach Route.* Leave

d. To go slightly downhill. Cont at the next junction. Cont (Brecon 3). Cont (Llangorse). Pass under the flyover. Cont (Groesffordd ½). Reach

e. Join the Llangorse Loop, or cont. Leave

e (Llechfaen ¾). Cont at the next junction. L (Builth Wells 19¾, Hay-on-Wye 14¾). Pass **Ty'n-y-Caeau**. Reach

f. The Llangorse Loop rejoins the Llanfrynach Route. Leave

f. Leave on a 13' 9'' height limit road with the sign Single Track Road. L at the T junction with the main road.

Cwm Cynwyn Loop
adds 12 miles (19 km)
anticlockwise

This loop follows an untarmaced track for 4 miles (7 km). The first stretch is over fist-sized stones, and you will have to push your cycle over them for 300 yards (metres). Thereafter the going is generally easier, although rarely suitable for cycling on the ascent. At the summit is a very difficult part, only about 50 yards (metres) long, but up a steep gradient with boulders in the path. The descent is gradual; you will be able to cycle in parts and it is not too strenuous to wheel the cycle elsewhere. The track is clearly defined throughout, but do not attempt it through mist or in wet or snowy conditions when the rocks will be slippery. It is an exhilarating route for those willing and able to tackle at least 2½ hours of slow, hard going.

Leave

c. Leave in the direction *opposite* to 'Brecon 2¼'. R at the T junction. Cont past Bailea Farm. Cont onto an 'Unsuitable for Vehicles' track. Go through a gate to follow the track keeping to the right of a wall. Where the wall gives way to a wire fence, cont uphill do *not* bear L to go downhill. You are now ascending the valley of Cwm Cynwyn. Just beyond the summit the track veers slightly L to descend gradually. At a fork near a red-roofed house, take the R fork, then turn L in front of the fence—in law this is only a Right of Way on foot, and you will have to lift your cycle over a style at the end; but the L fork, which is the Right of Way for all traffic, involves the much harder crossing of a very steep gully. Having crossed the style, go down to the tarmaced road, on which turn L. L (Aber-Clydach 6½,

Talybont-on-Usk 7½). Cont at the next junction. Pass **Capel Glyn Collwn**. Pass through Aber. Where the road bends R to (Talybont-on-Usk ½), go straight ahead on an unsignposted lane. Cont downhill by a white farm. L (Llanfrynach 2¾, Brecon 5¼). Cont at the next junction. Reach

d **Pencelli** *telephone box. Rejoin the Llanfrynach Route.*

Llangorse Loop
adds 11½ miles (19 km) anticlockwise

Leave

e (Talyllyn 2½, Llangorse 3¾). R (Talyllyn ½). R (Pennorth 1). L (Bwlch 3¾). Cont (Bwlch 2½). L just before the pillar box coded Point Corner No. 391. L at the T junction by a Give Way sign. Cont at the next junction. Enter

Llangorse. Cont at the next junction. L (Brecon, Llangorse Lake). Cont (Brecon). *Otherwise detour for ½ mile (1 km) following Llangorse Lake signs for Langorse Lake and common.* Cont (Brecon 5½). L (Brecon 5). Pass through Llanfihangel Tal-y-llyn. Cont (Brecon 4¾). R (Llanwern ¾). Cont (Brecon 4½). Cont at the next junction. L at a T junction enclosing a small grass triangle. L at the T junction. Reach

f. Rejoin the Llanfrynach Route.

Stokesay Castle

THE SHROPSHIRE HILLS

These hills of Shropshire (and parts of Herefordshire) range from gentle 100-ft (30-m) swells of farmland near Leominster, to the barren summit of Long Mynd which is 1700 ft (500 m) high. Most of the rides have strenuous parts, sometimes on long, steep slopes, so if you want to explore the countryside from north to south without riding it all check with British Rail for trains between Ludlow and Leominster, and Church Stretton and Stokesay, which will offer short cuts.

The farmlands everywhere are lush and fertile, and when ploughed show a rich burgundy red soil. The hedgerows surrounding the fields of cattle and corn harbour plenty of wild flowers and are often tall.

Though homely, the hamlets and villages do not rank as 'beauty spots', so motor tourists rush on in search of the picturesque, leaving the lanes threading through these lovely landscapes as a cyclists' tranquil paradise. Few tourists means few places serving food though, so it is best to take a picnic. The southern rides are better explored on a Sunday, when you can avoid the traffic and enjoy Leominster in relative peace.

Fairly strenuous cycling. Very quiet with a few busy miles.

LUDLOW

Location: 35 miles (57 km) west of Birmingham.

Trains: Ludlow Station is on the minor line from Shrewsbury to Hereford both towns having main line connections to other cities. Birmingham: 2 hours (change at Shrewsbury); Manchester: 2 hours 15 mins (change at Crewe); Bristol: 3 hours (change at Newport).

Tourist Information Bureaux: Castle Street, Ludlow, Shropshire, tel: (0584) 3857 (summer service only); District Library, South Street, Leominster, Herefordshire, tel: (0568) 2384; The Square, Shrewsbury, Shropshire, tel: (0743) 52019 (accommodation service).

Accommodation: Hotel and bed and breakfast accommodation is available in Ludlow. There is a YH in Ludlow, and another at Wilderhope Manor, 3 miles (5 km) from the Long Mynd Loop near Rushbury. There is a campsite at North Farm, Ludlow, Shropshire, tel: (0584) 2026. Other sites are near Church Stretton and Little Stretton on the Long Mynd Loop, and Mortimer's Cross. Advance booking is recommended.

Cycle-hire: The nearest is at 11a St John's Hill, Shrewsbury, Shropshire, tel: (0743) 65150.

Cycle-shop: Cowgills, 12 Old Street, Ludlow, Shropshire.

Maps: OS 1:50 000 (no. 137 and no. 149 just for the Leominster Loop); Bartholomew's 1:100 000 (no. 18); OS 1:250 000 (no. 7).

Ludlow

This fascinating town owes much to the Normans, who not only built the massive eleventh-century castle (open) but planned the town too. The castle is sited on an impressive bluff beside the River Teme, and has a circular chapel nave. The streets of the town still follow the Norman grid pattern, although the earliest surviving houses now date from the fourteenth century. An ancient wooden door with 350 studs still opens into the Feathers, one of England's oldest and loveliest inns first used as such in the reign of Henry VIII.

Ludlow church has some boldly carved misericords, and in St Giles, just across the river in Ludford, the oval churchyard suggests a site of great antiquity. Canoeists revel in the river's rushing waters below St Giles, but you can hire more sedate boats near the swimming baths. Riverside walks

123

pass below the castle, and benches on a little green behind Ludlow church enjoy expansive views.

It is little wonder that tourists flock to Ludlow, especially during the summer festival fortnight, when the castle makes a superb setting for Shakespearian plays and other events. Many cafés, restaurants, antique and craft shops vie for the tourist trade, and the old Butter Cross building is now used as the local museum.

CLEE ST MARGARET ROUTE

Tucked in a fold high in the hills, **Clee St Margaret** is a timeless hamlet of red-stone houses. The cobbled ford is very long, for the river flows not across but down it. It is difficult to cross so it is prudent to use the raised footpath instead. Look up from the bend a little beyond the ford to the ditch, rampart and entrance to Nordybank, a prehistoric hill fort set on a strategic spur.

The hardest part of this quiet route comes early, as you will probably have to walk the first, steep 400-ft (125-m) climb into the hills, whose folds make the going slow as far as Clee St Margaret. The views are ample reward though, across fertile lowlands to distant barren summits.

The chapel at **Upper Heath** stands in a field, and seems rather barn-like with its massive stones and slit windows, until the carved Norman doorway gives its purpose and age away. A key can be obtained from a nearby farm if you wish to look inside.

The riding is easy from Upper Chapel all the way back to Ludlow with views to far horizons alternating with those of the immediate valley. In Corve Dale, which is an almost flat patchwork of fields, you cycle towards the landmark of Ludlow's church tower, and pass a pleasant group of Georgian and black-and-white farmhouse buildings at Lower Hayton.

The Wenlock Edge Loop

Wenlock Edge is a long, narrow, range of hills rising some 400 ft (125 m) above the surrounding lowlands. It has many fine woods, with a way-marked footpath trail in Edge Wood and a display explaining the forest wildlife.

Although narrow, the Edge hides tranquil farmland valleys within its folds, one of which shelters Middlehope. Here the road climbs 300 ft (90 m) before taking you past a castellated tower and down to Dinchope.

Stokesay Castle (open) was one of England's earliest fortified manor houses, and is certainly one of the loveliest. The thirteenth-century banqueting hall, is spanned by huge roof timbers and lit by exceptionally large windows for the time. The adjacent church is interesting too, with dark canopied pews and a mounting block by the lych-gate.

The A49 is busy around Craven Arms, but otherwise this loop is peaceful, the lane through Bache even having grass down its middle.

The Long Mynd Loop

Each of this day's rides introduces you to a new range of hills: Long Mynd, Clee Hills and Wenlock Edge. The smooth moorlands of the Long Mynd range are broken by tightly curving stream valleys, and softened by wooded hollows. There is a coffee shop and restaurant in **Church Stretton** where the ancient church has a Sheila-na-Gig, or female fertility carving, over the north door, and a curious morte-safe in the yard. Prized mineral waters flow from Cound Dale Spring beside your road through **All Stretton**.

Little Stretton's church is thatched, but its bold black and white walls are in fact early twentieth-century work. Many older, timbered cottages lie behind the Ragleth Inn where a stream flows from Ashes Hollow. Even a half-mile walk into this wild little valley is worthwhile—for it is far more peaceful than the popular Cardingmill Valley near Church Stretton. A 200-ft (60-m) climb from Little Stretton to Minton repays your effort by penetrating unspoilt Long Mynd country, and the following descent swoops down to a gated level crossing complete with old-style signals.

Rushbury and Cardington are both pleasant villages, set in farmlands beneath Caer Caradoc and its neighbouring hills. The going here is quiet but strenuous, taking you below bracken-clad hill tops, past grazing sheep and cattle and alongside hedgerows which in autumn bear hazelnuts.

Teas can be bought near The White House (open) at **Aston Munslow**, a twelfth-century homestead with buildings ranging from a Norman dovecote and a fourteenth-century cruck hall to other eighteenth-century parts. There are many old domestic and dairying tools here, but further on, at **Acton Scott**, you can visit a working farm museum where old crafts and techniques are still practiced, Shire horses are still used, and home produce is sold at the café. Acton Scott lies in a lowland enclave between the Long Mynd and Wenlock Edge, whose wooded scarp flanks your lazy winding ride beyond Alcaston.

THE ASTON ROUTE

Steep, convoluted and pine-forested hills rise south west of Ludlow, where this route starts with an arduous ascent. It does, however, climb past an educational forest footpath trail, and offer you a fine view over Ludlow, which is neatly laid out below beside its castle.

Little pockets of farmland shelter within the higher woods, and near Aston, a broad plain surrounded by hills opens out before you. The freewheel to **Aston** is delightful, but a halt at St Giles is worthwhile to see the twelfth-century tympanum which is wonderfully carved with beasts symbolising God and the evangelists. Inside, the walls are painted with a cheerful floral design. 'Eloquent silence' is a symbolic painting adorning **All Saints**, a recently built church with doors that are bound in a bold, sweeping design of metal.

Beyond Elton, 300 ft (100 m) of steep ascent bring you to the ride's highest point, before taking you down a narrow winding valley to Ashford Bowdler. Peaceful lanes passing orchards and pretty cottages take you back through the Ashfords to Ludlow to complete this quiet route.

The Mortimer's Cross Loop

Explore this loop on Sunday if you can, for the B roads can be busy on weekdays. That aside, the ride to Mortimer's Cross through open country-side and then winding valleys is tranquil. **The Grange** is one of several isolated farms, but its large size and ancient timbering belie its twelfth-century abbey origins. The lanes are generally easy, although a steep slope leads to Upper Lye.

The Royal George at Lingen sells food, as does the pub at **Mortimer's Cross**, whose attractive sign symbolises the historic battle fought here; the victor later becoming King Edward IV of England. An eighteenth-century London merchant built **Lucton's** public school, and its facade with the clock and statue of the founder is typical of the date.

Croft Castle (NT, open) is still in the hands of the Croft family, just as it was during the Domesday survey of 1086. The 24-acre iron-age hill fort of Croft Ambrey stands in the spacious grounds. Beyond Croft Castle you can either climb a 200-ft (60-m) hill on rural lanes to Orleton, or avoid it by continuing on the B4361 to All Saints.

The Leominster Loop

England's last legal and recorded use of the ducking stool, occurred in **Leominster** in 1809. Today, the stool and a fine Gothic chalice are kept inside the priory church by the green. Also on the green is the black and white town hall, called The Grange. There is a fish and chip shop in the town, as well as a teashop and a local museum.

The classified roads near Leominster are not very busy, and elsewhere quiet lanes cross gently swelling farmlands, making this an easy but some-times dull ride. Occasional orchards and riverside willows bring variety to the scenes, and copper beeches shade the parklands of **Berrington Hall** (NT, open). The grounds of Berrington Hall were landscaped by Lancelot 'Capa-bility' Brown, one of the first designers to move away from the formal European-style layouts so loved in the seventeenth century, and to introduce a more romantic, natural-looking landscape. The eighteenth-century house has remarkable plaster ceilings, and there is a tea-room.

The seventeenth-century manor at **Eye** (open) was built and lavishly furnished with wealth accumulated from slave-trading. Alabaster effigies and carved-wood griffins grace the church next door, whilst **Yarpole's** church has a separate bell tower of unusual shape. There are some pretty black and white houses in the village and one near the church has a glass panel set in the wall showing the inner construction of woven wood.

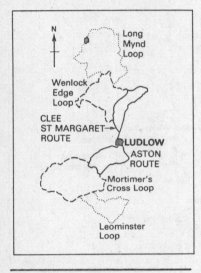

d. The Wenlock Edge Loop rejoins the Clee St Margaret Route. Leave

d (Ludlow). Cont at next junction. R at end of Fishmore Road. Go under railway bridge, then first L.

Wenlock Edge Loop
adds 13½ miles (22 km) anticlockwise

Leave

a (Diddlebury, Craven Arms). L (Diddlebury, Craven Arms). R (B4368, Bridgnorth 15½). Reach

b. Join the Long Mynd Loop, or cont. Leave

b (Middlehope 1¾). Pass through Middlehope. Keep R at woodland edge near summit. Reach

c near a 'Picnic Area ½ mile sign'. The Long Mynd Loop rejoins the Wenlock Edge Loop. Leave

c. Pass **Edge Wood**. Cont at next junction. R by a pillar box, having just passed a 'Picnic Area ¾ mile' sign for the road back the way you came. Cont at next junction. Take care to follow road where it kinks L, *not* going ahead on a no through road. R (Craven Arms 1¾, Strefford 1¼). Cont (Craven Arms 1¾, Strefford 1¼). Cont (Craven Arms 1½). L at T junction. R at T junction by a Give Way sign. Enter Craven Arms. L (Leominster, A49, Ludlow 7). Cont (Leominster, A49, Ludlow 7). Pass signposted drive on your R to

Stokesay. First L beyond Stokesay drive. R at T junction. R (Norton ¾, Burley 1¼). L (Bache ¾, Burley 1¼). Cont at next junction. Cont (Culmington 1¾, Ludlow 5¼). R (Ludlow). L (Stanton Lacy). Bear R by telephone box. Reach

CLEE ST MARGARET ROUTE
18 miles (29 km) anticlockwise

LUDLOW. Leave going downhill past The Feathers. R (Kidderminster, A4117, Bridgnorth, B4364). Go under railway bridge, then L on Fishmore Road. R (Hayton's Bent 2½). Cont at next junction, where sign was broken during route-testing. Cont (Clee St Margaret 4). L (Clee St Margaret 2). L (Abdon 2, Ditton Priors 4½). Enter

Clee St Margaret. L (Abdon 1¾, Ditton Priors 4¾). L (Bouldon 2, Peaton 2¼). Pass through

Upper Heath. L (Peaton 1, Ludlow 9) Reach

a Peaton. *Join the Wenlock Edge Loop, otherwise cont.* Leave

a (Sutton, Ludlow). Cont (Ludlow). Cont at next junction. Reach

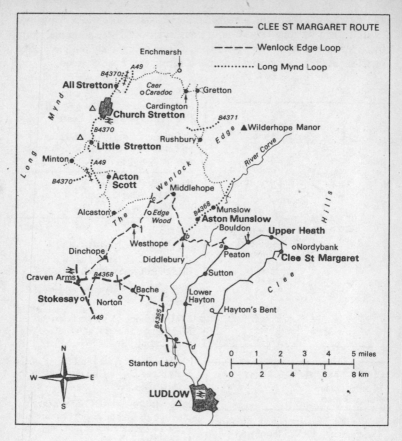

CLEE ST MARGARET ROUTE
Wenlock Edge Loop
Long Mynd Loop

d. Rejoin the Clee St Margaret Route.

Long Mynd Loop
**adds 18 miles (29 km)
anticlockwise**

Leave

b. Cont, *not* L 'Middlehope 1¾'. Pass through

Aston Munslow. L (Rushbury 3, Church Stretton 7¾). L (Rushbury 2½, Church Stretton 7). R (Longville 2¼, Much Wenlock 8½). L (Church Stretton 4½). R (Gretton 1½, Cardington 2). L (Cardington ½, Leebotwood 4½). Enter Cardington. R (Leebotwood 3¾, Church Stretton 5). L (Leebotwood 3½, Church Stretton 5). L at fork to take the less uphill road. Cont (Leebotwood 2¾, Church Stretton 4). L (Church Stretton 3). Cont (All Stretton ¾). Cross railway. L at T junction. Enter

All Stretton. Cont at all junctions. Enter

Church Stretton. Cont at all junctions. Enter

Little Stretton. R by Ragleth Inn. L at T junction onto streamside road. Next R, going through speed de-restriction signs. Enter Minton. L (Marshbrook

1). L to cross level crossing. R (Acton Scott Farm Museum). L (Acton Scott Farm Museum). R (Henley 1¼, Craven Arms 4¾) *otherwise detour 200 yards (metres), continuing straight on, for* **Acton Scott** *farm museum.* Next L at a fork with a small pillar box. Cont (Wolverton 1¼, Harton 2¾). R at **T** junction by woodland edge. Reach

c near 'Picnic Area ½ mile' sign. *Rejoin the Wenlock Edge Loop.*

ASTON ROUTE
14 miles (23 km)
anticlockwise

LUDLOW. Leave from river bridge, going away from town. R (Burrington 5¼, Wigmore 7½). Cont at next junction. Pass through

Aston. Reach

e. Join the Mortimer's Cross Loop, otherwise cont. Leave

e (Wigmore). L (Richards Castle). Reach

h by small pillar box on post. *The Mortimer's Cross Loop rejoins the Aston Route.* Leave

h (Richards Castle). Cont (Ludlow 4). Pass **All Saints.** L at T junction. 1st R, crossing white lines. Bear L at fork. Cont (Ashford Carbonel ½, Caynham 3, Clee Hill 6). Cont at next junction. L (Ludlow 2). R (Ludlow). Bear L at next junction. L opposite 'Steventon New Road' sign.

Mortimer's Cross Loop
adds 17 miles (27 km)
anticlockwise

Leave

e (Burrington, Leintwardine). Cont at next junction. Cont (Leintwardine 2½). Cont at next 2 junctions. L (Wigmore). L (Wigmore). Pass **The Grange** on

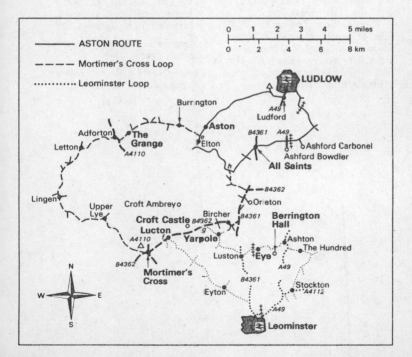

129

your L. R (Knighton 8, A4113, Leintwardine 2). L just past church. Cont at next junction. L at T junction. Cont at next junction. Cont (Lingen, Presteigne). Cont at next junction. Bear L with white lines at next junction. Enter Lingen. R (Presteigne 5, Kington). L (Limebrook, Upper Lye). L (Upper Lye, Aymestrey). R (Mortimer's Cross). L at T junction. Enter

Mortimer's Cross. Cont (Ludlow, A49, Tenbury, A456). Cont at next junction. Reach

f **Lucton** school tennis court. *Join the Leominster Loop, otherwise cont.* Leave

f. Cont in same direction. Reach

g near **Croft Castle** *park entrance. The Leominster Loop rejoins the Mortimer's Cross Loop.* Leave

g (Orleton 2¼, Richards Castle 4). Cont at next 2 junctions. L (Orleton 1½, Richards Castle 3, Ludlow 6½). L (Orleton 1, Richards Castle 2½, Ludlow 6). Cont (Ludlow 5½, B4361). Cont at next 2 junctions. L (Orleton Common, Goggin). R to cross white lines, very soon passing a house with an unusual pointed window. Cont (Goggin, Elton). Reach

h by small pillar box on post. *Rejoin the Aston Route.*

Leominster Loop
adds 13 miles (21 km), including
Leominster detour.
anticlockwise

Leave

f. Turn R to pass tennis court. Cont at next junction. Cont at cross-roads with Give Way sign. Cont (Leominster). R at T junction. R at T junction. L (Shrewsbury, A49) *otherwise detour ½ mile (1 km), R (Town Centre), for* **Leominster**. R (Leysters 3½, A4112, Kimbolton 1). Cont at next junction. L (Pateshall). Cont at next junction. Cont (Middleton on Hill). L (Leominster). R (Shrewsbury, A49). L (Eye Manor 1). pass drive to **Berrington Hall** on your L. Cont at next junction. Enter

Eye. Cont (Leominster). R at T junction with Give Way sign. L (Yarpole 1½). R (Yarpole). Enter

Yarpole. L (Cockgate, Mortimer's Cross). Reach

g near **Croft Castle** *park entrance. Rejoin the Mortimer's Cross Loop.*

The Cheshire Plain

THE CHESHIRE PLAIN

Many have dreamt of lazy days spent bowling along peaceful country lanes. Here that idyll is matched in a countryside as soothing on the eye as it is on the leg muscles, where cows graze in rich pastures, the hedgerows are dotted with ancient oak trees and, in haytime swathes of drying grass pattern the fields. At any time of year big skies give a sense of freedom.

The Cheshire Plain (extending into the county of Salop) is renowned for its multitude of reedy meres and tiny ponds caused in some cases by subsidence following mining of Cheshire salt.

Whitchurch was once called 'Westune', meaning that it was at the westernmost edge of England at the border with Wales. The Cheshire Plain has some low yet impressive hills with cliffs of red sandstone. Each set of routes includes such a range, where wooded slopes contrast with the dairylands, but where the lanes skirt the slopes or seek out the gentlest gradients.

Although this area is delightful for cycling, it is not so interesting for motorists. The roads are therefore quiet, but it does mean that restaurants are infrequent. Never mind: on such easy terrain you wouldn't even notice the weight of a bottle of wine for the picnic!

Easy cycling. Quiet, with some busy road crossings.

WHITCHURCH

Location: 20 miles (32 km) west of Stoke-on-Trent.

Trains: Whitchurch Station is on the line from Crewe to Shrewsbury. Manchester: 1 hour 15 mins (change at Crewe); Birmingham: 1 hour 30 mins (change at Crewe); London: 2 hours 30 mins (change at Crewe).

Tourist Information Bureau: Brownlow Street, Whitchurch, Salop (accommodation service).

Accommodation: Hotel and bed and breakfast accommodation is available at Whitchurch. A YH might be established shortly. The nearest campsites are near Beeston and Wem.

Cycle hire: The nearest are: Border Holiday Tours, 11a St John's Hill, Shrewsbury, tel: (0743) 65150 and Roy Swinnerton, 69 Victoria Road, Fenton, Stoke-on-Trent, tel: (0782) 47782.

Cycle shop: 7 Claypit Street, Whitchurch.

Maps: OS 1:50 000 (nos 117, 126, 127 and 118 for the Shavington Loop). Bartholomew's 1:100 000 (no. 23). OS 1:250 000 (no. 7).

Whitchurch

The Romans built a strategic fortress at **Whitchurch,** and some of the street names in the busy market town of today have Latin origins. Follow the town trail (leaflets being available at the tourist information centre), and you will discover that the ugliness of the town hides much of interest and even beauty, such as a Victorian cast-iron framed building. As a thriving dairy centre Whitchurch has an excellent cheese shop, sharing a fifteenth-century black and white building with a tempting coffee and cake shop; a cheese-making museum is planned for the near future. There are plenty of shops, restaurants and fish and chip shops, from which to buy food.

The 'white church' which gave the town its name collapsed in the eighteenth century, but its Queen Anne replacement is beautiful inside, and contains some work of Randolph Caldecott, the Victorian illustrator and cartoonist, and an unusual modern etched window.

THE BROWN MOSS ROUTE

This route captures the contented atmosphere of rich dairying country with lanes winding past big, prosperous farms like Old Hall at Alkington. The flat roads are peaceful but become busier near **Prees,** (where the New Inn serves food), and **Brown Moss** where the lakes are an attraction.

The Wem Loop

The wooded hills towards **Hodnet** lend variety to this loop, which starts out over flat farmland, and is crossed by a disused branch of the Shropshire Union Canal.

Lowe Hall was once the home of Judge Jeffreys, who sent so many to their deaths in the Bloody Assizes after Monmouth's Rebellion. He was the Baron of **Wem**, a town now well-known for the ales it brews; it also has a Chinese restaurant and a fish and chip shop.

The easy terrain throughout the Cheshire Plain is emphasised beyond Aston by a 'Steep Hill' sign. In thousands of cycling miles I have never found another slope of such gentleness bearing that warning. Impressive and easily defensible, the red Sandstone cliffs beyond **Lee Brockhurst** were used as a hill fort by prehistoric man. Your route into the hills passes bracken woods and splendid beeches, and rises gradually by 200 ft (60 m).

Hodnet church has an octagonal tower, and inside can be seen a fifteenth-century bible made in Germany shortly after the invention of printing. Hodnet Hall Gardens (open) are enhanced by a string of lakes— and by the provision of tea-rooms!

The road to **Weston**, through a pretty valley, rises to give a magnificent view over farmlands to distant hills. The Citadel is an imposing red-stone mansion sited to enjoy the view. Should it rain, you will thank the family who live there, for in Weston they have built a shelter and bench 'for the use of all who pass by'. The village has some attractive half-timbered houses and the stocks still stand near the church.

The Shavington Loop

If you are in the mood for dreaming, this loop will suit you perfectly. There are neither many points of interest to tax your mind, nor many junctions to demand your concentration.

There are graceful sweeps of English parkland near **Shavington Hall**, much of it now under corn, and cattle graze by the lake which is covered with yellow water-lilies in summer. Otherwise you can coast through open farmland along flat and peaceful lanes.

THE WRENBURY ROUTE

This set of routes is more hilly than the Brown Moss set. Even so, none of them are difficult, the hardest climb on the Wrenbury Route taking you up 250 ft (75 m) into Wirswall, and the higher points giving views not only of the Welsh mountains, but also the Peckforton Hills, and occasionally the Pennines some 30 miles (50 km) away to the east.

Most of the riding is through flat dairylands studded with oaks, a fine avenue of which lead you to **Wrenbury**. The church has a musicians' gallery, a pleasingly painted organ, and a notice telling of the unusual duties of the one-time dog-whipper.

Wrenbury Mill stands beside the Shropshire Union Canal, planned in 1791 to connect iron and coal fields and limestone quarries in east Wales with the Mersey. It is now popular for holiday cruises, and you may have to wait whilst the bridge is raised to let the colourful narrow boats pass. Near Wrenbury Mill the Cotton Arms serves food.

The Malpas Loop

The riding continues to be easy here, the only significant climb being one of some 200 ft (30 m) up to Hampton Post. In places the pastures give way to cornfields, or orchards and fruit bushes. Where the loop skirts the parkland (open) of **Cholmondeley Castle**, you can catch glimpses of the nineteenth-century castle's drum-towers, and you may see some of the deer too. Inside the park is a farm which stocks rare breeds of cattle; there is also an ancient private chapel, with a notable screen.

The ride to **Malpas** is not very inspiring but you are amply rewarded by the beauty of the church. Among its treasures are a magnificent thirteenth-century chest, iron-bound by a local blacksmith, sixteenth-century Flemish roundels of delicately painted stained glass, and the exceptionally elegant effigies of the Breretons. The town itself, centred around a many-tiered market cross, has some pleasing half-timbered buildings. Food can be found at pubs and the fish and chip shop.

The Beeston Loop

This loop skirts the Peckforton Hills, whose slopes are sometimes gentle and dark with woods, and sometimes steep. Although the ride avoids hard slopes, the highest rise being a gradual one of some 200 ft (30 m), the hills rising abruptly from the plain almost demand that castles be built upon them. **Beeston Castle** (DoE, open) surmounting a craggy hill top, was built in the thirteenth century, later becoming a Royal stronghold. It withstood attack for a long time in the Civil War, but after its eventual surrender was deliberately ruined. Its battlements and drum towers are echoed by those of **Peckforton Castle** on the opposite valley-side, although the latter was built as a mansion by Salvin, a famous nineteenth-century architect.

Peckforton village has a castle of a rather different kind, being sculpted on the back of a massive elephant statue in a garden to the left of your road. The village houses are predominantly half-timbered above red-stone ground floors; a style distinctive to this corner of England.

The Bickerton Poacher on the A534 near Gallantry Bower serves food, and a small snack bar dispenses drinks and home-made cakes below **Beeston Castle**.

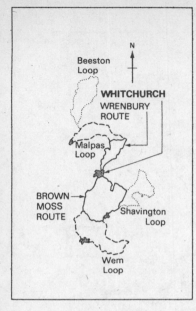

N

Beeston
Loop

WHITCHURCH
WRENBURY
ROUTE

Malpas
Loop

BROWN
MOSS
ROUTE

Shavington
Loop

Wem
Loop

BROWN MOSS ROUTE
19 miles (31 km)
anticlockwise

WHITCHURCH. Leave from the bottom end of High Street (A525, Wrexham). Soon turn L on Watergate Street. R on Bark Hill. Cont on Alkington Road. Cont at a junction by a VR wall pillar box. Cont at the next junction. R (Welsh End 2¼, Northwood 6½). Bear L where the road going R has a 5 ton limit. Cont at the next junction. Cont (Welsh End, Wem). Enter Welsh End. Cont (Dobson's Bridge, Ellesmere). L (Bostock Hall, Wem). Cont at the next junction. Reach

a Bostock Hall. *Join the Wem Loop, or cont.* Leave

a (Prees, Whitchurch). R (Braynes Hall). L (Whitchurch, Wem). R at the T junction. R (Wem 3, Shrewsbury 13½). Next L, to pass in front of a row of white houses. L at a T junction by a big farm. Reach

b. The Wem Loop rejoins the Brown Moss Route. Leave

b towards a large farm, with an estate of houses just visible to its left. R at the T junction. Enter

Prees. Cont on Church Street. L by the war memorial onto Moreton Street. Cont at the next junction. Cont (Calverhall 3, Ightfield 3). Cont (Calverhall 2¾, Ightfield 3). Reach

c near Millenheath farm. *Join the Shavington Loop, or cont.* Leave

c (Ightfield 2). Reach

d Ightfield. *The Shavington Loop rejoins the Brown Moss Route.* Leave

d on The Townsend. Enter Ash Magna. L on a lane, not signposted but almost opposite a 'No Through Road' finger-post. Cont at the cross roads. Next R at a junction around a small grass triangle. Pass **Brown Moss**. Cont at the junction by Brown Moss Cottages.

Wem Loop
adds 14 miles (23 km)
anticlockwise

Leave

a Bostock Hall (Waterloo, Wem). R at the T junction. R (Waterloo, Wem). Cont (Northwood, Wem). Cross the Canal Bridge. L (Lowe, Wem). Cont (Creamore 1½, Whitchurch 9½). Cont at the next junction. Reach

Lowe. L at the T junction. R (Wem). L at a T junction to pass The Fox. Enter

Wem. Follow the Station signs through Wem. Cross the level crossing. R (Aston 1, Barkers Green 1½). Cont at the next junction. R, to cross the river. Cont past a pillar box and telephone box. Enter

Lee Brockhurst. Bear R just past the church. L (Whitchurch, A49). R (Booley 2½, Stanton 3½). L by Moston Farm and opposite Rose Cottage. L at the T junction. There are views L to **Bury Walls**. L just before a 'West Midlands Shooting Ground' sign. R

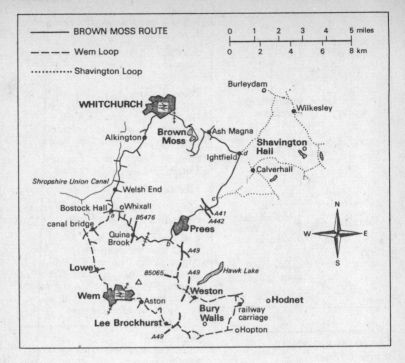

beside a pond. At first this road can be so mucky that you might mistake it for a track. Cont at the next junction. Pass an inhabited railway carriage. L at the T junction *otherwise detour 1 mile (1½ km) R at T junction, R (Hodnet ½) for* **Hodnet** Cont at the next junction. Cont (Weston 1½, Wem 5½). Enter

Weston. Cont (Wem). R (Wem). Cont (Wem 3¾, Ellesmere 12¼). R (Prees 2, B5065). L (Whitchurch, A49, Prees 1). Cont at the next junction. First L, after a farm and before a white house. Reach

b. Rejoin the Brown Moss Route.

Shavington Loop
**adds 11 miles (18 km)
anticlockwise**

Leave

c near Millenheath Farm (Calverhall 2, Market Drayton 8). First R to cross a

white line, at an unsignposted junction. L at the next cross roads, where a 'Willaston' sign points back the way you came. Enter Calverhall. Cont at the next junction. R (Market Drayton 6). L (Adderley). L at the 'Tittenley' signpost to pass between two lodge houses, entering the parkland of **Shavington Hall**. L (Wilkesley 2). R at the 'Shavington Gardens' sign. Cont (Burleydam 1¾, Whitchurch 6¼). Cont at next junction *not* R to Aston & Wrenbury. L (Ightfield). Cont (Whitchurch 4½, Ash 2¾). Reach

d Ightfield. *Rejoin the Brown Moss Route.*

WRENBURY ROUTE
**12½ miles (20 km)
anticlockwise**

WHITCHURCH. From the parish

church of St Alkmund, leave towards the Horse and Jockey. Cont on Claypit Street. Cont (Marbury). Cont at the next junction. First R to cross white lines onto a lane, itself having a Give Way sign at the junction. L (Nantwich, Wrenbury). R (Wrenbury 2). Cont at the next junction. R (Wrenbury, Nantwich). Cont (Wrenbury). Enter

Wrenbury. L (Norbury, Bickley, Cholmondeley). Reach

e **Wrenbury Mill.** *Join the Malpas Loop, or cont.* Leave

e (Bickley, Norbury). Cont (Norbury ½, Bickley 2½). Reach

g. The Malpas Loop rejoins the Wrenbury Route. Leave

g (Marbury). L (Marbury, Whitchurch). R (Bickley, Malpas, Wirswall). L (Quoisley, Wirswall). R at a T junction with a Give Way sign.

Malpas Loop
adds 12 miles (19 km) anticlockwise

Leave

e (Wrenbury Frith & Cholmondeley). Bear L with the white lines at the next junction. Cont at the next junction. L (Cholmondeley, Tarporley 8½, Chester 16). Cont (Egerton 3, Bickerton 5). Pass the entrance to **Cholmondeley Castle.** Cont at the next junction. L (Malpas). R (Malpas). Reach

f Hampton Post. *Join the Beeston Loop, or cont.* Leave

f (Malpas). Cont (Malpas 1½). L at the T junction. Cont, or follow Malpas signs, at all junctions till reaching **Malpas.** L at a T junction to pass the Fire Station. L opposite The Crown (Nomansheath, Nantwich). Cont (Chester, alternative route for heavy

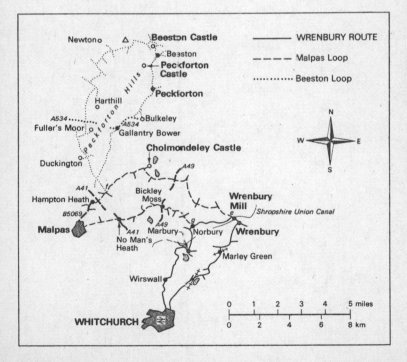

vehicles). Cont at the next three junctions. Cont (Bickley 1½, Marbury 4, Norbury 4). Cont (Wrenbury 5½, Nantwich 10¾, Beeston 9, Tarporley 11). Cont (Wrenbury, Nantwich). Cont at the next junction. Cont (Norbury 2, Wrenbury 4, Aston 5½, Nantwich 9¼). Cont (Wrenbury 4). L (Norbury, Wrenbury, Nantwich). Cont at the next junction. Cont (Wrenbury 3, Norbury 1). Reach

g. *Rejoin the Wrenbury Route.*

Beeston Loop
**adds 16 miles (26 km)
anticlockwise**

Leave

f Hampton Post (Chester, Broxton). R at the T junction. R (Tarporley). Cont at the next junction. R (Beeston 5, Ridley, Acton, Nantwich 10). Cont at the next junction. R (Nantwich). Cont at the next junction. Cont (A534, Tarporley, Nantwich). L (Beeston). Cont on Stone House Lane. Enter

Peckforton. Cont (Beeston, Tarporley). L (Tattenhall 3, Bolesworth 4, Burwardsley 5). R (Beeston Castle, Ancient Monument). Pass **Beeston Castle**. Cont at the next two junctions. R (Tattenhall 3, Burwardsley 4). Ignore two 'No Through Road' turn-offs. Cont (Tattenhall, Burwardsley, Harthill). Cont at the next junction. L (Burwardsley 1¼). R (Harthill 2, Broxton 3, Bolesworth 2). Bear R at the next junction. L (Harthill, Broxton). First R, at the summit of a short slope. Cont at a Give Way cross roads. Bear R *not* L on Broomhill Lane. R (Duckington). L (Duckington). Cont at the next two junctions. R (Malpas), then immediately L. Reach

f *Hampton Post. Rejoin the Malpas Loop.*

Freewheeling down the Llanberis Pass

SNOWDONIA AND ANGLESEY

This is the most varied set of rides in this book. They explore lush valleys, desolate moorlands, rugged mountains and rolling farmlands, with views to open sea and sheltered straits. The marks of man range from a serenely lovely moated castle to the vast and savage scars of mountain slate-quarrying. A gruelling pass at 1100 ft (350 m) above sea level contrasts with miles of near-flat roads beside the Menai Strait, and there is almost every sort of cycling terrain between the two extremes.

It is partly to enjoy the region's full variety and partly because of the limited choice of roads in the mountains that these routes necessitate your staying in a different place each night. It is best to start at Conway, deciding whether you still have the time and inclination to follow the Capel Garmon Loop on the first day when you reach Betws-y-Coed. Should the second day's weather be very bad you can return to Conway (Llandudno Junction) on a branch train line from Betws-y-Coed. Otherwise cycle to Bangor, adding the Anglesey Loop if you wish, and return on the Bangor to Conway (Llandudno Junction) train.

Large sections of these rides explore the Snowdonia National Park, so you will share the mountain roads with other tourists. There is little heavy traffic, however, as lorries prefer to use flatter coastal routes. By and large the lanes are very quiet, but many of the signposts have been removed (perhaps by Welsh Nationalists), so take great care in your navigation, and if in doubt, ask. Although the mountain population is sparse, quite a number of roadside places offer tourist accommodation and food.

Moderate cycling, strenuous in parts. Very quiet but with some busy streches of road including a bridge crossing.

CONWAY, BETWS-Y-COED AND BANGOR

Location: Bangor and Conway are both on the North Wales coast.

Trains: Bangor and Llandudno Junction are both on the main line from Crewe and Chester to Holyhead. Betws-y-Coed is on a branch line from Llandudno Junction. Manchester to Bangor: 2 hours 45 mins; Birmingham to Bangor: 3 hours 30 mins (change at Crewe).

Coach: Coaches run along the North Wales coast road through Colwyn Bay, Conway and Bangor, from Chester and Liverpool.

Tourist Information Bureaux: Snowdonia National Park and Wales Tourist Office, Castle Street, Conway, Gwynedd, tel: (049 263) 2248 (summer service only, accommodation service); The Tourist Information Bureau, Betwys-y-Coed, Gwynedd, tel: (069 02) 426 (accommodation service); Bron Castell, Bangor, Gwynedd, tel: (0248) 52786 (summer service only, accommodation service).

Accommodation: There is hotel and bed and breakfast accommodation in each of the three centres. Penmaenmawr YH is 3 miles (5 km) from Conway, and Colwyn Bay and Rowen YH are also fairly near. Oaklands YH is 3 miles (5 km) from Betws-y-Coed. There is a YH in Bangor. Other hostels are at Capel Curig and Llanberis on the Llanberis Route, and there are several others in the area. There are camp sites at: Morfa Beach Caravan Park, Conway, tel: (049 263) 2338; Bwlch Mawr Farm, Llanrwst Road, Conway tel: (049 263) 2856; Riverside Caravan and Camping Ground, Betwys-y-Coed, tel: (069 02) 310; Hendre Farm, Betws-y-Coed; Dinas Farm, Halfway Bridge, Bangor, tel: (0248) 4227. This site is 3 miles (5 km) south-east of Bangor. There are other sites at Brynrefail on the Llanberis Route, and at Llangoed and Llanfaes on the Anglesey Loop.

Cycle-hire: West End Cycles, 121 Conway Road, Colwyn Bay, Clwyd, tel: (0492) 30269, 5 miles (8 km) east of Conway, and Bryn Golau, Capel Curig, Gwynedd, tel: (069 04) 251, on the Llanberis Route.

Cycle-shop: West End cycles, as above; John Owen, High Street, Bangor; Barry Davies, College Road, Bangor.

Maps: OS 1:50 000 (nos 115, 116 and 124); Bartholomew's 1:100 000 (no. 27); OS 1:250 000 (no. 7).

Conway, Betws-y-Coed and Bangor

The nature of these routes means that you are unlikely to spend much time in any of the three centres. Nevertheless each has its charm and interest, and meals can be bought in them all.

Conway grew around its castle (DoE, open) on a strategic estuarine site. Much of the medieval town walls remains, and the railway bridge is built in a harmonizing gothic style. Thomas Telford, the famous early civil engineer, built the suspension bridge; its Old Toll House is now run by the National Trust as a museum devoted to him. Conway boasts not only Britain's smallest house, but also Wales' oldest. The latter, called Aberconwy House (NT, open) houses the Conway Exhibition.

Betws-y-Coed's stone bridge spans a river tumbling over wide rocky falls. The iron Waterloo Bridge was completed by Telford in the year of the famous battle that spelt final defeat for Napoleon. Once a peaceful Victorian honeymoon resort, Betws-y-Coed now caters for tourists and has a woollen mill, craft shops, a miniature railway and railway museum.

Bangor has many shops, a cinema and a theatre. There is an art gallery and museum of Welsh antiquities, and only 2 miles (3 km) away, you can visit Penrhyn Castle (NT, open), which is built of marble with a colossal keep. Standing in grounds graced with exotic trees and shrubs, the castle contains dolls from all over the world.

THE LLANRWST ROUTE

North of Ty'n-y-groes the Conway estuary curves lazily through well-tended farmlands, and passes the superb gardens at **Bodnant** (NT, open). Snowdonia's mountains rise beyond a profusion of colourful trees and garden shrubs, and there is a welcome snack bar there too. **Gwydir Castle** (open) is an historic Royal residence, still furnished in the Tudor style, and with lovely grounds that are famed for their exotic birds.

Between Ty'n-y-groes and Llanrwst there is a hard climb onto a 600-ft (200-m) high ridge, from which you can enjoy views over the wooded Conway valleyside to Snowdonia's barren heights in the west, and the gentler valley of woods and pastures in the east. The cycling here is fairly strenuous, and again many of the signposts are missing.

Llanrwst is a bustling little town set around a square, where you can find cafés and a fish and chip shop. Its fifteenth-century stone-built courthouse was later converted into two cottages (NT, open). The North Wales Museum of Wildlife specializes in Snowdonia's fauna, and birds of the South Pacific. The sombre richness of the church's wooden rood and loft contrasts with the adjoining chapel, where interesting monuments and carvings are bathed in the light which streams through large and elegant windows. Inigo Jones, the seventeenth-century Welsh architect, designed

141

both the chapel and the graceful triple-arched bridge over the Conway.

The work of the Forestry Commission (which was set up after the shortage of timber following the First World War), is explained and illustrated at the **Gwydir Uchaf** exhibition. A nearby chapel (DoE, open) has a notable painted ceiling.

The Capel Garmon Loop

This strenuous loop climbs high to desolate moorlands around Llyn Conway, the source of the river which accompanies you throughout much of the ride. Surging along its rocky, tree-clad course beside the A5, it passes below a graceful single arch bridge near Glan Conway. Sometimes it tumbles over low but picturesque falls; the Conway Falls are particularly fine but you have to pay to see them.

The A5 suffers bursts of heavy traffic, but the other roads are quiet, and on the farm road beyond Ysbyty Ifan the slow pace forced upon you by the gated farmyards suits the peace of the deep countryside.

Penmachno Mill is a craft and woollen shop where you can watch the machines being worked in the basement. It lies in a valley of woods and sheep pastures which becomes ever more open and lonely as you cycle easily towards the south-west. Near Carrog, steep slopes of bracken, boulders and scrubby trees, give way to dense pine woods at the point where your 1000-ft (300-m) uphill struggle begins.

Seven miles of freewheeling towards Ysbyty Ifan follow the young river Conway over heather moorland with low mountains in the distance, and along roads where sheep wander freely.

Bronze Age man buried his dead in **Capel Garmon chamber** (DoE, open), 400 ft (120 m), above the Conway valley on steeply rolling hills now covered with fields. Capel Garmon village has a pleasingly compact centre and some sturdy outlying cottages. Beyond it is a leafy but very steep descent which requires special care in the wet, and which should be walked if the road is icy.

THE LLANBERIS ROUTE

Snowdon's craggy summit at 3850 ft (1085 m) is the highest in all England and Wales. It dominates the eastern part of this ride, yet in the low-lying farm country near Bangor no mountains can be seen.

At first you must follow the A5, which can be busy with both lorries and tourists, many of whom pay to see the attractive but commercialized Swallow Falls. **Ty-hyll**, the 'ugly house', was built of ungainly boulders in the fifteenth century. The tranquil lane to Pont Cyfyng passes leafy woodlands and pastures where a sparkling river flows.

At Capel Curig and its café the route leaves the A5 to become quieter, climbing gradually past two lakes which shimmer below sweeping, grassy valley-sides. The massive and rugged Snowdon range rises straight ahead. John Hunt's 1953 Everest expedition team practised on the range, using **Pen-y-Gwryd** hotel as their base. A stiff 250-ft (75-m) climb takes you to Pen-y-Pass at the road's summit, where the café is a welcome sight, especially if a chilling mist has descended. Bad weather can come to Snowdonia very quickly, so always carry extra warm and waterproof clothing, and remember that both Pen-y-Pass and the high moorlands on the Capel Garmon Loop may be under snow, even when the lower lands are clear.

Footpaths from **Pen-y-Pass** climb a further 2400 ft (730 m) to Snowdon's summit. The ascent is exhilarating for the properly equipped, but do not attempt it without a 1:50 000 map, a compass, spare food and clothing, and several remaining hours of daylight. Do not attempt the knife-edge Crib Goch path unless you are very experienced.

The Pass of Llanberis is a dramatic rocky ravine the sides of which dwarf the occasional whitewashed farmstead. A superb freewheel takes you to **Llanberis**, where the mountain-sides have been eaten away by slate-quarrying. Slate-dressing sheds, a foundry and a 50-ft (15-m) water-wheel are amongst the North Wales Quarrying Museum's exhibits. A new power station here will be Britain's biggest pumped-storage scheme. Llyn Padarn offers boating and fishing, and you can ride on the narrow gauge railway along its northern shore. The lazy way to the top of Snowdon is to take the mountain railway from Llanberis, where cafés and craft shops cater for the many tourists. **Dolbadarn Castle** (open) is a grim pele tower where the Welshman, Owen the Red, was held captive for twenty-three years by his own brother.

Beyond Llyn Padarn you enter softly undulating farm country, with rocky knolls and marshy patches where wild yellow irises bloom in early summer. Twentieth-century houses are thickly scattered in the landscape, yet ancient field boundary walls, built with massive boulders, still stand. Purple slate from the nearby mountains is even made into fences, a fine example surrounding **Pen Dinas**. This was a prehistoric camp, 'Pen' being welsh for 'top' and 'dinas' meaning 'hill fortress'.

The Anglesey Loop

Celtic druids held this island sacred and called it Mon, whilst Celtic Christians used it as a base for their missions to foreign lands. Vulnerable to attack by sea, the island was captured from the Welsh by an Anglo-Saxon king, after which it was called 'Angles Ea', the 'Isle of the English'.

Fields and woods now chequer the island, and the cycling is moderately easy, on quiet, undulating lanes. Llandona (which has a café) is your highest point at 500 ft (120 m), but beyond it a ridge-top road commands views over the sea to Snowdonia's mountains and the Great

143

Orme's Head peninsula near Conway. From here it is easy to understand why Norse sea-farers likened it to the head of a terrible sea serpent or 'orme'.

Some of the island's many recent houses are pleasingly built with traditional slate roofs and whitewashed walls. A seventeenth-century dovecote at **Penmon** (DoE, open) has hundreds of nesting holes, and a thick central pillar to support the ladder during collection of eggs or young birds (called squabs—hence the term 'squabbling') for food. The priory remains (DoE, open), include a huge cross showing Scandinavian influence, a fish-pond, and Saint Seriol's clear-water well. Sea-birds wheel around **Puffin Island** (also called 'Priestholm', as it was a religious settlement in Celtic times), where there is a café in the pilot house.

Beaumaris is a popular yachting town, with several restaurants and cafés. Seek out the pair of old, elaborately boxed-in water-pumps. The thirteenth-century castle (DoE, open), is beautifully proportioned, its drum towers reflected in a moat which is connected to the sea by a canal. The name of Beaumaris is Norman in origin, meaning 'lovely flat land', and indeed the cycling near it is easy. Milestones beside the road to Menai Bridge are unusually accurate, giving distances in miles and furlongs.

Built by Telford in 1826, the **Menai Bridge** was the first suspension structure to bear heavy vehicles. It is narrow for today's busy traffic, which unfortunately accompanies you between here and **Bangor**. Walk across the bridge on the footpath so that you can admire its metalwork structure, and the tubular railway bridge to the south-west. Menai Bridge Town has a Museum of Childhood and several cafés.

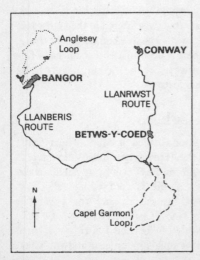

LLANRWST ROUTE
16½ miles (27 km)
north to south

CONWAY. Leave through gate between castle and Guildhall. L (Llanrwst 11, Betws-y-Coed 14). Cont at next 2 junctions. L (Taly Cafn Bridge). Cont at next junction. L to cross river and railway. L on main road then immediately R, opposite Tal y Cafn Hotel. L at T junction to continue climbing. Cont at next junction. Cont (Eglwysbach). R (Eglwysbach) *otherwise detour ½ mile (1 km) following Bodnant signs for* **Bodnant**. Cont past a pillar box on a telegraph pole. Enter Eglwysbach. Cont through village. Cont (Llangernyw 5). R by Bryn Gosol cottage on a lane with a 'road narrows'

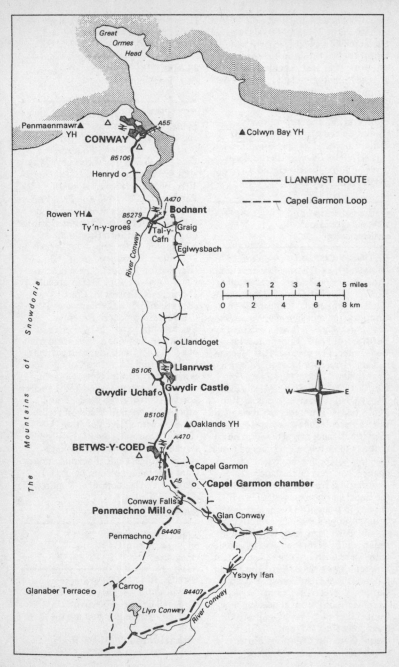

sign. Cont at next junction. Cont by Pen y Graig Farm. R at cross-roads to pass a telephone box. Next L to cross a little hump-backed bridge in 100 yards (metres). Bear L at next junction. Cont at next 2 junctions. Cont by pillar box, number 44. Cont at next junction. Enter

Llanrwst. R on Abergele Road. L (Betws y Coed 4). R (Capel Gwydir Uchaf Chapel). L (Capel Gwydif Uchaf Chapel). Pass **Gwydir Castle**. Pass drive on R to **Gwydir Uchaf**. Cont on to **BETWS-Y-COED**.

Capel Garmon Loop
23½ miles (38 km)
anticlockwise

BETWS-Y-COED. Leave on the A5 going south-east (Llangollen direction). Cross Waterloo Bridge. R (Llangollen 32, Dolgellau 33). Cont (Pentrefoelas 6, Cerrigydrudion 11). R (Penmachno 2). Cont past the mill sign *otherwise detour 100 yards (metres) following mill signs for* **Penmachno Mill**. Cont at next junction. Enter. Penmachno. Pass Machno Inn and cross river bridge. L (Cwm Penmachno 3). Cont (Festiniog 7½ MLS). L (Yspytty Ifan 7 MLS). Enter Ysbyty Ifan. L at cross-roads *not* R to Pentrefoelas. From the next turning to the A5 the ride follows a tarmaced farm road which is not a right of way. You are unlikely to be refused permission to use it, but if you prefer not to take the chance, continue on the lane you are now on till it reaches the A5 very near the Capel Garmon turn-off. Turn R passing in front of a bench, and soon going through a gate. Pass through several gated farmyards. R at T junction near a conifer plantation, and by a stone with 'Ochr Cefn Isa' marked on it. L at T junction with main road. Cont at next junction. Pass Glan Conwy. R (Capel Garmon 2, Nebo 2¾). Cont (Nebo, Capel Garmon). Cont at next junction. Cont (Llanrwst). Pass a signposted track for a 500 yard (metre) walk to **Capel Garmon Chamber**. Enter Capel Garmon. Cont past chapel. L

(Betws-y-Coed). L at T junction with main road. Follow (Betws-y-Coed) signs.

LLANBERIS ROUTE
26 miles (42 km)
east to west

BETWS-Y-COED. (Bangor 20). L just before main road swings R to cross the river *otherwise cont on main road for 100 yards (metres) to* **Ty hyll**. Cross river, then L at T junction with a Give Way sign. Enter Capel Curig. L (Llanberis 10¼, Beddgelert 11½. Caernarfon 17¾, Porthmadog 19, A4086). Pass **Pen-y-Gwryd**. R (Llanberis 5, Caernarfon 12, A4086). Pass **Pen-y-Pass**. Pass drive on R to **Dolbardarn Castle**. Cont (Cwm-y-glo 3, Llanrug 4¼, Caernarvon 7¾). Enter **Llanberis**. Cont (Caernarfon 7). Cont at next junction. Cont (Caernarfon 7). R (Brynrefail ¼, Deiniolen 2, Bangor 8). Cont (Brynrefail ¼). L (Penisarwaun 1). Cont at next junction. Enter Penisarwaun. Straight over cross roads with a line of pylons to the L. R in front of a big chapel with Glasgoed written on it. R opposite Penygroes Cottage; there is a sign for (Pentir, Bangor), but it points between the two roads. Pass **Pen Dinas**. Cont at cross-roads. L at T junction, then immediately R at T junction with a Give Way sign. L (Pentir, Caerhun). Bear L by Vaynol Arms. Bear R just after crossing a stream bridge. Cont at next junction. Cont past pillar box number 243. L (Bangor 1). R at bottom of Hendrewen Road, to

BANGOR

ANGLESEY LOOP
26 miles (42 km)
clockwise

BANGOR. Leave following signs for Holyhead till reaching the Menai Bridge. The bridge is narrow and busy; it is best to dismount and use the foot-path. Enter
Menai Bridge. R (Menai Bridge Town, Beaumaris, A545). Cont at all

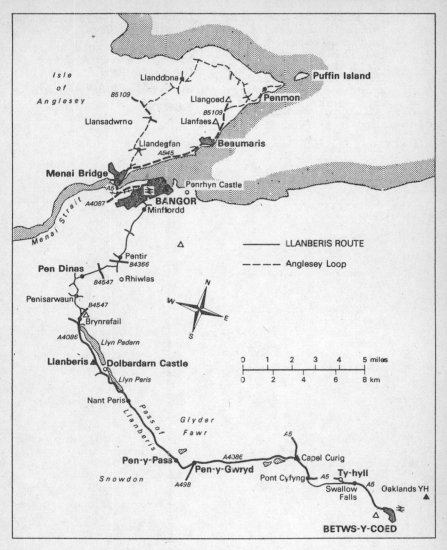

Map legend:
—— LLANBERIS ROUTE
---- Anglesey Loop

junctions through Menai Bridge. L (Llandegfan). At top of slope, L on 4 ton limit road. Cont at next junction. L (Beaumaris 3¼ M). L (Pentraeth, A5025). Cycle down a dip then up again to turn R crossing white lines. R then L (Pentraeth). R (Llanddona 2M). R (Llanddona, Beaumaris). L (Llanddona, I'r Traeth, to the beach). Enter Llanddona. R by telephone box (*not* ahead 'to the beach'). Cont (Glan yr Afon 2½, Llangoed 3½). Cont (*not* L on to Single track road with passing places). Cont (Glanrafon, Llangoed). Sharp L to pass an 'Unsuitable for lorries and coaches' sign. Cont at

147

junction by another 'Unsuitable for lorries and coaches' sign. Cont at all junctions still keeping L by an old signpost with its arms taken off, to pass along R edge of a small wood. R then L (Penmon Priory). R (B'maris) *otherwise detour 2 miles (3 km), L (Penmon Priory and Dovecote), for* **Penmon**, *and the shore opposite* **Puffin Island**. L

(Porthaethwy, Menai Bridge, A5). Cont at next junction. Enter

Beaumaris. Cont through town, to leave on the waterside A545. Cont (Bangor, A5). Enter

Menai Bridge. Follow signs for

BANGOR

Stannage Edge

THE PEAK DISTRICT

The high hills of the Peak District are of two kinds. Those of the Dark Peak have broad heather-moorland summits, which rise above farmed slopes and are made of millstone grit; so called because it was used for millstones. Field walls are made of it too, and it stands out in higher ground as 'edges' whose deeply fissured cliff-faces run for miles.

The White Peak by contrast, is limestone country where, emerald pastures are patterned with walls and field barns of rough white rock. Britain offers no scenes more fresh and vibrant than a sunny day in the White Peak. The dividing line between the two regions is not a neat one, but roughly speaking the White Peak lies south of Eyam and the Dark Peak to its north.

Although the rides are short, they are amongst the most exhausting in the book, for the hills are high, steep and frequent. Make sure you choose rides which are not too long for your ability. Some of the lanes are almost deserted, but you will meet heavier traffic on other roads, as well as lorries from the big limestone quarries of the White Peak. Food is easy to come by.

Rain soaks rapidly through porous limestone, and so the rambling, stone-built villages which are built higher up the hills rarely have streams close by. For this reason, the village well used to be of vital importance, and was 'dressed' each year with floral pictures in thanksgiving for its waters. Well-dressings continue to be a strong tradition, each village having its own well-dressing day which is often related to the church's patron saint. Ask the information bureau for a listing of villages and their dates for the year.

Strenuous cycling. Quiet but tourist traffic at times. One track needs wheeling at times.

EYAM

Location: 12 miles (20 km) south-west of Sheffield.

Trains: A line from Manchester to Sheffield runs through Edale, Hope, Bamford, Hathersage to Grindleford, which is 3 miles (5 km) from Eyam. Manchester: 1 hour; Leeds: 1 hour 30 mins (change at Sheffield); Birmingham: 2 hours 30 mins (change at Manchester).

Tourist Information Bureaux: The nearest are run by the Peak District National Park in Castleton and Edale. For information in advance of your visit contact St Ann's Well, The Crescent, Buxton, Derbyshire, tel: (0298) 5106 (accommodation service).

Accommodation: There are a few bed and breakfast houses in Eyam but no hotels. Youth Hostels can be found at Eyam, Hathersage, Edale, Castleton, Bretton, Bakewell, Youlgreave and Hartington. Two miles (3 km) west of Eyam is a campsite at Brosterfield Farm, Foolow, Eyam, Sheffield, tel: (0433) 30958. Other sites can be found near Hope, Winnats Pass, Edale, Ashford and Over Haddon. Most villages and some isolated farms also offer accommodation.

Cycle hire: Monsal Head Cycle Hire, Little Longstone, Derbyshire, tel: (062 987) 505. This is 5 miles (8 km) south-west of Eyam. For an extra charge they will deliver and collect the cycles to other places.

Cycle shop: P. Hebden, Matlock Street, Bakewell, Derbyshire, and several in Sheffield, which is accessible by train.

Maps: OS 1:50 000 (nos 110, 119). Also the 1":1 mile Tourist Map of the Peak District covers all the rides; Bartholomew's 1:100 000 (no. 29); OS 1:250 000 (no. 5 or no. 6).

Eyam

Eyam is famed as 'the plague village', for the disease reached here in 1665, brought from London in a box of clothes. When the first victims fell, the Rector, William Mompesson, urged the folk neither to leave the village nor to meet other people, and their heroic, self-imposed isolation kept the plague from spreading. A cupboard made with wood from that very clothes box is inside the church. There is also an eighteenth-century sundial which tells the time throughout the world, and a carved ninth-century Anglo-Saxon cross.

Despite decimation by the plague, the village recovered and prospered because of local mining and quarrying. It is a typical Peak District village in that it is loose-knit with stark yet friendly stone houses. There is a café and a pub serving food, and the fish and chip shop opens on Saturdays. Although tourists are attracted to the village, Eyam has escaped commercialization. There is little bad-weather amusement here, but **Hathersage** (described on the Eyam Moor Route) is only 5 miles (8 km) away along fairly flat A roads.

THE EYAM MOOR ROUTE

During the plague, the trading of goods with outsiders had to be done with care. The things they needed would be left at **Mompesson's Well**, and the villagers would leave the money for them in the water, hoping that it would thus be cleansed. You will appreciate their efforts all the more when you climb the steep 300-ft (100-m) slope to the well.

The high moorlands are dark with peat and heather, and in a good September you will find plenty of bilberries to pick and eat. Hucklow Edge is 700 ft (200 m) above the Plough (at *a* on the map), and your long ascent climbs the side of a particularly sequestered valley. From the summit's other side you may see gliders soaring in the air currents. Another reward for your efforts is a 'top of the world' ridge road through Bretton, with marvellous views on either side.

Your only chance of finding food on this ride is to go into **Hathersage**, which also has a swimming pool. Little John, one of Robin Hood's faithful band, is buried by the church, which contains fine brasses, together with replicas and materials for rubbing: some of them are detailed and yet small enough to be carried rolled-up on a bicycle. Charlotte Brönte stayed awhile in Hathersage, modelling her 'Morton' of *Jane Eyre* upon it, and even finding the name of 'Eyre' upon a medieval church brass.

The Stannage Edge Loop

Cottages at **Hathersage** have doorsteps made of millstones, perhaps old 'seconds' hewn from Stannage Edge. A hard 500-ft (150-m) ascent takes you to a windswept waste of peat and bracken below the Edge, where your only shelter for miles is the Mountain Rescue hut. Stannage Edge is a gaunt 3-mile (5-km) fissured cliff but even so, the Romans found a footway up it, building a road whose stone slabs are still in place above the Edge (you can reach it on the footpath which starts near a 'Boundary of Open Country' sign past the Mountain Rescue Post).

Sombre but exhilarating, the Stannage Edge area is in stark contrast to limestone country around **Castleton,** when white walls divide the valley pastures and white crags break through the hillside turf. One rugged bluff is surmounted by Peveril Castle (DoE, open), a ruined Norman stronghold whose site was given to the Peverils by William the Conqueror himself. Many tourists visit the castle and the awe-inspiring cave-system dissolved out of the limestone by aeons of seeping water. A passage is reputed to link the castle to Peak Cavern, where the villagers used to barricade themselves when under attack.

Many locals are employed in quarrying the limestone for cement. A slender chimney and white dust in the air marks the modern **Hope Works** from afar, although a little, tall-chimneyed building on the left of your road shows that limestone has been worked here for a long time. Beyond a hard ascent out of Castleton, the near-level lanes to Little Hucklow pass above the grimy grandeur of Hope's huge quarries.

The **Ladybower Reservoir** also adds a vigorous element to the landscape, though at the cost of two drowned villages. Your leafy lanes from Stannage Edge through Thornhill to Hope pass below the reservoir's stone retaining-wall.

The Mam Tor Loop

The Peak District's superb limestone scenery is at its most impressive in the gorge of Winnats Pass, where crags tower over a lane so steep that even a walking ascent is hard. Nearby are more cave systems: you can tour the Speedwell Cavern by boat via tunnels dug in the eighteenth-century by leadminers. The unique Blue John stone found in the cavern of the same name is renowned for its beauty. Some fine examples are in the Vatican library, and you can buy objects made from it in tourist shops close by.

If you want a rest at the Winnats Pass summit you have an excellent excuse: study the undulating horizon to your right, and it betrays the sixteen-acre fort, built in the Iron Age above **Mam Tor's** massive, barren face. Here you re-enter dark-stone country, where the unstable rock layers of Mam Tor cause frequent landslips, earning it the nickname of 'Shivering Mountain'. You can reach the summit and hill fort earthworks on foot from the ride's highest point—over 1000-ft (300-m) above Castleton. From there, however, the view over a great green ampitheatre ringed by mountains is wonderful, as is the descent down to it. Edale valley is an unusual Peak District delight, with miles of easy riding below sweeping grassy slopes.

Pennine Way walkers start their 250-mile (400-km) journey to the

Scottish border from **Edale** village. All are welcome at the National Park information centre, where displays tell of Peak District life past and present, human and wild, and evocative twentieth-century music enhances the slide shows.

THE MONSAL HEAD ROUTE

The country around Foolow is fresh and fertile, with tiny pastures grazed by sheep, and enclosed by white walls. Limestone causes both this beauty, and the dusty ugliness of Cavendish Mill's quarries. In rain the dust becomes a slimy mud, making the road by the Mill very slippery. Natural cliffs flank your road out of **Stoney Middleton**, and some of its houses even use the cliff-face as a wall. Stoney Middleton church is unusual, being octagonal in shape.

A narrow, sinuous dale beyond the B6465 has just enough room for a lane to snake beneath steep slopes of turf or rock or trees. Such dales are typical of the White Peak, and their delightful freewheels make all the uphill struggles worthwhile. This one leads to the Wye valley. There you will probably have to walk the 200-ft (60-m) climb to **Monsal Head,** from where you can see the arched viaduct which used to carry the trains en route from London to Manchester; there is a café here.

Your 500-ft (150-m) climb to Longstone Edge overlooks four circular ponds. Because of the lack of streams in these high limestone areas, dew water is collected for the livestock by allowing it to run into waterproof-bottomed little dewponds. Apart from the stiff ascents to Monsal Head and Longstone Edge, and another back into Eyam, the cycling on this quiet route is moderately easy.

The Bakewell Loop

Strenuous cycling takes you through dark gritstone hills of pasture and forest, as well as over gentle limestone country and secluded White Peak dales. The Lathkill Dale is especially known for its riverside walks, reached on foot from **Over Haddon** on the hill above.

This ride passes several attractive buildings and villages. **Ashford** church has a Norman carving of beasts sporting amongst foliage above its door, whilst inside stands a marble table of many colours inlaid in black 'Ashford marble', which is really a local limestone that darkens when polished. Beside the old Sheepwash Bridge it is easy to imagine sheep being coaxed down the ramp, through the river and into the stone-built pen on the opposite bank.

Bakewell was once a spa town, where Jane Austen often stayed in the Rutland Arms. The Bakewell tart—or 'pudding', as it is called in this town of its origin—was an accidental invention, the result of a misunderstanding whereby the cook put the egg mixture on top of the pastry instead of

153

mixing it in as instructed. You can treat yourself to delicious puddings at the shop in the square, where they have been baked since early Victorian times. A Victorian kitchen, together with collections of costume, toys and craftsmen's tools can be seen in the early tudor Old House Museum (open).

Chatsworth House (open) is one of Britain's loveliest stately homes. Visitors flock to see the magnificent architecture and furnishings, and to stroll in the spacious grounds. The Emperor Fountain has a 290-ft (88-m) jet, powered only by the natural head of water from a lake on the hilltop above. Old **Edensor** village was razed to the ground simply to improve the views from Chatsworth. It was rebuilt in the nineteenth-century and is worth seeing for its odd assortment of foreign and past architectural styles of housing.

The Youlgreave Loop

By Peak District standards this is an easy ride, the only two significant climbs being a long one of 600-ft (180-m) up to **Long Rake**, and a short, strenuous one on the B5054. You could even cut out the latter, by using the **Tissington Trail**, an old railway line now surfaced with cinders and open to walkers, horse-riders and cyclists. If you do this however, you would miss the long, peaceful, and lazy freewheel between the smooth-curved slopes of Long Dale.

You must add a few pence to a bucket full of coins to gain entry to **Arbor Low** stone circle. Erected in the Bronze Age, the pitted limestone slabs are no longer upright, but their expansive site undoubtedly has atmosphere.

Lead has been mined for centuries in the White Peak, often in long 'rakes' following veins where they lie near the surface. Grass grown on land poisoned by mining—locally called 'belland land'—is harmful to livestock, and has mostly been replaced by trees; **Long Rake** being an example of this.

Beyond the fairly busy A515, leafy lanes descend to the hamlet of Middleton, continuing to **Youlgreave** where the wells are dressed in late June. The stained glass window behind the church's altar is by William Morris and Burne-Jones, both famous artists of the pre-Raphaelite era. Also of interest is a small medieval effigy of a knight; it is small because as he died before his father, he did not receive the heritage of lands and title.

EYAM MOOR ROUTE
11½ miles (19 km)
anticlockwise

EYAM. Leave up Hawkhill Road, passing car park. Bear R at junction. Cont (Grindleford 2). Pass

Mompesson's Well. L just before a '1:6, low gear for ½ mile' sign on road ahead. L at T junction with main road. Reach

a The Plough. Join the Stannage Edge Loop, otherwise cont. Leave

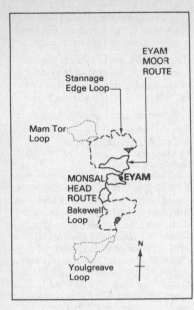

*a Detour 1 mile (1½ km) following
Stannage Edge Loop for* **Hathersage**.
Leave The Plough (Abney 2½, Gliding
Club). Pass through Abney. Reach

*c. The Stannage Edge Loop rejoins the
Eyam Moor Route.* Leave

c. Turn L if coming from Abney, or
cont if coming from Great Hucklow.
Cont to pass The Barrel Inn. Bear R
with chevrons below a summit with a
mast. R (Eyam 1¼).

**Stannage Edge Loop
adds 11 miles (18 km)
anticlockwise**

Leave

a The Plough. Cont along main road *not*
L to 'Abney 2½, Gliding Club'. Enter

Hathersage. R at junction by The
George. L on School Lane *otherwise
detour L up steep Church Bank for
Hathersage church.* Cont up The Dale. L

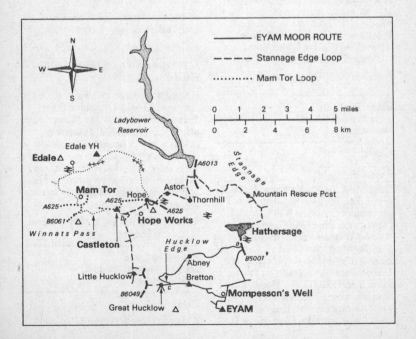

(Ladybower 5). Views R to Stannage Edge. R (Ladybower 4). Pass footpath on your R to Stannage Edge and Roman Road. L (Ladybower 3). R (Ladybower). L at T junction with main road *otherwise detour ½ mile (1 · · R to* **Ladybower Reservoir**. R (Thornhill 1½). L immediately past bridge. R by telephone box onto a road marked 'Unsuitable for Motors'. Pass to R of a chapel Cont at next junction, where the road you have just come along is signposted 'Unsuitable for motor vehicles'. R (Hope ¼, Castleton 1¾). Enter Hope. Cont at next junction. L (Pindale, Cement Works). Cont (Pindale). Pass near the **Hope Works**. R (Pindale). Reach.

b. Join the Mam Tor Loop, otherwise cont. Leave

b (Little Hucklow 3) *otherwise detour ¼ mile following Mam Tor Loop for* **Castleton**. Ignore 2 roughish roads, one to the L then one to the R. Follow 'Little Hucklow' signs to Little Hucklow. Descend through village. R at cross roads, where road ahead has a 3 ton limit. L (Gliding Club). L (Gt Hucklow ½, Gliding Club). Cont (Grindlow, Gliding Club). Cont (Gliding Club, Bretton 1½). Reach

c. Rejoin the Eyam Moor Route.

Mam Tor Loop
adds 11 miles (18 km)
clockwise

Leave

b (Castleton). Enter

Castleton. At Market Place, L past the green then R on Castle Street. L at T junction opposite the Bull's Head. L (Speedwell, Blue John Caverns). Ascend Winnats Pass. Views R to Mam Tor. R (Blue John Cavern). L (Chapel-en-le-Frith, A625). R (Barber Booth, Edale). Pass access points on foot to Mam Tor. Cont (Edale, Hope). Cont at next junction *otherwise detour ¼ mile (1 km) L on road with 'No Coaches 150 yards ahead' sign to* **Edale**. Cont (Hope 5).

Cont at all junctions. Enter Hope. R at T junction by church. Cont (Car Park, Toilets). Cont on main road. Enter

Castleton. L by The Castle pub onto Castle Street. From Market Place green, leave uphill, to soon pass footpath sign for Cave Dale. Reach

b. Rejoin the Stannage Edge Loop.

MONSAL HEAD ROUTE
13 miles (21 km)
anticlockwise

EYAM. Leave from the church so as to pass a cottage marked with a plaque as the place where the first plague victim died. Cont through village, passing Rose and Crown, and ignoring all turn-offs. L (Wardlow, Middleton). R (Wardlow 1½). R (Wardlow 1, Peak Forest 5). L (Cavendish Mill). R (Longstone Edge 2¼, Ashford 4). Cont at next junction. Cont at next junction *not* L to Longstone Edge. Cont (Upperdale, Cressbrook). L (Monsal Dale, Ashford). Reach

d **Monsal Head**. *Join the Bakewell Loop, otherwise cont.* Leave

d (Great Longstone 1, Calver 5). Reach

f. The Bakewell Loop rejoins the Monsal Head Route. Leave

f (Longstone Edge 1¼). Cont at next junction. Ascend Longstone Edge. *Ignore* an 'Unsuitable for Motors' turn-off. R (Cavendish Mill 1, Stoney Middleton 4). Cont at next junction. R (Cavendish Mill). Cont at mill to go up a short slope. The descent into Stoney Middleton is extremely steep, and is better walked if conditions are wet or icy. Enter

Stoney Middleton. L by The Moon. R (Eyam, B6521).

Bakewell Loop
adds 14½ miles (23 km)
anticlockwise

Leave

d **Monsal Head** (Ashford, Bakewell,

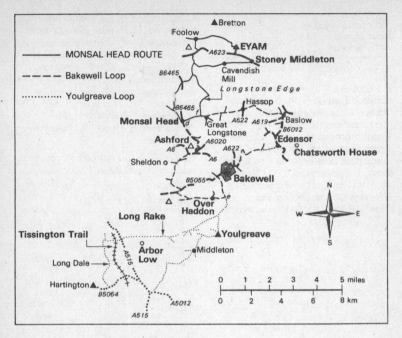

MONSAL HEAD ROUTE

----- Bakewell Loop

.... Youlgreave Loop

B6465). Cont at next cross-roads, going with white lines. Enter

Ashford. R opposite Devonshire Arms. Dismount in front of Riverside Hotel, to walk over an old stone bridge. R on main road. L (Sheldon 1½). Cont at next junction. Cont (Flagg 3¼). L (Bakewell 2½). R (Monyash 2½, B5055). L (Over Haddon, Lathkill Dale 1½). L (Over Haddon, Lathkill Dale 1). Enter

Over Haddon. Cont at all junctions through village. L (Bakewell 2, Youlgreave 2½) *otherwise detour R, (Lathkill Dale), for walks in Lathkill Dale.* R (Youlgreave 2½). Reach

e. Join the Youlgreave Loop, otherwise cont. Leave

e. (Bakewell 1½). Bear R onto a 30 mph limit road. Bear L by a telephone box. R at T junction at end of Yeld Road. Enter

Bakewell. Follow Chesterfield signs through town and over bridge. R on Station Road. Ascend steep hill, then R on track with sign 'Unsuitable for Motors'. The track is firm throughout, although sometimes bumpy with stones, ruts and rain-gullies. Most of its length can be cycled with care. Enter

Edensor. Cont to emerge through gates onto main road, on which turn L *or detour 1 mile (1½ km) R for* **Chatsworth House.** R (Baslow, B6012, Sheffield, A621). Cont (Baslow, B6012, Sheffield, A621). Cont (Chesterfield, A619, Sheffield, A621). Enter Baslow. L (Bubnell). First L on road marked Unsuitable for Coaches. L (B6001. Longstone 1¾, Bakewell 2½). R (Great Longstone). Cont (Great Longstone 1). Cont (Great Longstone ¾). R (Little Longstone). Cont (Little Longstone ½). Reach

f. Rejoin the Monsal Head Route.

Youlgreave Loop
**adds 16 miles (26 km)
anticlockwise**

Leave

e. (Youlgreave 2). Pass footpath up
Lathkill Dale on R just before river
bridge. Cont (Newhaven 4¾). Cont at
next junction. Cont (Monyash 4¾).
Cont (Monyash 4¾). Pass alongside
Long Rake. Cont (Monyash 4). Pass
signposted farm drive on L to **Arbor
Low**. L (Newhaven 2½). L (Newhaven
2½). R (Parsley Hay, Pilsbury 2¾).
Pass drive to Parsley Hay and
Tissington Trail. L (Hartington 2¾).

L (Hartington 2¼). L (Ashbourne,
B5054, A515). Pass an access drive to
Tissington Trail. Cont at next junction.
R (Ashbourne, A515). L (Cromford,
A5012, Matlock, A6). L (Friden ¼,
Middleton 3, Youlgreave 4). R
(Middleton 1). Cont (Middleton by
Youlgreave ½). Cont at next junction. L
(Youlgreave 1, Bakewell 6). R
(Youlgreave 1, Alport 1¾, Bakewell
5½). Enter

Youlgreave. L by church (Over
Haddon 2½). R (Over Haddon 1¾).
Reach

e. Rejoin the Bakewell Loop.

The crumbling church at Wharram Percy

THE LITTLE HILLS OF YORKSHIRE

This part of Yorkshire maybe little known but it is lovely with a variety of gentle hills. The Wolds offer easy cycling along breezy ridges and snaking valleys whilst to their west lie the Howardian Hills, more wooded and more crumpled, so that the lanes must rise and fall, though rarely through more than 150 ft (50 m).

The marshy Vale of Pickering has been drained for use as lush pasturage but is still kept empty of buildings by threat of flood. Nevertheless, villages have grown on upswellings of land sometimes but a few yards in height. Only the Helmsley Loop in this set of rides takes you briefly through harder and wilder country.

The lanes and most of the classified roads are quiet, but there are a few moderately busy stretches. Many of the rambling villages are picturesque, with greens flanked by red-roofed, brown-stone houses.

Fairly easy cycling though a little strenuous in parts. Quiet with a few busy miles.

MALTON

Location: 17 miles (28 km) north-east of York.

Trains: Malton Station is on the Scarborough to York line. Leeds: 1 hour (change at York); Newcastle-upon-Tyne: 1 hour 45 mins (change at York); London: 2 hours 45 mins (change at York).

Coaches: One coach links Sheffield, York, Malton and Whitby. Another runs from Leeds through Malton to Whitby.

Tourist Information Bureaux: The nearest is at Pickering Station Information Centre, Pickering, North Yorkshire tel: (0751) 73791 (accommodation service). A national bureau is at De Grey Rooms, Exhibition Square, York, North Yorkshire tel: (0904) 21756 (accommodation service).

Accommodation: Hotel and bed and breakfast accommodation is available in Malton. There is a YH in Malton, another in Helmsley on the Helmsley Loop, and a third at Thixendale on the Thixendale Route. There is a camp site 5 miles (8 km) west of Malton at Castle Howard Estate Ltd, Coneysthorpe, York, North Yorkshire, tel: (065 384) 366. There is also a small site at Appleton-le-Street, and another at Thorpe Hall ½ mile east of Rudston.

Cycle hire: The YH at Malton hires cycles to YHA members who stay at least one night in the hostel. Freedom of Ryedale, 23a The Market Place, Helmsley, tel: (0439) 70775, also hires them.

Cycle shop: H. Simpson, 7 Commercial Street, Norton, Malton, North Yorkshire.

Maps: OS 1:50 000 (nos 100, 101); Bartholomew's 1:100 000 (nos 33, 36); OS 1:250 000 (no. 6).

Malton

There are pretty corners to **Malton**, but essentially it is a busy town with pens for livestock sales, a market square and warehouses down by the river Derwent. Tetley's the brewers have big old buildings here, and St Lawrence's spire rises behind a yard full of beer-barrels. A whitesmith who enjoyed a tipple himself, fashioned his own memorial to warn us against his vices: the plaque is inside the church.

Attractive and substantial buildings of several eras line the market place, where the Milton Rooms contain a museum of local history. It has many Romano-British finds, for a Roman station was nearby. The river divides Malton from Norton, and the two towns share facilities including a cinema, a swimming pool, and several tea-rooms, restaurants and fish and chip shops.

Old Malton is a mile (1½ km) to the north-east on the A169. The country's only Gilbertine monastery still in use is Old Malton's stark and sombre priory church which has some fantastically carved misericords.

THE THIXENDALE ROUTE

Fertile rolling lowlands south-east of **Malton** slowly rise to the barer

Wolds' edge near Birdsall and North Grimston. On the Wolds themselves this route tackles two ascents of some 400 ft (120 m), both taken so that a mile (1½ km) of hard climbing is rewarded by several miles of gradual free-wheeling. The valley through Thixendale to Burdale is especially delightful: twisting and scrubby at first, later broadening out to more pastoral scenes.

Horses swish their tails under copper beeches in Birdsall House Park, which is set in the lush lowlands below the Wolds' more barren flanks. White scars reveal the chalk of which the hills are formed, and where the land has been ploughed the soil is pale with chalk rubble. The Yorkshire Wolds harbour many of England's deserted medieval villages, usually detectable now as ground made bumpy by the building foundations below. One cause of village abandonment throughout the country was the loss of about one third of the population in the fourteenth-century plagues. Whereas before, the growing population forced the clearing of forest for farmlands, afterwards, there were insufficient people to tend it and survivers in less fertile regions often moved to greener pastures. Nevertheless, the reasons for a particular village's desertion remain uncertain unless an answer is found in old records or by excavation, as is happening at **Wharram Percy**.

Chalk is quarried in the Wolds, and you must share the B1248 with occasional lorries. The easy descent is compensation, though, with wide views over rolling lowlands. Food cannot be bought anywhere on this route.

The Sledmere Loop

Two unusual memorials honour the dead of the two World Wars in **Sledmere**, a pleasing village comprising many turretted and gabled estate buildings.

Sledmere House (open) is a Georgian mansion in grounds landscaped by Capability Brown. It has a room gorgeously decorated with Turkish tiles, and the 100-ft (30-m) long library has vaulted ceilings of intricate plasterwork. There is a restaurant for visitors to the house.

Sir Christopher Sykes of Sledmere House worked the estate lands energetically in the late eighteenth century, creating a landscape that has changed little today. He planted trees and hedgerows, laying out a chequerwork of expansive grainfields that are dotted with scarlet poppies in summer. Comfortable red-brick or whitewash isolated farms stand in country which is otherwise empty, save for the earthworks of prehistoric man. On your left just before Duggleby a tumulus—or 'howe' as they are called hereabouts—can be seen on the horizon.

Gradients on this ride are few, and are low or very gradual. The lanes are almost deserted, but the B1251, although mostly quiet, carries fairly heavy traffic bound for the sea-side resort of Bridlington.

161

The Rudston Loop

Although this loop is long, you can ride it with little effort before returning up a shallow valley which rises almost imperceptibly through 400 ft (120 m) in 15 miles (24 km). The countryside everywhere is expansive, with broad slopes patterned by straight hedges and big fields. There are very few buildings on the ridge, but a bumpy pasture above Swaythorpe Farm marks the site of old **Swaythorpe** village.

The B1253 carries you easily down into **Rudston**, where a huge sinister monolith dwarfs the tombstones in the churchyard. Perhaps Ice Age glaciers swept the great rock on to these chalklands, where prehistoric man might have set it upright. A number of England's Christian churches were built on sites already sacred in pagan times, a clue being their circular churchyard such as the one at Rudston.

Need for water kept most of the villages in the valley by the stream. Geese can be seen on Weaverthorpe green and you may find horses grazing around **Wold Newton's** pond. This is a good village for stopping to eat; there are benches on the green a bus shelter in case it rains, and the Anvil Arms serves food. So, too, does the Star at **Burton Fleming**, where a pair of unusually tall old water-pumps are both double-handled.

THE CASTLE HOWARD ROUTE

The Vale of Pickering was a broad lake during the Ice Age era, since when it has slowly drained and silted into marshes. Man has continued the job, cutting channels to drain the marshes into pasturelands. Even so the Vale is liable to flooding, so it is little surprise that an old roadway (now the B1257) and a string of villages keep a critical few yards above the Vale at the foot of the Howardian Hills. The B1257 can be fairly busy, so it would be wise to make this your Sunday ride. The road is generally level giving views over the Vale's emptiness to the North York Moors which rise some 8 miles (12 km) to the north.

A riot of original and Victorian Norman-style carving adorns St Michael and All Angels in **Barton-le-Street** with geometric patterns, scenes, and heads both true to life and fantastic. In the earlier days of the postal system the Post Office added extra bits onto frequently occurring village names to differentiate addresses. 'Le' was often used in Yorkshire, distinguishing, for example, Appleton-le-Street from Appleton-le-Moors only 9 miles (14 km) to the north.

Hovingham's sturdy houses ramble picturesquely around irregular greens and the Hall's riding school archway bears dragons and an admirable motto. **Terrington** is also spacious and pleasing: look out for the topiary work, so finely trimmed as to spell out the village's name.

Quiet lanes twist and turn through the Howardian Hills' fields and forests, frequently swooping over 200-ft (60-m) hills. One is surmounted by the colonnaded Temple of the Four Winds which, however elegant, is but a tiny part of **Castle Howard's** splendour. The eighteenth-century house (open) was the first major work of Vanbrugh, who later designed Blenheim Palace. Colossal and magnificient, the facade with its central dome rises beyond a reedy lake beside your route. The richly furnished house contains a wealth of art treasures and a large collection of eighteenth- to twentieth-century dress. A restaurant caters for the many tourists.

The Gilling Loop

At its western end, the Vale of Pickering splits into fingers of flat land, splayed between low ridges and hills. This is the area you will explore on this ride, leaving **Hovingham** past the hall's parkland where even the livestock cross a stream on a pretty little bridge of stone. From there you climb 200 ft (60 m) through woods of conifers and silver birch, to descend again to **Gilling**. The Castle (open) has an original Norman keep with additions from later centuries. It is not very clearly signposted, so look out for its drive on the left of your road through the village.

At **Oswaldkirk**, which straggles beneath a wooded cliff, the Malt Shovel sells food, as does **Gilling's** Fairfax Arms.

Nunnington is a charming stone-built village, tiered upon the flank of a low ridge stretching into the Vale of Pickering. Summertime swifts swoop and dive for insects over the river Rye, which flows past **Nunnington Hall** (NT, open). The seventeenth-century manor house has some fine panelling, and there is a tea-room. Beyond the village an avenue of trees climbs 150 ft (450 m) to the ridge-top, where a sudden vista reveals Hovingham away across the flatlands.

The Helmsley Loop

Both the hardest and the busiest stretches of road are on this loop. It rises 600 ft (180 m) through steep woods above Wass to the A170 which free-wheels all the way to **Helmsley** with lovely views over both that town and open moors and fields.

Prosperous old buildings of ivy-clad stone or black and white half-timbering flank Helmsley's big market place, where cafés and a fish and chip shop cater for the tourists. The church has fascinating murals with heraldic devices, tracing the history of Christianity in the area. The ruined thirteenth-century castle (DoE, open) withstood a three-month seige in the time of the Civil War.

Ampleforth College was founded in 1802 as a Roman Catholic public school. Some parts are harsh and ugly, but below a slope to your left lies the abbey church. Its simple white interior sets off the finely worked altars, and the oakwood furnishings are 'signed' with a mouse, the master crafts-man's emblem.

From Oswaldkirk, the lane roller-coasts below woods and past elder-berry bushes. In the distance, as you approach **Wass,** you will see the haunting yet elegant ruins of **Byland Abbey** (DoE, open). In Wass the Wombwell Arms serves food, as do both the Swan and the White Horse in **Ampleforth.** Reached by easy lanes from Helmsley through the Vale of Pickering's fertile emptiness, **Harome** has some pretty roofs of thatch.

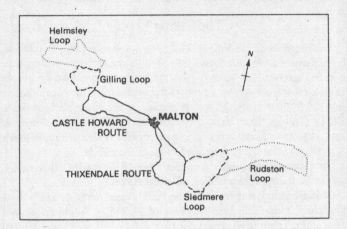

THIXENDALE ROUTE
20 miles (32 km)
anticlockwise

MALTON. Leave from the level crossing on Church Street. R (Langton 4, Birdsall 4). R (Langton 4, Birdsall 4). Cont (Birdsall 1½, Leavening 4½). R (Leavening 4, Pocklington 14). L (Leavening 3½, Pocklington 14). Cont (Leavening 3, Pocklington 13½). Cont (Pocklington 13). L (Thixendale 3, Burdale 5). Cont (Thixendale 3, Burdale 4). Enter Thixendale. Cont at next junction. L (Burdale 2½, Fimber 4½). Reach

a. Join the Sledmere Loop, otherwise cont. Leave

a (Wharram le Street 2½). Pass a ¾ mile (1 km) track to **Wharram Percy**. It is on your left just before Bella Farm. Where a wooden 'Wolds Way' sign points along the road, dismount and walk downhill along a white stone track.

Follow the path where it becomes covered with earth, down to an old rail-way cutting, from where Wharram Percy is signposted. L (Malton 7, B1248). Reach

d Wharram le Street. *The Sledmere Loop rejoins the Thixendale Route.* Leave

d (Malton 6½, B1248). Cont following Malton signs at all junctions.

Sledmere Loop
adds 11½ miles (19 km)
anticlockwise

Leave

a (Fimber 1¾, Fridaythorpe 2¼). Cont at next junction *not* R to 'Fridaythorpe 1½'. Cont (Fimber). L (Sledmere 4, Bridlington 20). L (Sledmere 4, Bridlington 20, B1251). Cont (Sledmere 3). Cont (Sledmere 1). Cont (Bridlington, B1253, Driffield, B1252). Enter

Sledmere. Cont at next junction. Reach

b. Join the Rudston Loop, otherwise cont. Leave

b. (Luttons 3, Weaverthorpe 5). L (West Lutton 1, Malton 13). Reach

c. The Rudston Loop rejoins the Sledmere Loop. Leave

c. (West Lutton, Malton 12). Cont (West Lutton, Duggleby 6). Cont at next junction. R (Kirby Grindalythe 2, Duggleby 4). L (Kirby Grindalythe 1½, Duggleby 3½, Malton 11). Enter Kirby Grindalythe. Cont (Duggleby 2, Malton 9). Fork L into a lane with a Duggleby village name sign by a hedge. Cont (Wharram 1). Cont at next junction. Reach

d. Detour 2 miles (3 km) to **Wharram Percy** *L (Beverley 21½, B1248). R (Burdale 2). Pass Bella Farm then walk track on your R as described in Thixendale Route. Rejoin the Thixendale Route.*

Rudston Loop
adds 21 miles (34 km)
anticlockwise

Leave

b (Driffield 8, Bridlington 16, B1253). L (Bridlington. B1253, Scarborough, A64). Cont (Rudston 8, Bridlington 14, Scarborough 17, B1253). Cont following Rudston signs at all junctions. Beyond 'Rudston 4' sign, and just past Swaythorpe Cottages on your L, pass views R to **Swaythorpe**: a sign 'A Conner and Sons' marks the modern-day farm drive. Cont following Rudston signs. Enter

Rudston. Leave village on road sign-posted (Grindale 5, Burton Fleming 3, Hunmanby 6). Cont at next junction. Cont (Burton Fleming 1½, Hunmanby 4½). Enter

Burton Fleming. L (Hunmanby 3, Malton 21½). Cont (Wold Newton 2½, Malton 21½). R (Wold Newton 1, Malton 20). L (Wold Newton 1, Malton 20). Cont (Foxholes 2, Malton 19). Cont

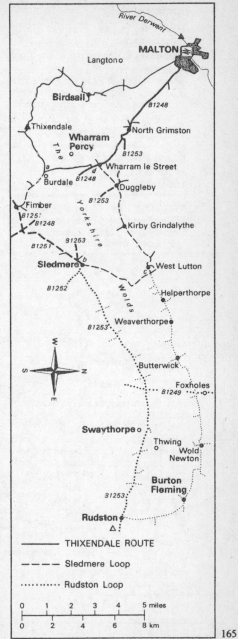

THIXENDALE ROUTE

- - - - Sledmere Loop

········ Rudston Loop

| 0 | 1 | 2 | 3 | 4 | 5 miles |
| 0 | 2 | | 4 | 6 | 8 km |

(Foxholes 2, Malton 19). Cont
(Foxholes 1, Malton 17½). Cont at next
junction. Cont (Weaverthorpe 4,
Malton 18). Enter
Butterwick. Cont (Weaverthorpe 2,
Malton 15). Cont at next junction. Cont
(Sledmere 4, Malton 13). Cont
(Helperthorpe, Malton 13). Cont
(Luttons 1, Sledmere 3). Cont (Lutton
1½, Malton 12). Cont at next junction.
Reach

c. Rejoin the Sledmere Loop.

CASTLE HOWARD ROUTE
20 miles (32 km)
anticlockwise

MALTON. Leave from traffic lights on
Wheelgate. Cont (Kirkbymoorside 13,
Helmsley 16, B1257). Cont at next
junction. Cont (Amotherby ¾,

Helmsley 14, B1257). Cont (Helmsley
13¼, B1257). Cont at all junctions
through Appleton-le-Street. Enter

Barton-le-Street. Cont (Slingsby,
Hovingham) *otherwise detour 200 yards
(metres) R into village to church*. Cont
(Helmsley 10, B1257). Cont
(Hovingham 2). Cont (Helmsley 9,
B1257). Reach

e **Hovingham**. *Join the Gilling Loop, or
cont*. Leave

e. (Sheriff Hutton 6, York 16). Cont
(Terrington 2, Malton 10¼, York). L
(Terrington 1¼, York 13½). Cont
(Terrington ¾, Malton 8¾). R
(Terrington, Malton 8). Pass through
Terrington. L (Castle Howard 3½,
Malton 7½). Cont (Malton 5) *otherwise
detour 1½ miles (2½ km), following
Castle Howard signs, for* **Castle**

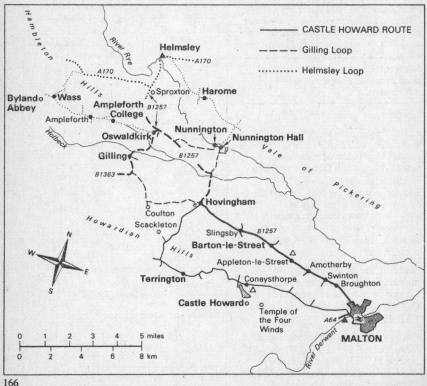

Howard. Pass view to R of Temple of the Four Winds. Cont (Malton 3). Cont (Malton 2).

Gilling Loop
adds 12 miles (19 km)
clockwise

Leave

e **Hovingham**. (Helmsley 8, Kirkbymoorside 8, B1257). L (Coulton 2½, Easingwold 10). R (Gilling 2, Helmsley 7). R (Gilling ½, Helmsley 6, B1363, B1257). Enter

Gilling. Cont (Helmsley 5¼, B1363). Reach

f Oswaldkirk. Join the Helmsley Loop, otherwise cont. Leave

f (Helmsley 3½, Hovingham 4½, Malton 13). R (Malton 12½, B1257, Stonegrave 2, Hovingham 4). L (Nunnington 2). L just before church to follow road through village. Reach

g **Nunnington Hall**. *The Helmsley Loop rejoins the Gilling Loop.* Leave

g (Hovingham 2¾, York 19). Cont (Hovingham 2). L (Hovingham 1¼, Malton 9½, B1257). Enter

Hovingham. Cont (Slingsby 2, Malton 8, B1257). Reach

e. Rejoin the Castle Howard Route.

Helmsley Loop
adds 12½ miles (20 km)
clockwise

Leave

f (Ampleforth 2½, Coxwold 7). Pass through **Ampleforth College**. Cont (Ampleforth ½, Coxwold 4½, Thirsk 11½). Cont (Wass 2, Coxwold 4, Thirsk 11). Cont at next junction. Enter

Wass. R (Helmsley 6), via (Wass Bank 1 in 6) *otherwise detour ½ mile (1 km), turn L by Wombwell Arms, to* **Byland Abbey**. Cont (Helmsley 4, Thirsk 10). Follow Scarborough signs as far as **Helmsley** market place. Leave (Scarborough, A170). R (Harome 2). R (Wombleton 2½, Nunnington 3½). L (Wombleton 2, Nunnington 3¼). Cont at next 2 junctions. R (Nunnington 2½, Malton 13). R (Nunnington 1, Malton 11½). Reach

g **Nunnington Hall**. *Rejoin the Gilling Loop.*

A peaceful lane in the North York Moors

THE NORTH YORK MOORS

The land which is now the North York Moors National Park was once a plateau, but rivers have since eroded long valleys deep into it, dividing the moorland into ridges or 'riggs', a word deriving from the Norse for *back*.

The valley sides sweep nearly 1000 ft (300 m) up to the riggs where sheep forage in bracken and heather. Cycling the near-level riggs or valley bottoms is easy, but the slopes between them are long and arduous, requiring low gears, good brakes and stamina.

Before roads were built, finding one's way over the featureless plateau was tricky, especially in mist and so waystones and crosses were erected many of which exist today. The exposed ridge-tops, are exhilarating in fine weather, but can be cold and windy, so be prepared to wrap up well.

Sheltered by the riggs, the vales are a different world of trees, hay-fields and grazing black and white cows. The red-tiled roofs of villages, hamlets and isolated farms are set above glowing brown walls, the blocks roughly patterned in a distinctive local style. The Westerdale Routes are basically moorland in character, whilst the Danby Routes explore the rolling, green Esk valley.

The Eskdale lanes remain peaceful because the road network is too tortuous for easy motoring, but tourist traffic to the National Park will be

encountered near Blakey Ridge and Rosedale on the Westerdale Routes.
Strenuous cycling. Very quiet except near Whitby. One easy riverside track.

CASTLETON

Location: 35 miles (56 km) north of York, and 13 miles (21 km) west of Whitby.

Trains: Castleton Moor Station is only ½ mile (1 km) away, on the Middlesborough to Whitby line. Leeds: 2 hours 45 mins (change at Darlington), and Newcastle-upon-Tyne: 2 hours 45 mins (change at Darlington).

Tourist Information Bureaux: Danby Lodge National Park Centre, Lodge Lane, Danby, North Yorkshire, tel: (028 76) 654 (summer service only, accommodation service), and New Quay Road, Whitby, North Yorkshire, tel: (0947) 2674 (accommodation service).

Accommodation: Limited hotel and bed and breakfast accommodation is available in Castleton. The nearest YH is Westerdale Hall, 2½ miles (4 km) from Castleton. There is also a YH at Whitby. Camping is sometimes allowed at The Broadgate Farm Caravanserai, Westerdale, North Yorkshire (contact them in advance), but there are also sites at Whitby, and Rosedale Abbey on the Hutton-le-Hole Loop.

Cycle-hire: None.

Cycle-shop: nearest are G & M Cycles, 50 Flowergate, Whitby, North Yorkshire, and Blenkeys, 6 Flowergate, Whitby, North Yorkshire.

Maps: OS 1:50 000 (no. 94) or alternatively the OS 1'':1 mile Tourist Map of the North York Moores covers all the routes; Bartholomew's 1:100 000 (no. 36); OS 1:250 000 (no. 6).

Castleton

Typical of the North York Moors, Castleton is a loose-knit village set on the flank of a hill. Amongst its big houses are a few shops, and the Downe Arms which serves food. Castleton stands near the head of Eskdale, from where the riggs and dales fan out ahead. There is little to do in Castleton if it rains, but trains run to Grosmont and Whitby (both described in the Whitby Loop), where there are many attractions.

THE WESTERDALE ROUTE

Short but strenuous, this route is a sampler of the Moor's varied scenery. From Castleton an easy lane keeps close to the young river Esk, but beyond

Westerdale you climb a steep 750-ft (200-m) hill over 2½ miles (4 km), first looking down on the pastures below, then passing through bracken until you reach the silent purple moors. From there you descend quickly down Castleton Rigg's long and narrow back.

Grouse eat the seeds and shoots of heather and are a common sight on the moorlands. Grouse shooting is a popular sport and you may pass patches of heather which have been burnt to encourage more palatable young growth for the birds. As you climb above **Westerdale** you will pass a row of shooting butts, low stone and turf shelters, from which marksmen fire at the grouse, driven towards them by beaters. In Westerdale, the dark towers of Westerdale Youth Hostel, which was originally a hunting lodge, peep over the trees.

'**Fat Betty**' was named after Prioress Elizabeth of Rosedale Abbey. Legend tells that when she came with an assistant to confer on a matter of boundaries with Westerdale delegates, all parties got lost in a thick moorland fog which, when it eventually lifted, revealed the Prioress and assistant standing at the places now marked by their respective crosses. The original **Ralph Cross** (named after the assistant), had a hollow on top where the rich could put coins for poorer wayfarers in need, but the present one is too tall for that.

The Hutton-le-Hole loop

Fat Betty stands on the sombre moorland plateau, silent except for the sound of the wind and the curlew. Looking across the moors to your left, where the long freewheel into Rosedale crosses a cattle grid, you can see the weird white spheres of Fylingdales Ballistic Missile Early Warning Station.

After the Dissolution of the monasteries, stones from **Rosedale Abbey** were reused in the village's houses and in the church, where, the credence table is carved with a realistic lizard as the craftsman's signature. Anyone may buy meals at the nearby campsite restaurant, and the isolated Blacksmith's Arms 2 miles (3 km) further down the valley serves food.

The gorse-covered slopes of Rosedale have rocky scars, relics of the ironstone mining and smelting boom of the nineteenth century, when a railway line linked Rosedale to Teeside. From Blakey Ridge you can see across the valley to the pillasters that bore the rails over difficult terrain. The remote Lion Inn at **Blakey House**, once patronised by iron and coal miners, now serves bar meals. A half mile south, by a turn-off to Farndale, there is access to the old line now surfaced with cinders. It makes a very peaceful albeit slow cycling detour, although in law it is a walkers' right of way only.

Beyond Rosedale the road descends through forestry plantations to cornfields, rising again through 250 ft (75 m) to **Appleton-le-Moors**. There is an ancient Low Cross by the junction there, whilst a High Cross stands by the road a little further on. Waystones on Blakey Ridge bear odd inscriptions, some using unfamiliar spellings for well-known place names.

Your first view of **Lastingham** is of red roofs nestling in a tree clad dip below the sweeping moorland skyline. The church boasts one of England's rare Norman crypts, a complete little church in itself, which is dank yet beautiful. The nearby Blacksmith's Arms sells food, and there is a tea and lunch shop in **Hutton-le-Hole**, a seventeenth-century village founded by Quakers. It is a picturesque village, its cottages loosely arranged about a hummocky green, with a clear stream winding through. The sheep graze steadfastly, oblivious to the many tourists looking at the blacksmithy and the Elizabethan glass furnace which are amongst the Ryedale Folk Museum's fascinating exhibits.

Gather your strength in Hutton-le-Hole for the laborious climb up some 800 ft (250 m) onto Blakey Ridge. With a headwind the going is hard to Ralph Cross, but otherwise the ridge-top offers exhilarating riding and views.

The Farndale Loop

There is little to say about this loop, yet its pleasures are great, despite occasional hard gradients. Few bother to explore the dead-end valley, but Farndale is a nature reserve, aglow with daffodils in springtime, and in late summer you may find bilberries on the heathlands at its southern end. Looking south you can see the Vale of Pickering, flat and vast below the moors.

THE DANBY ROUTE

The Danby and Whitby rides follow the Eskdale railway line which, with its closely-spaced stations, enables you to take the train on the outward or return journey if you wish. Trains run infrequently, though, so check your plans against the timetable.

The river Esk flows beneath fourteenth-century **Duck Bridge**, emblazoned with a carved coat of arms, down to the **Beggar's Bridge**, supposedly built by a man of fortune returning to claim the sweetheart of his younger, poorer days. Both bridges are single arches, simple and elegant but needing low gears for cycling over their humps.

Great fingers of highland reach towards Eskdale from the south, and as you ride past the mouths of the successive dividing dales, their slopes open to your view.

Isolated farms dot a landscape so quiet that a farmer shouted his thanks to me when I scared crows from his crops as I cycled past. **Danby Castle** is now a farm, but a gaunt wall with only the smallest of windows hints at its fourteenth-century origins. Henry VIII was Catharine Parr's third husband: it was her second who owned Danby Castle.

The nearby **Danby Lodge** was a shooting lodge, and is now used as a National Park Centre. For a fee you are admitted to extensive grounds encompassing formal gardens and a woodland trail; the lodge has displays and films which describe many aspects of North York Moors life. Refreshments are available, the Mitre at Glaisdale sells snacks, and Ye Horseshoe Inn at Egton serves meals.

Egton is the scene of an August Gooseberry Fair. The area was a seventeenth-century Roman Catholic stronghold, and Nicholas Postgate, the last English martyr, who was arrested for baptising a child and hung at the age of 83, lived here.

The Whitby Loop

This loop continues through country similar to that of the Danby Route, except that the roads are busier. There are cafés and boats for hire near **Ruswarp**, where a riverside mill, built in 1752, is still in use.

Whitby itself was a whaling centre in the eighteenth century, and is still a fishing port. Holiday makers can choose between many sorts of meals, the fish and chips, of course, being of the freshest. The ruined abbey (DoE, open) standing above the jumble of quayside houses is still a landmark to those at sea. Founded in the seventh century, it was one of England's most important religious houses, and a great centre of learning for both men and women.

The Sutcliffe Gallery in Flowergate, exhibits photographs of nineteenth century life in Whitby by Frank Sutcliffe. Many British artists including Turner are represented in the Pannett Art Gallery, whilst the Whitby Museum includes an outstanding fossil collection and relics of Captain James Cook, explorer and discoverer of the Hawaian Islands. His house still stands in Grape Lane.

The coming of the railways to the North York Moors opened up markets for its high grade ores. An iron-working village grew beside **Grosmont** station, where the earliest trains were horse-drawn. After falling to the Beeching axe in 1965, the Grosmont to Pickering line has been re-opened for the use of steam trains and the sheds where they are maintained are open to visitors. The station, level crossing and rolling stock at Grosmont are all delightfully old-fashioned, and needless to say several cafés cater for its tourists.

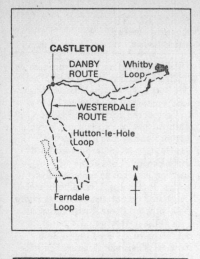

CASTLETON

DANBY ROUTE

Whitby Loop

WESTERDALE ROUTE

Hutton-le-Hole Loop

N

Farndale Loop

Rosedale Abbey. Cont (Pickering 10).
Cont (Pickering 10). Cont (Pickering 7).
R (Lastingham 1¾, Kirkbymoorside
6¼). L (Appleton-le-Moors 1½). Reach

Appleton-le-Moors. R (Lastingham
1½, Hutton-le-Hole 3). R (Lastingham
½). Enter

Lastingham. L (Hutton-le-Hole 2,
Kirkbymoorside 5). R (Hutton-le-Hole
1½, Kirkbymoorside 4½). Cont at the
next junction. Enter

Hutton-le-Hole. R (Farndale,
Castleton 12). Reach

WESTERDALE ROUTE
**9 miles (15 km)
anticlockwise**

CASTLETON. Leave from the junction
between High Street and Station Road
(Westerdale 2½, Rosedale 10, Hutton-
le-Hole 12). R (Westerdale 2,
Commondale 2½). L (Westerdale).
Enter

Westerdale. L (Farndale 5, Hutton-
le-Hole 10½, Kirkbymoorside 14).
Cont at the next three junctions. Reach

a **Ralph Cross.** *Join the Hutton-le-Hole
Loop, or cont.* Leave

a (Castleton 4) *otherwise detour 500 yards
(metres) following the Hutton-le-Hole
Loop for* **Fat Betty**. Cont at the next two
junctions. R (Danby 2, Guisborough
9½, Whitby 17½).

Hutton-le-Hole Loop
**adds 23 miles (37 km)
clockwise**

Leave

a (Farndale 2½, Hutton-le-Hole 8,
Kirkbymoorside 11½). L (Rosedale
Abbey 5½). Pass **Fat Betty**. Cont
(Rosedale 3¼, Pickering 13). L
(Rosedale 1, Pickering 10). Enter

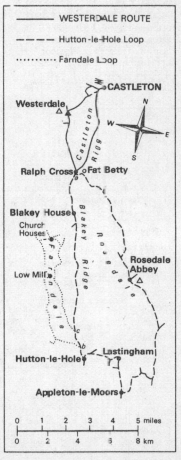

———— WESTERDALE ROUTE

– – – – Hutton-le-Hole Loop

·········· Farndale Loop

CASTLETON

Westerdale △

Castleton Rigg

N W E S

Ralph Cross · Fat Betty

Blakey House

Church Houses

Blakey Ridge

Rosedale

Low Mill

Farndale

Rosedale Abbey △

c

b

Hutton-le-Hole

Lastingham

Appleton-le-Moors

0 1 2 3 4 5 miles
0 2 4 6 8 km

b. Join the Farndale Loop, or cont. Leave

b (Castleton 11½). Reach

c. The Farndale Loop rejoins the Hutton-le-Hole Loop. Leave

c (Castleton 10½). Cont (Castleton 6½). Pass **Blakey House**. Cont (Castleton 4¼). Reach.

a. Rejoin the Westerdale Route.

Farndale Loop
adds 9½ miles (15 km)
clockwise

b (Gillamoor 1¾). R (Farndale). Enter Low Mill. L (Farndale, West Side). R (Church Houses ½, Castleton 8). R (Hutton-le-Hole 6, Castleton 8). R (Hutton-le-Hole 6, Gillamoor 6). R (Hutton-le-Hole 5¼, Gillamoor 5½). Cont (Hutton-le-Hole 3¾). Reach

c. Rejoin the Hutton-le-Hole Loop.

DANBY ROUTE
18½ miles (30 km)
anticlockwise

CASTLETON. Leave from the junction of High Street and Station Road (Danby 1½, Botton 3, Whitby 17). Cont at the next junction. R (Ainthorpe 1, Fryup 4). Cont at the next two junctions. Cont (Danby ½, Whitby 13). Next R on Easton Lane. Views R to **Danby Castle**. L to cross the very humped **Duck Bridge**. Cont at the next junction, *not* L to go under a railway bridge. R (Fryup). L (Lealholm 1¾, Glaisdale 3). Cont past the 'Great Fryup Dale' turn-off. Bear R with the white lines at the next junction. Cont at the next cross-roads. Pass Busco Beck Farm. R (Glaisdale 1). Enter Glaisdale. Cont (Rly Stn ½, Egton 2). Cont at the next two junctions. Pass the **Beggar's Bridge**. Bear R with the white lines at

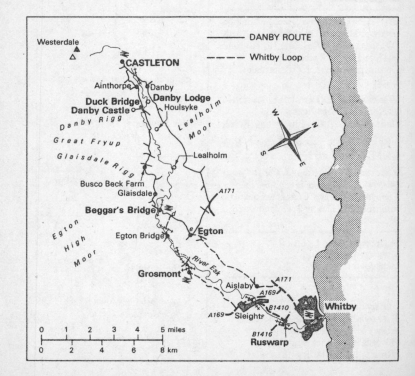

174

the next junction. Reach

d. Join the Whitby Loop, or cont. Leave

d (Egton 1¼). Reach

e **Egton**. *The Whitby Loop rejoins the Danby Route.* Leave

e (Guisborough 16½). L on the main road, then immediately L (Lealholm 2½, Glaisdale 4½). Cont at the next junction. Cont (Lealholm 1, Glaisdale 3). R just beyond the '1 in 6, low gear for ½ mile' sign, where the road ahead is signposted 'Lealholm, Rosedale'. L by the chevron sign. Cont at the next two junctions. Cont (Danby ½, Castleton 1¾) *otherwise detour 200 yards (metres) L for* **Danby Lodge**. Cont (Castleton 1¼). Cont (Castleton ¼, Guisborough 9½).

Whitby Loop
adds 15½ miles (25 km)
anticlockwise

Leave

d (Egton Bridge 1, Goathland 6¼). L (Egton 1, Whitby 8). Immediately turn R between gateposts bearing the sign 'Private, road closed, bridle path only, Egton Estates Company'. In law bicycles are allowed on bridleway Rights of Way. However, this is only a permissive bridleway and, although it is very unlikely to occur, the landowners would be within their rights to turn you back. The track is firm and able to be cycled throughout despite a few puddle-holes, and there will probably be awkward muddy ruts under the railway bridge. On reaching the road turn R, and immediately keep L to cross the river. Enter

Grosmont. L (Sleights 2½, Whitby 7). L (Sleights 2½, Whitby 6½). L (Whitby 4, A169). Cont at the next junction. R (Ruswarp 1½, B1410). Cont at the next junction. Enter

Ruswarp. R (Scarborough, B1416 A171). Cross the river then go L onto a '13' 0'' height limit road. Cont at the next junction. Cont (Abbey, East Whitby). Enter

Whitby. Leave from Whitby's river bridge (A171, Guisborough, A169, Pickering, A174, Saltburn). Follow (Teeside) signs for 2 miles (3 km) until you reach the (Aislaby 1) turn off, onto which turn L. Fork L by the church and war memorial onto Egton Road. Cont at the next two junctions. L at the T junction near a farm with a large yellow-brick-walled building. Cont at the next junction. Reach

e **Egton**. *Rejoin the Danby Route.*

Hawes

THE YORKSHIRE DALES

Soft plumes of smoke rising from grey village houses; gaunt fells; solitary farms beneath majestic moorland: comfort amidst harshness is the character of the Yorkshire Dales.

Make no mistake, this is an area where roads either rise long and hard, or descend in steep curves that are treacherous in bad weather. You need low gears, excellent brakes and determination to cross the passes, but the valleys are long and level.

The Vikings settled here, and their influence can still be seen in the place names. Many hamlets end in *sett*, from the Norse for 'summer pasture', and even 'fell' recalls the Norwegian *fjell* for 'mountain'. It was the Vikings, too, who first built the grey stone barns that dot the lowland pastures. Long drystone walls divide the barren uplands, where shaggy sheep graze the rough grass.

The dales between the fells are fertile and tranquil, each with a clear yet peat-brown river sometimes tumbling over beautiful falls.

The roads are moderately quiet but the region's popularity brings bursts of tourist traffic as well as some advantages: virtually every village offers food, and many have boards with snippets of interesting local information erected by the National Park authorities.

Strenuous cycling with long easy stretches. Quiet but tourist traffic at times.

HAWES

Location: 30 miles (50 km) north-east of Lancaster.

Trains: There are no stations nearby. The closest to the routes is Skipton Station, 15 miles (24 km) by road from Kettlewell on the Wensley Route.

Tourist Information Bureau: The Market Place, Askrigg, North Yorkshire, tel: (0969) 50441 (accommodation service).

Accommodation: There is hotel and bed and breakfast accommodation in Hawes. There are YHs at Hawes, Keld, Grinton and Kettlewell, all on or very near the routes. Camping is available at the Bainbridge Ings tel: (096 97) 354, and Brown Moor sites tel: (096 97) 338, which are in Hawes itself, and there are several other sites on the routes. Hawes is not only popular with tourists, but with walkers doing the Pennine Way, so prior booking is advisable.

Cycle-hire: The nearest is 51 Belmont Street, Skipton, North Yorkshire, tel: (0756) 5932, and Craven Cottage, 44 Main Street, Grassington, near Skipton, North Yorkshire, tel: (0756) 752205.

Cycle-shop: The nearest is in Sedbergh, 15 miles (25 km) to the west.

Maps: OS 1:50 000 (nos 92, 98, 99); Bartholomew's 1:100 000 (no. 35); OS 1:250 000 (no. 5).

Hawes

Hawes is the market town of Upper Wensleydale, where a small factory makes the famous Wensleydale cheese and the Upper Dales Folk Museum has a display showing how it is done. With the exception of the market day bustle on Tuesday, Hawes has a village atmosphere. Thick-walled grey stone houses cluster near the church, where the graveyard is kept neat by grazing sheep. Hill walkers, other cyclists and tourists mingle in the streets, the many pubs and cafés catering for all.

If you feel like a break from cycling, visit the National Park Centre in Station Yard, and they will give you information on nearby recreations such as fishing and pony-trekking.

THE BUTTERTUBS ROUTE

This route links the pastoral valleys of the Ure and the Swale, and crosses the open ridge between them via passes of nearly 1000 ft (300 m). As you walk up parts of the Buttertubs Pass, you will see some rocky spoil heaps and ruined buildings to your right. Lead mining was carried out in the

177

Yorkshire Dales for centuries, and even the Romans worked veins in Swaledale.

A few hundred yards beyond the summit are **The Buttertubs**, deep holes in which rain-fretted limestone columns stand 18 ft (6 m) tall.

Crossing the barren pass, the road is flanked by dark poles (which mark its course in the winter snows), before it descends to flower-covered meadows in the valley below. Near **Thwaite** the land is thickly patterned with walls and Norse field barns, *Thwaite* itself meaning 'clearing' in Norse, just as **Muker** comes from the Norse for 'small cultivated enclosure'.

On the strenuous rise to the stark limestone cliff of Oxnop Scar, it occasionally becomes a struggle even to push a bicycle. From the summit, the impression of Wensleydale is of a tranquil valley amidst ranks of desolate hills. Semer Water, visible on the opposite valley side, was the site of lake dwellings in prehistoric times. The descent enjoys a charming view over **Askrigg**, a former lead-smelting village which now has a tourist information centre.

Beyond Askrigg both the riding and the valley views are restful. Hardrow Force is a few hundred yards behind the pub in **Hardrow** village, and is accessible from there by footpath. It is England's highest single-drop waterfall, the torrent rushing over the lip of 90-ft (30-m) high amphitheatre of rock.

The Tan Hill Loop

The Yorkshire Dales are famed for their limestone country where the grass grows in stark contrast to the white limestone cliffs and walls. There are also sombre gritstone areas, with peat and heather, and brown building stone. This loop passes through both types of terrain, the road from Tan Hill to Whaw being one of the bleakest in this book, and devoid of any shelter.

Near **Keld** bridge the Swale tumbles over clean limestone slabs, and at Ivelets the same river flows beneath an elegant single-arch bridge, before curving placidly through pastoral Swaledale, alongside the reasonably quiet and level B6270.

From Keld an open lane rises gradually up some 700 ft (200 m), into more open and desolate country; exhilarating to some and dismal to others. The Pennine Way runs parallel to your road and you may well see walkers trudging towards the **Tan Hill**, England's highest inn at 1732 ft (525 m) above sea-level. Cars mark the **Bowes Road**, once the trans-Pennine Roman road, seen to the north over unrelieved dark moorlands.

Beyond the desolation near Tan Hill you enjoy a long and gradual descent, passing occasional fields reclaimed from the moorlands. The hamlet of Whaw understandably shelters beneath a natural limestone scar, but further down the valley the scars are man-made by leadmining.

Reeth was a leadmining centre in the nineteenth century, but earlier inns and shops flank the broad hillside green. There is a little Swaledale Folk Museum, and the roomy shelter at the top of the green is ideal for bad weather picnics.

The track up **Gunnerside Ghyll** goes deep into silent moorlands. Follow it on foot or bicycle for nearly 3 miles (5 km), and you will find ruins of old leadmine buildings. The great gouges in the hillsides are hushes which were formed by the damming and then sudden release of stream water to wash away rock and expose any veins of lead beneath.

THE LANGSTROTHDALE ROUTE

Whichever of the two routes you choose in this set, you will be faced with two big passes. The one to Oughtershaw rises some 1000 ft (300 m), the B6160 goes up about 600 ft (180 m), and the one from Kettlewell to Bradley about 900 ft (270 m). The passes are so steep in places that you will have to walk, but the freewheels down again are long and exhilarating.

South out of Hawes the lane rises up a smooth contoured valley, its emptiness emphasized by a single farm sheltering by a clump of trees. The track by the summit was a **Roman Road**, used in their control of the conquered Britons; an ancient British defensive hill fort was on the summit of Ingleborough, the distant flat-topped mountain to your half right as you pass the 1:6 gradient sign.

The Langstrothdale lane is one of England's most delightful riverside rides, where crystal water flows round fretted limestone boulders, and pale ash trees sprout from the river banks. Near Cray, you pass limestone cliffs and rocky knolls. A rest between the two passes is a good idea, and the George (at *c*) serves food.

The hamlets and isolated farmsteads of the mountains give way to villages in the gentler lowlands near the River Ure. **West Burton** has an unusual spire-shaped cross on its spacious green. There is a clogmarket in Aysgarth village, and a museum of horse-drawn carriages, both not far from **Aysgarth Church** with its colourful screen, said to have been brought from the dissolved Abbey at Jervaulx. Notice the rebus carved on a chair: it is a pictorial pun on the name Heslington, with a hazel tree depicted above a tun, or cask. A footpath passing the church follows the River Ure downstream, passing three broad and beautiful falls within the space of half a mile.

The stocks that stand on **Bainbridge** green were already in use in Elizabeth the First's reign. Beside them is a plaque telling the story of the village's history. On the peaceful lanes between Aysgarth and Bainbridge, gradients are very low or short, and they continue thus on the A684.

The Wensley Loop

If you follow this loop your day's ride will be long and tiring but full of variety. The steep-sided, limestone-scarred valley through Starbotton contrasts with the darker-hued Coverdale, whilst there are richly rural lowlands near Middleham.

The rise out of Kettlewell is extremely steep and long, and there is a gradual 300-ft (90-m) climb from **Wensley** up to **Castle Bolton**, where the castle guards Wensleydale's wide mouth. Otherwise the riding is easy and quiet, even on the A6108, where the gateway to the bridge of the Ure, is wide enough for only one car at a time, but can still cope with the traffic.

Middleham grew around the castle (DoE, open), in which King Richard III once lived. He gave Middleham its market rights, and his badge of the white boar adorns many a sign in the town. The church bells are renowned among bell ringers for their tone and many travel here especially to try them. Inside the church is a tombslab carved with a rebus for the name of Thornton.

The monks of Jervaulx Abbey at Middleham began a tradition of horse breeding and **Horsehouse** is still known for excellent breeding and training today. Walk up the track from the river bridge below **Coverham** church, and you will pass beneath an old stone arch, before reaching a house and garden incorporating the remains of Coverham Abbey.

The church at **Wensley** contains a fourteenth-century brass, and the red-curtained pews of the Bolton family. A Viking burial and sword were found in the churchyard.

Beyond Wensley and across the valley from Castle Bolton, Penhill's austere silhouette dominates the countryside—'Pen' being one of the Yorkshire Dales' rare name fragments to survive from Celtic times. The partly ruined castle (open) rises starkly at one end of **Castle Bolton's** broad, single street, yet it was luxuriously modern in its day, being one of the first to have chimneys. Mary Queen of Scots was imprisoned here and managed to escape, only to be recaptured a couple of hours later. Next door in the church, evocative photographs illustrate a display about Wensleydale's early settlers.

THE BUTTERTUBS ROUTE
18 miles (29 km)
clockwise

HAWES. From the end of the main street near the church, follow the one-way signs to pass to the L of the Midland Bank. L (Hardrow 1½, Muker 7). L (Hardrow ½, Muker 6). R (Muker 6). L at the next junction, following the white dashes running down the middle of the road. Pass **The Buttertubs**.

Reach

a near **Thwaite**. *Join the Tan Hill Loop, or cont.* Leave

a (Muker 1, Richmond 20, B6270). Pass through

Muker. Reach

b. The Tan Hill Loop rejoins the Buttertubs Route. Leave

b on the lane signposted (Askrigg 5) and 1:4 gradient). Cont at the junction

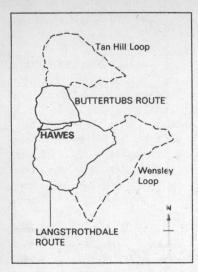

Tan Hill Loop

BUTTERTUBS ROUTE

HAWES

Wensley Loop

LANGSTROTHDALE ROUTE

Gunnerside. Cross the bridge over the stream, and go ahead on an unsignposted road, passing to the R of 'East View' and 'Greystones' houses. A track with the sign 'Private Road, no unauthorised vehicles beyond this point' doubles back to the R of your road, leading to **Gunnerside Ghyll**. The track is clear and firm but bumpy with stones. Before it reaches the hill shoulder its gradient forces you to dismount, but beyond that it is able to be cycled in parts. L (Weight limit 2 tons, ½ mile ahead). Pass through Ivelets. R at the T junction with the main road to cross the bridge labelled YNR 350. Reach

b. Rejoin the Buttertubs Route.

where a 'Muker 4' sign points back the way you came. Cont at the next junction. Enter

Askrigg. R (Hawes 5½). Cont through the village to pass to the L of the church. Cont at the next junction. Cont (Hardrow 4¼, Hawes 4½). Cont at the next two junctions. L (Hawes 1) *otherwise detour 1 mile (1½ km) following 'Hardrow' signs for* **Hardrow**.

The Tan Hill Loop
adds 23 miles (37 km)
clockwise

Leave

a (Keld 2, Kirkby Stephen 12½, B6270). Pass through

Thwaite, and then reach

Keld. L (Tan Hill 4, K Stephen 10¼ B6270). R (W Stonesdale ¾, Tan Hill 3¾). R (Reeth 11). Pass Tan Hill. Cont (Reeth 10, Bowes 7). Cont at the next junction. Cont (Reeth 3½). Cont at the next junction. Enter

Reeth. R by the Buck Hotel, to follow signs for Gunnerside till you reach

LANGSTROTHDALE ROUTE
30 miles (48 km)
anticlockwise

HAWES. Leave from the top end of the main road (Gayle ½, Kettlewell 15). L (Kettlewell). R (Kettlewell 14½). Reach the **Roman Road**. L (Kettlewell 11½). Keep L where a road goes R to Greenfield. Reach

c The George Inn. *Join the Wensley Loop or cont.* Leave

c. Go L to cross the river. L at the next junction, just beyond a stream bridge. L at the T junction, where the lane you have just come up has a 'Heavy vehicles prohibited ¾ mile ahead' sign. Cont at the next junction. Cont (W Burton 1½, Aysgarth 3, Leyburn 8¾, B6160). Cont at the next junction. L (Aysgarth 1¾, Leyburn 7½, B6160) *otherwise detour ¼ mile (½ km) R (West Burton ¼), for* **West Burton.** L (Aysgarth 1½, Hawes 10½). L (Aysgarth ¾, Hawes 10, A684). Pass the drive to **Aysgarth Church** bearing a wooden Aysgarth Parish Church sign which is easily missed. R (Aysgarth Falls ¼, Carperby 1, Bolton Castle 4, Redmire 4¼). Reach

d. The Wensley Loop rejoins the Langstrothdale Route. Leave

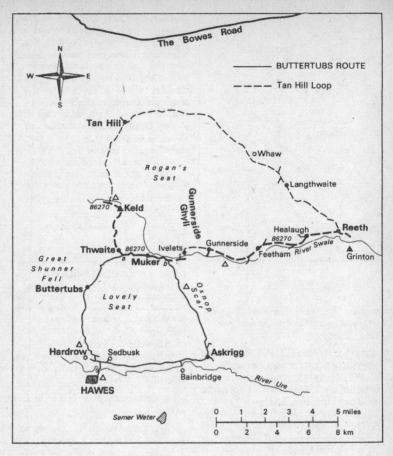

d (Askrigg 4¼, Hawes 9¾). Cont at the next three junctions. Bear L at the next junction i.e. *not* R to Newbiggin ¼. Cont Tourist Information. Enter

Askrigg. L (Hawes 5½). Cont through the village to pass to the L of the church. Cont at the next junction. L (Bainbridge ½). Enter

Bainbridge. R to pass in front of the Rose and Crown. Cont (Hawes, A684). This A road can be reasonably quiet, but if it is too busy for you, complete the route on the lane to the north of the river, as on the Buttertubs Route.

**Wensley Loop
adds 18½ miles (30 km)
anticlockwise**

Leave

c. Cont past the George i.e. do *not* cross the river. Enter Buckden. R (Kettlewell 3½, Grassington 10¼, Skipton 17¾, B6160). L just beyond the Bluebell Hotel in Kettlewell to pass the telephone box. Cont (Leyburn 16, gradient 25%). L (Leyburn, gradient 1 in 4). R (Leyburn). Cont past the 'Arkleside only' turn-off. Pass through

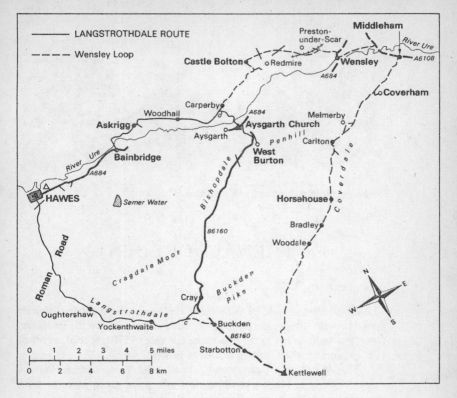

LANGSTROTHDALE ROUTE

Wensley Loop

Horsehouse. Cont (Middleham 5, Leyburn 6). R in Carlton village i.e. *not* L onto the 'Unsuitable for motors' road. Cont (Middleham 4, Leyburn 6½, Masham 12½). Cont (Coverham 2, Middleham 3½). Cont at the next two junctions. Cont (Middleham 1¾, Leyburn 4) *otherwise detour downhill a few hundred yards (metres), R (Caldbergh 1, W Scrafton 3), for* **Coverham**. Enter

Middleham. L (Leyburn, A6108). L (Wensley 1¾, Hawes 17, A684). Enter

Wensley. R (Leyburn 1½, Bedale 12, Richmond 12½, A684). L (Castle Bolton, Aysgarth Falls, Preston 2, Redmire 3½, Carperby 6). Cont at the next junction. Cont (Redmire 2). Cont (Redmire 1, Carperby 3½), then, before reaching a 'Z bends for 1 mile' sign, turn immediately R onto a tiny lane. Cont (Castle Bolton ¾). Enter

Castle Bolton. L (Redmire 1¼, Aysgarth Falls 3½). R (Carperby 2½, Aysgarth Falls 3, Askrigg 6½). Cont at all junctions through Carperby village, passing to the L of the big cross. Reach

d. Rejoin the Langstrothdale Route.

183

Pendragon, the legendary Castle of King Arthur

THE VALE OF EDEN

The subtitle here should be 'Mountains made easy', for the Vale of Eden's fertile breadth divides the rugged heights of Lakeland from the Pennines' moorland wall. Views to the fells make the Vale of Eden special, so try to visit in summer when the risk of misty weather is lowest.

The Vale of Eden's gently undulating sandstone lowlands are famous dairy country, so black and white cows grazing in green pastures are a common sight. Big, solitary farms are built from local red sandstone, as are the village houses, although some are colourwashed with their massive lintels and corner-stones picked out in black. By contrast the Pennines are scarred white with limestone, and the lower slopes are dotted white with sheep. The easy-riding routes keep mostly close to the Pennines, with the jagged Lakeland skyline rising to the west.

Easy cycling but occasionally a little strenuous. Very quiet with a few busy miles. One moderately easy track.

APPLEBY

Location: 30 miles (50 km) south-east of Carlisle.

Trains: Appleby Station is on the Leeds to Carlisle line. Leeds: 1 hour 45 mins; Glasgow: 2 hours 15 mins (change at Carlisle); Manchester: 3 hours 15 mins (change at Leeds).

Tourist Information Bureau: The Moot Hall, Boroughgate, Appleby-in-

Westmorland, tel: (0930) 51177 (accommodation service).

Accommodation: Hotel and bed and breakfast accommodation is available in Appleby. There are YHs at Dufton, 4 miles (7 km) from Appleby on the Temple Sowerby Route, and at Kirkby Stephen, on the Brough Loop. There are big camp sites near Great Ormside south-west of Appleby and at Ousby on the Long Meg Loop. There are cheaper sites at Brow Farm and Dufton Hall Farm in Dufton, 4 miles (7 km) from Appleby on the Temple Sowerby Route. Advance booking is recommended during the Appleby Horse Fair in June.

Cycle-hire: The nearest are Harpers Cycles, 1—2 Middlegate, Penrith, Cumbria, tel; (0768) 64475 and Treetops Ltd, Pooley Bridge, Cumbria, tel: (085 36) 267. Penrith is 12 miles (20 km) north-west of Appleby and 5 miles (8 km) from the Long Meg Loop at Langwathby. Pooley Bridge is 4 miles (7 km) south-west of Penrith.

Cycle-shop: The nearest is Harpers as above.

Maps: OS 1:50 000 (nos 91, 90 just for the Long Meg Loop, and 98 for the Pendragon Loop); Bartholomew's 1:100 000 (nos 38, and 34 or 35); OS 1:250 000 (no. 5).

Appleby

Centuries ago when borderland raids between Scots and English were frequent, **Appleby** grew up within a loop of the river Eden. It was a natural defensive site, for the town's single street had to cross the river at one end and pass the castle at the other. Even so, the thick walls of St Lawrence's church were a frequent refuge, and still show signs of burning. The organ dates from Tudor times, and was one of the few to escape demolition when Oliver Cromwell's parliament declared them idolatrous. A tomb shows the family tree of the local Clifford family: Lady Anne Clifford built the seventeenth-century almshouses, which can still be seen around their cobbled court today. The town's original sloping street is now Boroughgate, graciously lined with trees and with a Regency column sundial at each end. The castle's Norman keep (open) contains unusual collections including rare nineteenth-century bicycles, and you can see many unusual animals kept by the Rare Breeds Survival Trust in the grounds.

At Boroughgate's lower end, the black and white Moot Hall is now the information bureau where you can get town trail leaflets. The horse fair held here in June is the largest in the country.

There are open spaces and walks by the river, and Bongate Mill is now a pottery and craft shop. Tea-shops and restaurants are there in plenty, and the town has a swimming pool.

THE TEMPLE SOWERBY ROUTES

Between Appleby and Dufton lie two low ridges with a pretty white, river-water mill between them. Notice the house called **Bampton Tower** on the first ridge-back. It presents a smart castellated front to the south-west, whilst the back, not built for show, is quite ordinary in rough red stone.

From Dufton to Milburn easy lanes run below the Pennine scarp, which rises steeply to 1500 ft (500 m) high. Both Dufton and Knock are backed by their pikes—bare conical hills that stand a little apart from the Pennines.

The region is noted for its big village greens, where livestock could be watched in times of unrest. Three excellent examples lie on this route. On **Dufton** green there is an unusual circular horse trough with a latin inscription, and a house nearby which has a niche sheltering a statue sculpted from the local red sandstone. Two straight rows of houses, each one a different example of simple country architecture, face each other across the green at **Milburn**. A weathervane surmounts a huge maypole both here and at Temple Sowerby, a spacious and rambling village where the King's Arms serves food.

The garden at **Acorn Bank** (NT, open) is small but charming, with creeper-covered walls, old-fashioned flowers and a herb garden. At the Norman church in **Bolton**, look for the ancient carving on the outside back wall which shows two knights jousting, the one of higher rank—as shown by the pennant on his lance—about to receive a mortal blow from his inferior.

A fairly steep 150-ft (50-m) hill rises just before Appleby, but otherwise the route near the river Eden is gently undulating.

The Long Meg Loop

This loop continues the pattern of the Temple Sowerby Route, the lanes rising and falling gently with the land, first below the Pennine fells, and then near the meandering river Eden.

You climb 150 ft (50 m) towards **Kirkland** and the Pennine wall whose upper slopes are bare even of the drystone walls that pattern it lower down. And yet the indomitable Romans built a road over it, the Maiden Way, which connects the Vale of Eden with the Tyne and Hadrian's Wall.

Streams flow with force from the Pennines, the one through Melmerby flowing on to power the mill just past **Little Salkeld** where you can watch grain being milled by traditional methods. The flour is for sale, and is used in the bread and cakes which are sold in both the mill's own teashop and Melmerby's bakery. The latter has a small restaurant, and the nearby Shepherds Inn serves food.

At the junction where you leave **Gamblesby**, the low, metal stocks must have been exceptionally uncomfortable. **Long Meg** is a gaunt, red, Bronge Age monolith, and stands aloof from the circle of her many grey, lichen-covered daughters.

The B6412 is a quiet road, overlooking fields and tracts of conifers on its way to the pleasant village of Culgaith.

The Maulds Meaburn Loop

The land south-west of Appleby, folds into little dips and hills, and rises irregularly from the Eden valley's farmlands onto open moor some 700 ft (200 m) above. Near **Orton Scar**, on the hills' southern edge you pass bare areas of 'limestone pavement': they are not of the best, but still you can see how the water-soluble rock can be weathered into weirdly-shaped 'clints', with 'grykes' like tiny chasms between them, harbouring special plants which like this unusual habitat.

As you approach Orton Scar junction, you will notice that although turf and limestone line the road, heather starts neatly beyond a fence to your right. Many heather moors owe their existence to man's love of hunting game birds, and have been coaxed to suit his purpose.

Climbing up to Orton Scar, this loop is the hardest of the day's rides, although the ascent follows the pastoral valley of Lyvennet Beck, and is steep over the last two miles (3 km) only. The beck flows past fields and conifer plantations, and through **Maulds Meaburn's** attractive village green. Sheep graze by shady chestnuts, and although several bridges cross the water, you can try your luck on the old stepping stones. Flass House (open) contains an oriental exhibition.

Crosby Ravensworth, a village a little upstream, has a church with big gargoyles, and the Butchers Arms sells snacks. From Orton Scar the going along the B road is easy, with views to the Pennines ahead.

THE HILTON ROUTE

Penetrating further into high land than the Temple Sowerby routes, these rides go progressively deeper into the hills.

Once the new A66 bypass is left behind, a lonely lane rises 300 ft (100 m) to Hilton, snaking beside a beck which tumbles between banks of ferns and dark alders. Beyond Hilton the open road descends slopes, dotted with hawthorns, sheep and soldiers. This is the Ministry of Defence's Warcop Range, where I, for one, had to run the gauntlet of an 'ambush' of soldiers levelling their rifles at the road from both sides in mock battle.

Warcop itself lies in an area of rolling hedge-bounded fields and small woods; the Chamley Arms in the village sells food.

The **Helm Road** follows an almost level course, and is often lined by tangles of dog roses and slender silver birches. The word 'Helm' occurs

187

frequently in the Vale of Eden, and is associated especially with the Helm wind. When cold air comes from the east to rush down the Pennines' edge into the Vale, it blows a long bank of cloud over the fells' summit. Called the 'helm', it is echoed by a similar cloud 'bar' some 4 miles (7 km) out over the lowlands, which is caused by a re-rising of the air.

Several miles away on the Pennines is the mast of Great Dun Fell and its radar station. Beyond is the slightly lower Little Dun Fell, and beyond that, a flat-topped summit which was once called 'Fiends Fell'. It is now called Cross Fell, after the cross that was erected upon it to vanquish the fiends who were supposed to have sent the terrible Helm winds to the Vale. The Temple Sowerby Route passes close below these summits.

The Brough Loop

At first this loop passes through riverside pastures towards Brough Castle, the shell of which stands within the Roman earthworks at **Church Brough**. Both fortifications were strategically placed to guard the Stainmore Gap through the Pennines, once reputedly England's worst coaching road. The red castle walls contrast with the white of limestone scars and quarries on the Pennines' flanks. A cottage garden wall by Church Brough's little green is topped by strangely-shaped limestone clints.

Brough was once a coaching stop with many inns, some of which still serve food to travellers. There is also a café and a snack bar.

Peaceful lanes rise into more sombre country above Brough, where drystone walls enclose rough and sometimes swampy pastures. Both sheep and cattle graze here, and at the entry to **Winton** stands a circular drystone enclosure about as big as a room. It was probably the village pound for stray or confiscated livestock. The narrow road from Rookby to Winton is so rarely used that there are ridges of drifted earth in parts, so be careful not to skid.

Kirkby Stephen comes from the Norse meaning 'the town of the church of Stephen', yet the parish church's dedication is uncertain. Inside is a rare Anglo Saxon carving of Loki, a human embodiment of evil, and a pulpit built partly with the distinctive red granite from nearby Shap.

The small market shelter has a board stating old stallage fees (for each bushel of potatoes displayed, the fee was one dishful), and big benches which are ideal for wet weather picnics. There are many cafés and the Coast to Coast fish and chip shop is named after the unofficial, but popular, long-distance footpath which links the Atlantic to the North Sea through Kirkby Stephen.

From there, easy riding takes you to Soulby where you rejoin the Hilton Route.

The Pendragon Loop

Not far beyond Kirkby Stephen your road crosses a river bridge. Stop to look over and see the potholes, worn out by swirling stones. From near the bridge a group of cairns can be seen on the summit of Nine Standards Rigg to the east. Their true origins are not known but some say that raiding Scots were meant to mistake them for an army encampment.

The Black Bull at **Nateby** serves food, and on its wall is an early AA sign giving distances with impossible precision: London is 266¼ miles away, for example.

Mallerstang Common is a deep and barren-sided valley. It is said that England's last wild boar was hunted down on Wild Boar Fell, and the finding of a boar's tusk in a fourteenth-century Kirkby Stephen tomb adds substance to the tale.

Pendragon Castle's romantic ruin was supposedly the stronghold of Uther Pendragon, father of the great King Arthur. Only a big stone arch hints at past grandeur in **Lammerside Castle's** scant ruins, but in the hamlet above, a mullion-windowed cottage dated 1661 is still standing.

The track passes to the right of a kiln, built into the limestone hillside. The multi-coloured film that sometimes covers the swampy trackside puddles, shows that the special conditions under which plants decay to form oil are fulfilled here. Beyond the near-level track, a lane climbs some 200 ft (60 m) to the busier A road.

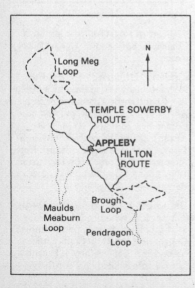

TEMPLE SOWERBY ROUTE
20 miles (32 km)
anticlockwise

APPLEBY. Leave from the river bridge (Penrith, A66). First R on Station Road. Veer R with the road, then L to cross the by-pass (which was still being built at the time of route-checking, so you might find the junctions altered). Cont (L Marton 2¼, Dufton 2¾, Knock 4¼, Milburn 5¼). Pass **Brampton Tower**. Cont (Brampton ¾, Dufton 2). Cont at the next junction. Cont (Dufton ½, Knock 2). Pass through **Dufton**. Cont (Knock). Cont (Silverband ½, Milburn 2½). Cont with road through all bends and past all turn-offs till a T junction is reached, where R (Milburn 1¼). Cont (Milburn ¾). R (Milburn). Enter

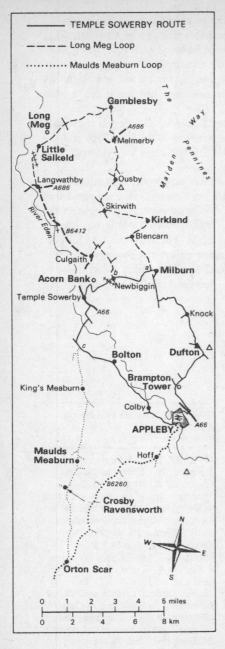

TEMPLE SOWERBY ROUTE

– – – – Long Meg Loop

· · · · · · · · · · Maulds Meaburn Loop

Milburn. L (Blencarn 1¾, Newbiggin 2, T. Sowerby 3¾). Reach

a. Join the Long Meg Loop, or cont. Leave

a (Newbiggin 2, T. Sowerby 3¾). R (Newbiggin 2, T. Sowerby 3¾). R (Newbiggin, Temple Sowerby). Reach

b. The Long Meg Loop rejoins the Temple Sowerby Route. Leave

b (Temple Sowerby). L (Temple Sowerby) *otherwise detour ½ mile (1 km), cont (Acorn Bank Garden), for* **Acorn Bank**. Cont at all junctions through Temple Sowerby. L (Brough, A66, Appleby 7). R (Morland 3½). R (Cliburn, Morland). L (Bolton 1½, Appleby 5½). Reach

c. Join the Maulds Meaburn Loop, or cont. Leave

c (Bolton 1½, Appleby 5½). R (Colby 2½) *otherwise detour 300 yards (metres), cont: Appleby 4, for* **Bolton** church. Cont (Appleby). L (Appleby ½, B6260).

Long Meg Loop
adds 18½ miles (30 km)
anticlockwise

Leave

a (Blencarn 1¾). Cont past Methodist Chapel. R (Kirkland 1). L (Kirkland 1). Reach

Kirkland. L (Skirwith 1¾, Penrith 9½). R (Ousby 1½, Melmerby 3, Alston 13). Cont (Ousby 1, Melmerby 2½, Alston 12½). L (Melmerby, Alston). Cont at next junction. R (Melmerby, Alston). Cont (Melmerby 1¼, Alston 11¼). Cont (Melmerby, Alston). Enter Melmerby. R (Gamblesby 1¼, Alston 10¼, A686). Cont (Gamblesby 1½, Renwick 4¼). Enter

Gamblesby. Cont at junction near church. L (Glassonby 2, Little Salkeld 3½). L (Maughanby 2, Langwathby 5). Cont at next junction. Cont (Little Salkeld 1½, Langwathby 3, Penrith 8). Cont (Little Salkeld ½, Penrith 6¾)

*otherwise detour 600 yards (metres), R
(Long Meg Druids Circle ½), for* **Long
Meg**. Cont (Little Salkeld ¼, Penrith
6½). Enter

Little Salkeld. Cont (Langwathby 1¾,
Penrith 6½). Cont (Langwathby 1¼,
Perith 5¾). Cont with white lines at all
junctions as far as Langwathby war
memorial. L (Melmerby 4¼, Alston
14½, A686). R (Culgaith 3½, Appleby
13½, B6412). Cont (Culgaith ½). L
(Penrith 7½, Appleby 8¾, B6412). L
(Skirwith 2, Blencarn 2¾). R
(Newbiggin 1½, Blencarn 2¼). Cont
(Newbiggin ¾, Appleby 7½). Reach

b. Rejoin the Temple Sowerby Route.

Maulds Meaburn Loop
adds 12 miles (19 km)
anticlockwise

Leave

c. (Morland 1¼, K. Meaburn 1¾,
Shap 8). Cont (K. Meaburn 1½). Cont at
junctions in Kings Meaburn. R
(Littlebeck, Maulds Meaburn). L
(Maulds Meaburn). Enter

Maulds Meaburn. Cont at next
junction. Cont (Crosby Ravensworth).
Enter

Crosby Ravensworth. Cont (Orton 4,
Kendal 17). L (Orton, Kendal). Reach

Orton Scar. L (Appleby 9, B6260).
Cont towards Appleby at all junctions.

HILTON ROUTE
16 miles (26 km)
clockwise

APPLEBY. Leave from river bridge
(A66, Brough). L (Hilton 3, Murton 4).
R (Hilton, Murton). Just past Express
creamery, L at T junction. Cont
(Hilton, Murton). Cross over bypass. R
(Hilton). Enter Hilton. Cont, crossing
white lines, at Cross Keys pub. L at T
junction with main road (lorries use this
narrow A road). R (Warcop ½). Cont at
next junction. Enter Warcop. Cont at
next junction. L by telephone box, then

R (Bleatarn 1¾). L just past Bleatarn
name sign and just before telephone
box. Reach

d. Join the Brough Loop, or cont. Leave

d Go R (*not* L to Musgrave). Reach

*f. The Brough Loop rejoins the Hilton
Route*. Leave

f (Ormside 3½, Appleby 6). Cont
(Ormside 3¼, Appleby 5¾). Cont
(Ormside 2½, Appleby 5). Cont (Gt.
Ashby 3, Appleby 3). Cont (Appleby
2¾). R (Appleby 1½, B6260). Cont
(Appleby ½, B6260).

Brough Loop
adds 17½ miles (28 km)
clockwise

Leave

d (Musgrave). Cont (Musgrave, Kirkby
Stephen). L (Gt. Musgrave 1, Warcop
2, B6259). R (Gt. Musgrave ¼, Brough
2). Cont at next junction. Cont at next
junction, passing to R of telephone box.
R (Brough ¼, Appleby 8). Enter.

Brough. R (Kirkby Stephen 4,
Appleby 8). Cont under flyover. Cont
(Kendal, A685). Cont at next junction
*otherwise detour 300 yards (metres), R
Church Brough, for* **Church Brough**. L
(South Stainmore 4). Cont at next
junction. R at T-junction, i.e. *not* L to
(Tanhill 6, Bowes 10½). L (Rookby,
Heggerscale). R (Winton). (Take care
not to slew on the drifts of earth.) Cont
at next junction. Enter

Winton. Pass school, then L to pass
Manor Cottage and Bay Horse pub.
Cont (Hartley ½). R (Kirkby Stephen
½). Reach

e **Kirkby Stephen** *Join the Pendragon
Loop, or cont*. Leave

e from main street (Soulby 2, Crosby
Garrett 4). R (Soulby, Crosby Garrett).
Cont at next junction. Cont (Appleby
8). Pass views a little to the R of straight
ahead to Great Dun Fell and Cross Fell
as you travel **Helm Road**. Cont at next

191

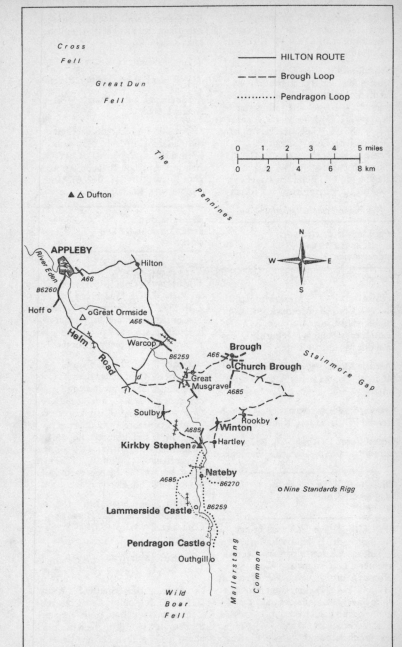

junction. Reach

f. The Brough Loop rejoins the Hilton Route

Pendragon Loop
adds 9 miles (15 km) clockwise

Leave

e from main street (Nateby 1½, B6259, Hawes 16½, A684). Cont (Nateby ½, B6259). Pass views L to Nine Standards Rigg. Cont at next junction. Enter

Nateby. Cont (Hawes 15, B6259). R by a wall pillar box, where the road you have just come on is signposted 'Kirkby Stephen 4, B6259'. Pass views L to **Pendragon Castle**. Cross a cattle grid, then immediately turn R on a track. (At first the track is bumpy with stones, but soon becomes turf-surfaced, and is slowly cyclable for much of its 1½ mile (2½ km) length.) Where the track descends to a level stretch leading to the river, turn L onto another track just before a telegraph pole. Your track roughly follows the line of the poles, eventually crossing a bridge, passing through a gate, and swinging L to a farm, whilst passing views R to **Lammerside Castle**. Go R on road by farm (the following stretch to a telephone box is not a Right of Way, but you are unlikely to be refused use of the tarmac drive on which you can damage no crops). R at T junction with main road. R (Kirkby Stephen 2, Brough, A685, Scotch Corner, A66). Pass views R to Nine Standards Rigg. Cont on the main road into Kirkby Stephen. Reach

e **Kirkby Stephen**. *Rejoin the Brough Loop.*

THE LAKE DISTRICT

The special charm of the Lake District lies in its happy combination of the wild and the homely. Although impressively rugged, the mountains are divided by peaceful valleys. A single scene encompasses so much: below crags and bracken-clad slopes, you will see copses where the famous daffodils bloom in spring, sturdy cottages of grey-green stone or white-wash, green fields and of course the lakes. The hardy Herdwick sheep have brown wool in their young years and white wool later on: hence the Lakeland expertise in working two-tone cloth.

No buildings remain to tell the tale of heavy raiding and settlement by the Vikings, but the Norse influence is still strong in the place names. 'Thwaite' comes from the old Norse for 'clearing'—for in those days the valleys still had most of their natural thick woodlands—and 'rigg' comes from their word for 'back'.

The Lake District has England's highest rainfall, and because the clouds can quickly roll in from the nearby Atlantic it is always wise to take waterproof clothing with you, even on a sunny day. Mist can also descend over higher ground, sometimes lending mystery to the landscape but at other times shrouding the mountains in a dreary pall. The risk of misty weather is greater in the cooler months, and in winter you might find roads blocked by snow.

You pay for the splendour of the scenery with hard work, for the Lake District is one of Britain's hardest cycling areas. All of the rides have some short, hard ascents that will make you walk unless you have very low gears, so take your time, and choose rides of lengths to suit your ability and inclination. The Grasmere rides have hard passes and very steep gradients. Make sure that you have not only the patience to walk up them, but also brakes in excellent condition for the descents; take extreme care in all conditions, but especially if it is wet or icy. The Hawkshead routes explore gentler scenery towards the southern fringe of the Lake District, where craggy mountains give way to lower, rounded and often wooded hills. All the rides have easy stretches along the flat valleys and despite the notoriety of Lakeland's busy tourist traffic, they were quiet over almost all of their lengths, even when tested on a sunny Easter bank holiday.

Strenuous cycling. Very quiet but heavy tourist traffic in parts. One particularly strenuous track with a road alternative.

AMBLESIDE

Location: 32 miles (52 km) south of Carlisle, at the northern end of Lake Windermere.

Trains: Windermere Station, 4 miles (7 km) away is on a branch line from Oxenholme, itself on the main London to Carlisle and Glasgow line. Manchester: 1 hour 30 mins (change at Preston); Leeds: 3 hours (change at Lancaster); London: 4 hours (change at Oxenholme); Glasgow: 3 hours (change at Oxenholme).

Coaches: Coaches run to Ambleside from many cities including Leeds, Newcastle-upon-Tyne, Manchester, Glasgow, Birmingham and London.

Tourist Information Bureaux: Old Courthouse, Church Street, Ambleside, Cumbria, tel: (096 63) 3084 (summer service only, accommodation service); Broadgate Newsagency, Grasmere, Cumbria, tel: (096 65) 245 (accommodation service).

Accommodation: There is plenty of hotel and bed and breakfast accommodation in Ambleside There is also a YH. Other hostels on the rides are at Coniston, Esthwaite Lodge (near Hawkshead), Grasmere, High Close, Elterwater, Eskdale and Duddon, and there are more not far away. Three miles (5 km) west of Ambleside is the Neaum Crag Caravan and Camping Site, Skelwith Bridge, Ambleside, Cumbria, tel: (096 63) 3221. Others are near the rides at Great Langdale, Hawkshead and Coniston. Although accommodation is plentiful it is in great demand and so booking in advance is recommended.

Cycle-hire: Ghyllside Cycles, The Slack, Ambleside, Cumbria, tel: (096 63)

3592; Windermere and Grasmere Cycle Hire, Black and White Snack Bar, Grasmere, Cumbria, tel: (096 65) 403 and 8 High Street, Windermere, tel: (096 62) 5553; Rent-a-Bike, 'Craig Lea', 72 Craig Walk, Bowness-on-Windermere, tel: (096 62) 2888; Station Buildings, Windermere, Cumbria, tel: (096 62) 4786.

Cycle shop: Ghyllside Cycle Shop, Bridge Street, Ambleside, Cumbria.

Maps: OS 1:50 000 (nos 90, 96, 97 and 89). Otherwise the 1":1 mile Tourist Map of the Lake District covers all the rides; Bartholomew's 1:100 000 (no. 34); OS 1:250 000 (no. 5).

Ambleside

Ambleside is an old town and present-day tourist resort at the head of Lake Windermere, England's largest inland water. Like all Lake District settlements, the buildings are made of stone, a delightful example being the tiny Bridge House (NT, open) built over a stream, supposedly by a Scotsman trying to avoid payment of ground rent.

Lakeland is outstandingly rich in literary associations. William Wordsworth, the Coleridges and Southey were the early nineteenth-century 'Lake District poets', whilst Walter Scott, Tennyson and Charlotte Brontë were amongst many others who visited the area. You can see the Wordsworth chapel in Ambleside church, which is one of the few in the Lake District to have a spire.

As a break from cycling you can take boat trips on the lake, or wander through the woodland garden of Stagshaw (NT, open) with its shrubs, springtime bulbs and views over Lake Windermere. Should it rain you can visit seventeenth-century Townend, a house with carved woodwork and collections of books, or you can visit the exhibition of lakeland life at the National Park information centre in Brockhole. Both Townend and Brockhole lie a couple of miles towards Windermere; other nearby places of interest are mentioned in the rides.

THE GRASMERE ROUTE

Although short, this route is typical of the beauty Lakeland can offer: from a riverside lane winding through lichened woods below Spy Hill, to views over serene waters and imposing mountains near Grasmere. The broken but sometimes very steep 350-ft (100-m) ascent from Skelwith Bridge to Red Bank passes near unfenced roads just west of **High Close** youth hostel. This is your best place to start a walking climb into lonely, bracken-clad slopes which eventually lead north west to wilder, higher ground. Do not explore far into the hills on foot without good shoes, a detailed map, compass and spare food and clothing, and certainly not in mist.

Houses built in local green slate add much to Lakeland's character, which is being carefully preserved today by compulsory use of the old materials in new buildings such as those at **Spy Hill**. **Grasmere** is popular with tourists but can nevertheless be recognised as Wordsworth's 'loveliest spot that man hath ever found'. It is a good place to take a break from the saddle: to stop and eat (try the local gingerbread), look around the art and craft shops, go boating on the lake, or visit the churchyard graves of William Wordsworth and Hartley Colderidge. Encircled by mountains, Grasmere is famous for fell sports, and as you continue towards **Dove Cottage**, look back past the village to see the famous crag, 'The Lion and the Lamb', so called because of the silhouette of rocks on its summit.

Seventeenth-century Dove Cottage was once Wordsworth's home, and is now a museum containing some of his manuscripts. Your track below Nab Scar was one of the poet's favoured walks between the village and his later home at **Rydal** (open), where he lived for thirty-seven years, writing, designing the garden, and eventually becoming Poet Laureate. Collections of his possessions and first editions are inside the house. From Rydal your road back to Ambleside is easy, curving by a clear river and through pastures below the hills.

The Langdales Loop

This loop takes you past inspiring views of Lakeland's most famous skyline: the craggy, Langdale Pikes. Great Langdale is an archetypal Lake District valley scoured out to its distinctive steep-sided, flat-bottomed shape by a powerful Ice Age glacier. Nowadays its lush, stone-walled pastures lie below rugged slopes, veined by mountain streams. The road is virtually level, but the 400-ft (120-m) Blea Tarn pass is steep on both sides. Bracken and rough grasses nearby vary their hues with the seasons, and are in contrast to the evergreen juniper bushes; a shrub rarely seen in such numbers in Britain. The passes and mountain views of both this an the Hardknott Loop are best appreciated on a clear day, so if your first day promises well, take the chance to explore this area.

The stone character of the Lake District is evident on this ride. **Elterwater**, where the Britannia serves food, was a quarrying community, and **Chapel Stile** still is. You will see scars over the nearby hillsides, where the 'Lakeland Green' slate has been quarried. Tiny **Slaters Bridge** is a charming example of craftsmanship in stone, set amidst Little Langdale's pastoral scenes. Later, when you have climbed the Blea Tarn pass, pause before swooping down again, to look at Pike o' Stickle, the conical and furthest left of the Langdale Pikes across the valley and the site of a Stone Age axe factory.

In Great Langdale you will find refreshments at the Old and New Dungeon Ghyll pubs. You will also notice how the Lakeland stone has been fashioned into smooth blocks for the town houses and the delightfully named chapel of 'Our Lady of the Snow'. It makes an interesting comparison to the rough boulders that can be seen in some outhouses; these boulders being taken from the land, as much to clear it for grazing as to provide building material.

The Hardknott Loop

This is an extremely strenuous loop, taking in four long, hard ascents. The 600-ft (175-m) Hardknott is Lakeland's most notorious pass: be sure to have brakes in excellent working order for the hairpin bends on the descent, and do not even attempt it in wintery or very wet conditions. Try this ride only if you know you can face a difficult physical challenge. If you do attempt it though you will be rewarded by a variety of scenery as you cycle through expansive, even desolate areas, through fertile Eskdale, and finally through the pine and larch forest of Duddon Valley. Population here is sparse, but the few stalwart stone houses enhance the landscape, some being protected by the National Trust.

An example of the hill farmers' struggle with the inhospitable higher land is an **old field** below the Wrynose Pass where a huge, almost circular stone wall was built at the expense of colossal effort. Nowadays the trouble to keep the land tended is no longer worthwhile, and it has been taken over again by bracken. Other examples can be seen on the moors between the Eskdale and Duddon Valleys where pockets of fields are still set amid the sombre, windswept waste from which they were won.

Mediobogdum (DoE, open) was a fort built high on the Hardknott's western side by the Romans. Its view along the valley towards the sea is both strategically and scenically super, as is the massive dry-stone walling of its ramparts and building remains. Further down Eskdale you can ride on the narrow gauge **Ravenglass Railway**, initially built in the nineteenth century to carry the Eskdale iron ore. There is a café there and food can also be found in the village of Boot, and at the George IV pub directly on the ride yet further down Eskdale.

Although the Lake District is now entirely in the county of Cumbria, it used to be shared by Lancashire, Cumberland and Westmorland, and this day's ride takes you into all three of the old countries. The B5286 bridge that you cross only about a mile out of Ambleside has a plaque showing that the river was the Lancashire—Westmorland boundary, whilst -the Duddon River descending the Wrynose Pass was the Lancashire—Cumberland boundary, meeting Westmorland at the summit where the three-shire **boundary stone** of 1816 still stands.

THE HAWKSHEAD ROUTE

This set of rides explores the Lake District's lower, southern hills, exchanging the grandeur of the Grasmere rides for the tranquility of lakes and woods and little farmland enclaves. Don't be lulled into thinking they are easy, though, for the roads are rarely level, and they sometimes climb 300 ft (100 m).

Serenely lovely is a fair description of the renowned beauty spot of 'The Tarns' or Tarn Hows whilst Windermere, on the other hand, is lively with yachts and water-skiers. **Wray Castle** on the slopes above Lake Windermere is now a Royal Marines school. It has a café, and a farmhouse at High Wray serves teas.

A tiny lane from Tarn Hows passes breathtakingly beautiful craggy mountains before it descends to **Monk Coniston**, so called because estate business was carried out here when monasteries owned great tracts of land. Now there is only a Holiday Fellowship guest house, and, on the right of the road a little downhill from the junction, the farm buildings of Boon Crag. One has an open gallery on its first floor, built so that spinning could be done in the moist Lake District atmosphere. The job often fell to the lot of unmarried women or 'spinsters'.

Prettily gabled **Hawkshead Courthouse** (NT, open) was part of the fifteenth-century estates held by Furness Abbey, and now it houses a museum of rural life. William Wordsworth went to school in **Hawkshead**, and many of the tourists who roam the village's narrow alleyways and courtyards go to see the desk where he carved his name. There are souvenir shops, but also sturdy old stone or whitewashed houses including that of Anne Tyson where Wordsworth lodged. Food can be bought in several places.

The Lake Coniston Loop

Donald Campbell died on Lake Coniston in 1967, in an attempt to break his own world water-speed record of 276.33 mph. The lake is usually kept free of motor boats though, so a row on its tranquil water beneath Old Man of Coniston mountain is a delight. Boats can be hired near **Coniston**. The Old Man is still worked for Lakeland green stone, and a lovely example can be seen in the churchyard where a stone cross commemmorates John Ruskin. Ruskin was a nineteenth-century critic and writer, and an ardent champion of quality in carefully crafted everyday objects. You can learn more about him in Coniston's local museum, as well as his old home of **Brantwood** (open).

This is a heavily wooded ride. Delicate birches and noble beeches flank the lanes and the hard 400-ft (125-m) climb to Oxen Park dips into a little valley by coppiced Sales Bank Wood. Coppicing is the technique of pruning trees hard back to the ground when they are still young, making them grow several very slender, supple trunks which are ideal for wicket fencing. Timber for furniture and paper is grown at **Grizedale** where the

Forestry Commission has planted acres of fast-growing conifers. You can learn about forestry work and woodland wildlife in displays at Grizedale, follow waymarked forest footpath trails, visit the forest nursery, and perhaps even see a performance in the little Theatre in the Forest. A rather dull 250-ft (75-m) climb through woods beyond Grizedale brings you to an exhilarating freewheel into Hawkshead from where there are superb views of distant rugged mountains.

The Graythwaite Loop

Scenically this ride is pleasant but not outstanding, except where it enjoys views over Esthwaite Water, and Windermere. Elsewhere, quiet but 'lumpy' lanes take you through ordinary woods and farmlands.

Lakeland stone might cleave cleanly into excellent building blocks, but it is not so easily carved. Softer red sandstone was sometimes brought into the area for decorative work, such as the carved plaque on the **trough**. At one time, exclusively local materials were used for building, creating a distinctive local style, but after the improvement of transport in the industrial revolution it became possible to use materials from other areas and new styles were evolved. The black and white half timbering of **Graythwaite Hall** (open), for example, is utterly untypical of Lakeland.

The Hall's estate was large, and the coat of arms that you see by its entrance is repeated in decaying splendour on big iron gates further along your ride. Metal used to be forged in woods by **Cunsey Beck**, and where you cross its bridge you can see old man-made channels and watergates by which men harnessed the power of flowing water.

Hill Top (NT, open) in **Near Sawrey** is the seventeenth-century home in which Beatrix Potter lived and wrote her Peter Rabbit books. The house is still much as she furnished it, except that some of her original drawings and writings are now displayed.

GRASMERE ROUTE
10 miles (16 km)
clockwise

AMBLESIDE. Leave following signs for (Coniston, A593, Langdale, B5343). Cross river bridge and keep L (Skelwith Bridge 2½, Coniston 8). L (Hawkshead, B5286, 4). R on a 6′ 6″ width restriction road, with small sign-post (Brathay Church). R (Skelwith Bridge). Enter

Spy Hill. Keep R at signless junction,

to cont descending. R (Ambleside, A593). Straight ahead on lane with 1:4 gradient sign, where no cars or motor bikes are allowed except for access. L at next junction, where there is no road sign, but a slate sign for 'Path to Elterwater and Langdale 330 yards'. Reach

a. Join the Langdales Loop, otherwise cont. Leave

a (Grasmere), *otherwise detour 300 yards (metres) west to* **High Close**. Reach

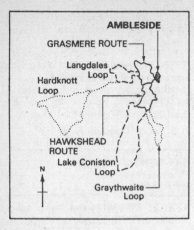

c. The Langdales Loop rejoins the Grasmere Route. Leave

c (**Grasmere**). Enter **Grasmere**. R (Ambleside). R at T junction to pass church. Cross A591 onto a 6′ 6″ width restriction road. Pass **Dove Cottage**, keeping L. L 'No through road for motor vehicles' (or cont. L onto main road to rejoin ride at Rydal if you do not wish to follow track). Follow tarmac, then cont on firm stony track. Pass to R of Brockstone Cottage gate. Go through small gate onto path which is clear but often bumpy. Short stretches are very tricky and strenuous, requiring the bike to be lifted over rocky knolls. Take care

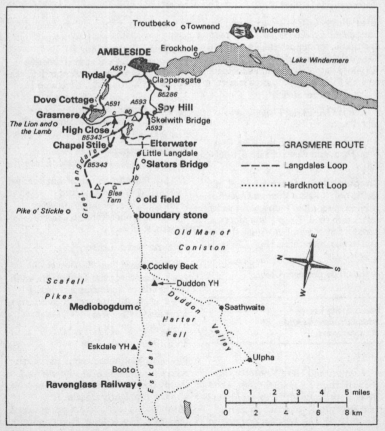

not to slip on rocks or tree roots if leaves cover them. At major track junction by buildings go R to descend. Reach

Rydal. L on main road, and in 200 yards (metres) R over bridge limited to 2 tons except for access. L (Ambleside ½).

Langdales Loop
adds 9½ miles (15 km) clockwise

Leave

a (Langdale). Keep R at next junction. R at 'Give Way' T junction, where house opposite is called Guide Stone. L (Elterwater ¼). Enter

Elterwater. L (Coniston 5, Little Langdale 2½). Keep L, *not* R on road unsuitable for motor vehicles. R (Little Langdale, Wrynose). R (Blea Tarn, Wrynose Pass). Pass a public footpath on your L, leading 500 yards (metres) to **Slaters Bridge**. Reach

b. Join the Hardknott Loop, otherwise cont. Leave

b. (Blea Tarn, Great Langdale). Pass Blea Tarn, and views of Pike o' Stickle. Enter

Chapel Stile. L (Grasmere 3¼, Light traffic only). Pass a Victoria Golden Jubilee water pipe. L on a 6' 6" width restriction road. Keep L at a junction with no fingerpost, but a stone sign in wall to Grasmere. Pass **High Close**. Reach

c. Rejoin the Grasmere Route.

Hardknott Loop
adds 26 miles (42 km) anticlockwise

Leave

b (Wrynose and Hard Knott Passes). Views L from 1:4 gradient sign to **old field**. Pass **Boundary Stone** on your R near summit. R (Eskdale via Hard Knott Pass). Pass **Mediobogdum** on

your descent. Pass **Ravenglass Railway**. L (Ulpha 6, Broughton 11). Cont (Ulpha 5½, Broughton 10½). Cont (Ulpha 3½, Broughton 8½). Cont (Ulpha, Broughton). L (Seathwaite 3, Langdale via Wrynose Pass). L (Seathwaite, Wrynose). L (Langdales via Wrynose 10). Pass Cockley Beck. R (Langdales via Wrynose Pass). Reach

b. Rejoin the Langdales Loop.

HAWKSHEAD ROUTE
15 miles (24 km) anticlockwise

AMBLESIDE Leave following signs for (Coniston, A593, Langdale, B5343). Cross river bridge and keep L (Skelwith Bridge 2½, Coniston 8). L (Hawkshead, B5286, 4). R on a 6' 6" width restriction road, with small signpost (Brathay Church). L (Hawkshead). Cont at next junction. Reach the Drunken Duck pub. R (Tarn Hows 3, Coniston 4½, Ulverston 18). Keep R, *not* L on a 6' 6" width restriction road. R (Coniston, Tarn Hows). R (Tarn Hows, Coniston). R (Tarn Hows). Pass Tarn Hows. Reach

d **Monk Coniston**. *Join the Lake Coniston Loop, otherwise cont.* Leave

d (Tarn Hows). Cont at all junctions to B5286/B5285 junction. R to (Hawkshead) *otherwise go 50 yards (metres) L to* **Hawkshead Courthouse**. Reach

e **Hawkshead**. Leave

e **Hawkshead** *Join the Graythwaite Loop, otherwise cont.* Leave from south end of village, following sign for (Sawrey 2¼, Windermere 6½ via ferry). L (Wray Castle, Wray 1¾). Reach

f. The Graythwaite loop rejoins the Hawkshead Route. Leave

f towards 'Colthouse' name sign. Cont with white lines at next 2 junctions. L (Wray Castle, Ambleside 4). Pass drive on your R to **Wray Castle**. R (Ambleside 2½, B5286). Cont at next 2 junctions. R at oblique T junction with

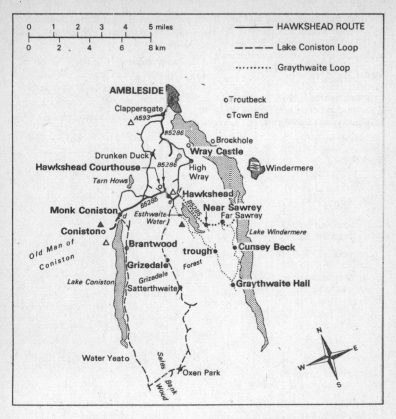

main road. Cont at all junctions towards Ambleside.

Lake Coniston Loop
adds 15½ miles (25 km) anticlockwise

Leave

d (Coniston 1¼). L (East of Lake, Brantwood) *otherwise turn R to detour 1 mile (1½ km) to* **Coniston**. Pass **Brantwood**. Pass alongside Lake Coniston. Cont (Newby Bridge 8). L (Oxen Park). Pass through Sales Bank Wood. L (Rusland, Grizedale, Satterthwaite, Hawkshead). Cont, *not* forking L to white and blue house. L at junction near Oxen Park Farm. L (Rusland 2, Grizedale 5, Hawkshead 8).

L (Rusland, Satterthwaite, Hawkshead). Cont (Force Forge ¾, Satterthwaite 2¼, Grizedale 3½, Hawkshead 6). L (Satterthwaite 1, Grizedale 2¼, Hawkshead 4¾). Pass through Satterthwaite. Pass **Grizedale**. L (Hawkshead ½, Coniston 4½, Ambleside 5½). Reach

e **Hawkshead** *and* **Hawkshead Court house** ½ mile (1 km) north. *Rejoin the Hawkshead Route.*

Graythwaite Loop
adds 10 miles (16 km) anticlockwise

Leave

e (**Hawkshead**). (Grizedale 3, Newby Bridge 8). Cont (Lake Side 7, Newby

Bridge 8, Ulverston 17). L (Lake Side 6, Newby Bridge 7, Ulverston 16). R (Lake Side 5½, Newby Bridge 6½, Ulverston 15½). Reach the **trough**. Cont (Lake Side 4½, Newby Bridge 5½). Reach

Graythwaite Hall. L (Cunsey, Sawrey, Ferry). Cross Cunsey Beck. R (Windermere by Ferry 4). L (Sawrey, Hawkshead, Coniston). Cont at all junctions through Far Sawrey. Pass through

Near Sawrey. Cont at all junctions. Pass alongside Esthwaite Water, then go ahead on lane, *not* bearing L with main road. Reach

f. Rejoin the Hawkshead Route.

Crag Lough below Hadrian's Wall

HADRIAN'S WALL COUNTRY

When Hadrian visited Britain in the year 122 AD, he ordered the building of a great wall to mark and protect the Roman empire's northernmost limit. Its position was well-chosen, as it is in expansive country whose shallow undulations offer little cover to enemies approaching from the north. The landscape has a forlorn quality in the higher windswept moors and reedy loughs, and you can often hear the curlew, the symbol of Northumberland's National Park. Elsewhere grey farms stand foursquare to the weather amidst bleak cornfields and pastures.

Woods and farmlands rise 700 ft (200 m) above the South Tyne, where the scenery may appear to be softer, but the rides are harder. The A69 and B6318 can be busy but the lanes are so quiet that some are even gated.

The Wall was associated with a network of forts, roads, signal stations, supply depots and temples, several of which have been excavated and can be seen en route. It is best to take food with you on these rides as you pass but few villages.

Fairly strenuous riding. Quiet to mildly busy.

HEXHAM

Location: 20 miles (32 km) west of Newcastle-upon-Tyne.

Trains: Hexham Station is on the line between Carlisle and Newcastle-upon-Tyne. Newcastle: 45 mins; Glasgow: 2 hours 30 mins (change at Carlisle); Leeds: 2 hours 45 mins (change at Newcastle).

Tourist Information Bureaux: Manor Office, Hallgates, Hexham, Northumberland, tel: (0434) 5225 (accommodation service), and The Vicar's Pele Tower, Corbridge, Northumberland, tel: (043 471) 2815 (summer service only, accommodation service).

Accommodation: Hotel and bed and breakfast accommodation is available in Hexham. Acomb YH is 2½ miles (4 km) from Hexham. 'Once Brewed' hostel is 2 miles (3 km) from the Stanegate Loop. The two camp sites near Hexham are: Fallowfield Dene Site, Acomb, tel: (0434) 603553 and Trax Campsite, Racecourse, Hexham (summer site only).

Cycle-hire: The nearest is: Sanders Brothers, 6a Brighton Grove, Newcastle-upon-Tyne, tel: (0632) 735045.

Cycle-shop: R. N. Taylor, 15 Priest Popple, Hexham.

Maps: OS 1:50 000 (no. 87); Bartholomew's 1:100 000 (no. 39 or no. 42); OS 1:250 000 (no. 4).

Hexham

Slate-roofed, plain-fronted houses give a feeling of strength to **Hexham**, which has faced many attacks from the north despite its strategic position above the river Tyne. The centre is still the market place, where columns support the open Shambles near the spot where the Duke of Somerset was beheaded after Hexham Battle in the Wars of the Roses.

Town trail leaflets are available in the information bureau, which is housed in a massive fourteenth-century stone building, once England's first purpose-built prison. Criminals could seek sanctuary in the abbey, for anyone arresting a prisoner there had to pay a fine, the amount depending on where in the abbey the capture was made. The twelfth-century abbey is well worth a visit, for it contains a tortuous Saxon crypt, a font fashioned from a Roman bowl and a Roman carving of a standard bearer, an eighth-century cross, a broad flight of monk's stairs and a number of art treasures.

The lovely designs of our pre-decimalisation coinage can be seen on the Midland Bank's stone frieze, whilst an intricate vine motif decorates the old pharmacy frontage. There are a number of cafés and restaurants, as well as an open-air swimming pool.

THE CORBRIDGE ROUTE

The hardest part of this ride comes first, on a long 700-ft (200-m) climb out of the Tyne valley to Portgate. Tranquil lanes rise between hawthorn hedges and pass fields and pastures and grey-stone farms.

The B6318 is an easy, high road, with views to distant northern hills. At first it is flanked by fine Roman earthworks; these have outlived the Wall which has long since disappeared, builders having used it as a handy source of ready-cut stones. Ancient Britons already inhabited this region before the Romans came, and the ramparts of one of their **hill forts** are still clearly visible, earthworks which although remarkable, seem small when compared to those of the Romans.

Troubled times came often to these English–Scottish borderlands, and the number of fortifcations reflect this. **Aydon** Castle was a fortified medieval manor house whose ruined walls still show a lot of defensive features. Tucked away in a gentle vale, ablaze with July poppies, it lies not far from **Halton** Castle the defensive tower of which is still used.

In **Corbridge** you can visit an almost unaltered fourteenth-century Vicar's pele tower, where people once barricaded themselves against border raiders. The ground floor was originally used for livestock, but now it houses an information bureau. A great flood in 1771 washed away all the Tyne's bridges except that of Corbridge; the town probably growing here because of the excellent river footing. The church incorporates a massive Roman arch, and contains the Manor Court's old halberd and staff. Attractive stone or whitewashed houses flank the market place, where food is easily available. Bottle **kilns** for firing pottery can be seen to the left of your road into Corbridge. Standing beside a farmhouse, they recall the days when transport was difficult and communities were far more self-sufficient, with people often dividing their time between two skills.

Easy cycling on quiet lanes below Beaufront Castle takes you back to Hexham. **Corstopitum** (DoE, open), built by the Romans at the junction of two of their roads, has been used as fort, supply base, arsenal and civilian settlement in turn. Ruins range from temples to granaries, and the museum contains articles found on the site, including the famous stone sculpture of the 'Corbridge Lion', and a replica of the largest hoard of Roman gold coins ever found in Britain.

The Bywell Loop

This is a peaceful, solitary ride, part of it running alongside the Tyne.

Bywell was a thriving riverside village 400 years ago, with fifteen shops, an inn, and several smithies making weapons. Now only cattle wander around the market cross which stands in a peaceful meadow spread below a plain fifteenth-century castle. Two ancient churches stand close together. St Andrew's was the 'white' one, served by white-robed canons from Blanchland; its superb Saxon tower built of rough rocks undoubtedly taken from Roman ruins. 'Black' St Peter's, served by the Benedictines, doubled as the parish school for centuries. Slots in the wall behind the tower door were for barricading it with huge timbers when villagers and animals sought refuge during border raids, and you can feel the pitted outside wall where arrows used to be sharpened.

This loop is easy all the way to Bywell, at first crossing near-level open farmlands near Matfen, and later allowing you to freewheel with gathering speed to the Tyne, and Ovington. From there a 400-ft (120-m) climb takes you back out of the valley past Bywell, but you can break it with a visit to the National Tractor and Farm Museum at **Hunday**. Displays include vintage tractors and engines, an Edwardian dairy and a working water wheel; there is also a café.

The Healey Loop

Folded hills south of the Tyne make this a slightly harder ride. It rises 600 ft (180 m) through an empty landscape of large woods and plantations, set amongst hedged or stone-walled fields. Later it swoops down through Broomley's pleasing hamlet, with lovely views of the northern Tyne valleyside.

A time-worn wooden bench for 'friends in council' leans against the wall by the **'Conversation Stone'**. Carved in 1901, it offers friendly advice on the art of conversation, its maxims fitting companionable cycling too. The name 'Lead Road' suggests industrial activity within the rural area, and indeed there are big rocky spoil heaps on the slope above.

Lanes on this loop are quiet, but none more so than the private road to **Healey**. There the modern church has a pleasing barrel-shaped roof, and a board in the porch that says that all the seats are reserved for the poorer parishoners; a far cry from older churches were they used to be owned by the landed gentry.

THE HEAVENFIELD ROUTE

Both this and the Stanegate ride use significant stretches of fairly busy classified roads, so they are best cycled on Sunday. The lanes are very quiet though: a gated lane above Acomb leads through a working farmyard and over heaths, whilst another which is deep and dank climbs through a leafy tunnel. This is the only ascent to break your 600-ft (180-m) freewheel from Heavenfield to the Tyne.

The ride has to start on the old A69 (not too busy now that a new bypass has been built), but once you cross the river you are in countryside. Further on, a level crossing is delightfully old-fashioned, with big white gates, red lamps and old-style signals.

Views over ample rounded slopes, can be seen from the 300-ft (100-m) climb near Fourstones. A prehistoric **hill fort** topped the conical hill to your right. Such sites were easily defended against marauding bands, but were no match for the organised Roman troops who later invaded the country.

Chesters (DoE, open) was a fort for 500 horsemen. The cavalry were the elite of the Roman army, and here enjoyed sophisticated bathhouse facilities with steam, dry hot, warm and cold rooms whose foundations you can easily trace; there is also an important museum of Roman finds. Chesters guarded a Tyne bridge, and you can see the gigantic building stones used by the Romans in the **bridge abutment** on the other side of the river. Many of Britain's historic sites were spoilt by incompetent excavation in the early days of archaeology, but the nineteenth-century owner of Chesters was a classics scholar, and ensured it was done carefully.

A hard 500-ft (150-m) climb beyond Chollerford ends by the austere wooden cross at **Heavenfield**. It commemorates another erected by the seventh-century Northumbrian King Oswald as his standard. St Oswald's is a simple church, standing amid fields on the battle site where miracles are said to have occurred.

The Stanegate Loop

This is the most 'Roman' of all the rides, its outward journey following the **Stanegate**, a Roman road which spanned the country from Solway to Tyne even before Hadrian's Wall was built. Although 'Roman' in its directness, the **Military Road** was built by order of Parliament after the 1745 Jacobite Rebellion in Scotland. Using stones from Hadrian's Wall, it was the single largest cause of the Wall's destruction.

Look out for the unusual old cross roads sign in **Newbrough** where the quiet Stanegate lane starts its 600-ft (180-m) rise to bleaker land, where waters of a lough lie amidst thistles and rough-grass.

From the near-level summit ridge you can see moorlands to your left, and a low, ragged edge topped by Hadrian's Wall on your right. Because the milecastles were ordered to be built on the Wall exactly one Roman mile apart you can see that some ended up in strategically ridiculous dips.

These heights can be desolate in bad weather, and there is a certain grim irony in the dedication of a temple at **Brocolitia** (DoE, open) to Mithras, the Persian sun-god. The Military Road bears fairly heavy traffic, and roller coasts over expansive low moorland.

Vindolanda (open) was once a 'behind the lines' fort, but today is a small museum which includes some touchingly personal remains. **Housesteads** (NT, DoE, open) is the finest fort on the Wall. It accommodated 1000 infantrymen, and later a community of wives, children and retired soldiers grew up on its protected southern side. Amongst the fascinating ruins are a granary with underfloor ventilation, latrines, a customs barrier, a hospital, and the 'murder house' where a man's skeleton with a sword through its ribs was discovered.

Hadrian's Wall is best appreciated walking along it. A very fine stretch runs west from Housesteads, although you have to imagine its original 15-ft (4½-m) height. A mile brings you to views of Crag Lough, lonely, beautiful, and overshadowed by a tree-topped cliff, part of the volcanic Whin Sill rock-sheet underlying much of northern England. Nature really played into the Romans' hands here by giving them England's narrowest width from Solway to Tyne (the Wall being 73 miles [116 km] long) together with Whin Sill cliffs and ridges from whose summits the Wall could dominate vast tracts of open wilderness.

The Wark Loop

Quiet but fairly strenuous, this ride takes you up 400 ft (120 m) past plantations to open moorland, where you can see the Wall from the 'Scottish' side.

Your descent off the moors is on a narrow gated road, twisting alongside a stream which is choked with hoary oaks. The rolling Tyne vale road passes rolling green hillsides, which shelter the castles and parklands of Chipchase and Haughton.

Wark was once Tynedale's capital, and its name means 'earthworks', although the Norman castle which once stood upon them has since disappeared. The village grew where the river is wide and shallow, the crossing point made yet easier by an eyot or river island, now supporting a nineteenth-century iron bridge. Several pub names recall the days when drove roads passed through Wark; pub food and tea and coffee can be bought.

Simonburn's thirteenth-century church of St. Mungo stands by the little village green. A slate-roofed building at **Keepershield Farm** was probably made circular so that a horse could power machinery by walking round and round inside it.

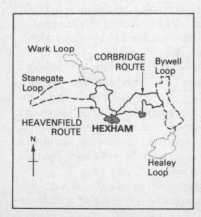

CORBRIDGE ROUTE
17 miles (27 km)
clockwise

HEXHAM. Leave from market place down Hallstile Bank. R at bottom. Follow (Newcastle) signs to roundabout, where take exit (Oakwood, Sandhoe, Anick). Cont (Oakwood ¼, Anick ½). L (Sandhoe 1¾). Cont (Sandhoe 1½). Cont (Sandhoe 1½). L (Stagshaw 3¼). R (Fawcethill 1). L (Fawcethill ¼). R (Fawcethill ¼). Cont (Stagshaw Cross Roads 1½). Go along gated road. R at T junction. Reach Portgate roundabout. Cont (Heddon on

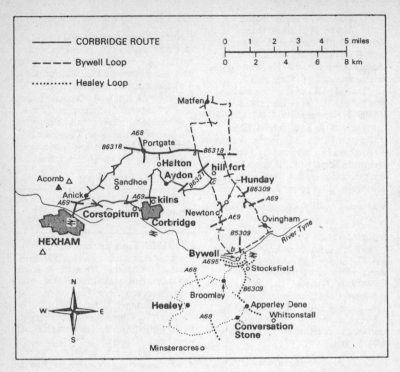

the Wall 9, Newcastle 17, B6318. Cont (Heddon 8¼, Newcastle 15¾, B6318). Reach

a. Join the Bywell Loop, otherwise cont. Leave

a Cont, *not* L to South Clarewood etc. R in 200 yards (metres). Cont at next cross-roads. R (Newton 1¾, Aydon 1¾, Corbridge 3½) with views L from junction to **hill fort**. Reach

c. The Bywell Loop rejoins the Corbridge Route. Leave

c (Aydon 1¾, Corbridge 3½). Cont (Aydon ¼, Corbridge 2). R (Wall Houses 2¼, Newcastle 15¼). L Aydon Castle 1 mile, Halton 2 miles, Stagshaw 2¾ miles). Bend R with road *otherwise detour 300 yards (metres)*, L (*Public Bridleway, Corbridge 2*), *for* **Aydon**. L at next junction *not* ahead 'Halton ¼'. Pass views R to **Halton**. 1st L, crossing

white lines, to go downhill. Cross ford and cont. Go below underpass. Pass **pottery** to your L. R at T junction to go down into

Corbridge. Leave from market place, on road passing L of church. Cont to pass L of the Wheatsheaf. L (Beaufront 1½, Hexham 4). Pass drive on your L to **Corstopitum**. Cont at all junctions, following Hexham signs where there are any, to a main road T junction, on which turn L.

Bywell Loop
adds 13½ miles (22 km)
clockwise

Leave

a (South Clarewood ¼, Clarewood 1, Whittington Mill 1½). Go through road gate, down slope, then R to go along bottom edge of field. L at T junction.

Cont (Ingoe 2¾, Stamfordham 3¾).
Enter Màtfen. R (Stamfordham 3¼,
Ponteland 10). Pass out of village, then
soon R on road with 'Gates' sign. Cont
(Stamfordham 4¼). R (Hexham 9½). R
at T junction. L (Stelling Hall 2,
Stocksfield 5). Cont (Stelling 1¼,
Stocksfield 5). Cont (Stocksfield 3¼,
B6309, Newcastle 13½). 1st L after hill
brow onto 3 ton limited road. Cont
(Ovington 1). Enter Ovington. L
(Ovingham 1¼, Wylam 3½). Fork R by
Ovington Social Club. R opposite
Ovington House. R at T junction to
cont downhill to river. Reach

b Join the Healey Loop, otherwise cont.
Leave

b (Stamfordham 8¼, Belsay 15, B6309,
Bywell ½). Cont (Newton 2¼, Styford
2¼, Corbridge 4½) *otherwise detour 500
yards (metres), L (Bywell ¼), for*
Bywell. R (Newton 1¾). Cont at next
junction. Cont (Newton ½). R (Stelling
1½). Cont (Stelling 1¼). L (Stagshaw 5)
*otherwise detour 300 yards (metres),
straight on, for* **Hunday**. R (Stagshaw
4¾). Reach

c. Rejoin the Corbridge Route.

Healey Loop
**adds 12 miles (19 km)
clockwise**

Leave

b (Stocksfield ½, Ebchester 6¼, B6309,
Riding Mill 2¾). R (Riding Mill 2¼,
A695, Hexham 9¼, A69). L (Ebchester
6, B6309, Hindley 1½). Bear R where a
path L is signposted 'Public Footpath,
Ridley Mill ¹/₈'. L (Durham 18½,
Whittonstall 2, Ebchester 4½, B6309).
R (Scales Cross 1¾, Staley 5¾). Reach
the **Conversation Stone**. Cont (Scales
Cross 1¼, Staley 5¼). Cont (Staley 4).
R through a big white gate just beside a
house, bearing the sign Private Road,
Public Footpath only. This road is not
legally a right of way for cyclists, so you
must turn back if you are asked to do so,
but it is most unlikely as you can do no
harm on the tarmac surface. Go down a
slope, then R at a T junction with a

white-gated drive opposite. Enter

Healey. L at T junction 100 yards
(metres) past church. 1st R *not* ahead on
single track road. R then L at staggered
junction (Broomley 1½, Whittonstall
4¼). Cont at next junction. Enter
Broomley. L just past telephone box on
a 13' 0'' limited road signposted
Unsuitable for heavy goods vehicles.
Under bridge then R at T junction.
Cont at next junction. L (Stamfordham
8¾, Belsay 15½, B6309). Reach

b. Rejoin the Bywell Loop.

HEAVENFIELD ROUTE
**13 miles (21 km)
clockwise**

HEXHAM. From market place, go
downhill past Arthur Boaden Antiques.
Cont down Market Street. L at cross-
roads near empty gas-holder. R at top of
Eilansgate, at a 'Give Way' junction. L
(Haydon Bridge, Carlisle, A69). R
(Warden ¾, Fourstones 2, Newbrough
3). L (Fourstones 2, Newbrough 3).
Reach

*d by Fourstones village name sign. Join the
Stanegate Loop, otherwise cont.* Leave

d on 3 tons unladen limited road. Pass
views R to **hill fort**. R at T junction.
Cont (Chollerford 2½, B6319). L
(Chesters ¾, Chollerford 1½, B6319).
Reach

*g. The Stanegate Loop rejoins the
Heavenfield Route.* Leave

g (Newcastle 22, B6318, Chollerford 1).
Cont at next junction. Pass entry to
Chesters. Take roundabout exit
(Newcastle 21, B6318). Pass signposted
gate for ½ mile (1 km) path to **bridge
abutment** on your R just beyond river
bridge. Cont (Newcastle 21, B6318).
Cont at next 2 junctions. Reach

Heavenfield. R opposite Heavenfield
cross. Enter Acomb. Cont (Hexham
2½). Descend slope, then 1st L to cross
stream. 1st R to go towards church. R
and soon R again (Hexham 1¼). Follow
Hexham signs.

Stanegate Loop
adds 14 miles (23 km) clockwise

Leave

d Near Fourstones village name sign, bear L. Cont (Newbrough 1, Haydon Bridge 4, B6319). Cont (Haydon Bridge 6, Heavy vehicles, Newbrough ½). Enter

Newbrough. Cont at all junctions through village. Cont (Settlingstones 1½, Haydon Bridge 5). Ignore fork to R. Cont (Bardon Mill 6, Light traffic only). You are following the course of **Stanegate.** Cont (Borcombe 2½, Bardon Mill 2½). R (Housesteads 2, Chollerford 10) *otherwise detour 1 mile (1½ km), L (Bardon Mill 2), follow Vindolanda signs, for* **Vindolanda.** R (Newcastle 32, B6318, Housesteads 1, Chollerford 9¾). Pass drive to **Housesteads**, and views and path to Crag Lough. You are riding along the **Military Road.** Cont (Newcastle 28,

B6318, Chollerford 7). Pass car park on your R for **Brocolitia**. Reach

e opposite footpath signposted 'Public Footpath, Walwick Fell, Newbrough 2½'. Join the Wark Loop, otherwise cont. Leave

e. Cont downhill on main road. Reach

f on the corner near King George wall pillar box. The Wark Loop rejoins the Stanegate Loop. Leave

f. Leave downhill towards a road sign. Reach

g. Rejoin the Heavenfield Route.

Wark Loop
adds 13 miles (21 km), including Wark detour clockwise

Leave

e. L onto lane, soon passing fine stretch of Hadrian's Wall. Pass through 2 gates, then R at T junction. Go through 3rd

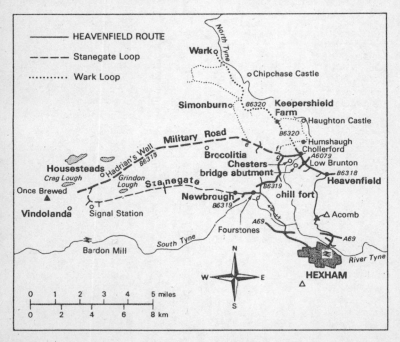

gate and cont. Cross stream, then R at T junction, *otherwise detour 100 yards (metres) L to* **Simonburn**. L at T junction. L (Stonehaugh 5½, Middleburn 5, Whygate 6). Pass summit views L to Hadrian's Wall. 1st R, opposite drive to Goatstones. R at T junction with main road *otherwise detour ½ mile (1 km) L to* **Wark**. Ignore all turn-offs till you reach 1st signposted L turn, where L (Haughton 1). Pass **Keepershield Farm**. R where drive to L is signposted 'Public Footpath, River North Tyne ¼'. Enter Humshaugh. R at T junction by the Crown. Cont (Walwick 1). Cont at next junction. Reach

f on the corner near King George wall pillar box. Rejoin the Stanegate Loop.

The Simonside Hills above Rothbury

THE NORTHUMBERLAND COASTLANDS

Northumberland's coast of lonely, dune-backed sands and huddling fishing villages is justly renowned. Inland, the hills are gentle, though rising to 1000 ft (300 m) above the sombre, craggy moorlands near **Rothbury**. The cycling is very easy near the coast, which is directly backed by low farm country, broken here and there by patches of woodland. Slopes get progressively steeper further inland, the longest rising 750 ft (225 m). The routes follow peaceful lanes where they can, and the B roads are moderately quiet.

Whilst comfortable manor houses were being built throughout the rest of England, the landed Northumbrians still lived in grim pele towers to protect themselves from Scottish raiders. Centuries of unrelenting strife have left these borderlands rich in superb castles. The country population is relatively sparse, many of the place-names on the map corresponding to hamlets or even single farms rather than villages.

A combination of mostly easy cycling with some shorter, fairly strenuous parts. Quiet to mildly busy roads.

ALNWICK

Location: 30 miles (50 km) north of Newcastle-upon-Tyne.

Trains: Alnmouth Station is 4 miles (7 km) from Alnwick, and is on the Newcastle–Berwick–Edinburgh line. Newcastle-upon-Tyne: 45 mins; Edinburgh: 1 hour 45 mins.

Tourist Information Bureau: The Shambles, Northumberland Hall, Alnwick, Northumberland, tel: (0665) 3120 (summer service only, accommodation service).

Accommodation: There is hotel and bed and breakfast accommodation in Alnwick and a Holiday Fellowship House in Alnmouth. There is a YH at Rock, on the Bamburgh Loop. There is no official camping site in Alnwick, but the Alnwick Rugby Club in Greensfield Park, 1 mile (1½ km) from the town centre, allows summer camping around its pitches and the use of the club house for a fee. Official sites on the routes are at Edlingham and Rothbury.

Cycle hire: The nearest are: 6a Brighton Grove, Newcastle-upon-Tyne, tel: (0632) 35045, and 17a Bridge Street, Berwick-upon-Tweed, Northumberland, tel: (0289) 6295.

Cycle shop: Whellens, 50 Bondgate Within, Alnwick, Northumberland. Wilsons, 8 Bondgate Within, Alnwick, are not specifically a cycle shop, but keep some spares in stock.

Maps: OS 1:50 000 (nos 75, 81); Bartholomew's 1:100 000 (no. 42); OS 1:250 000 (no. 4).

Alnwick

Alnwick is an ancient border town where history comes alive for a fortnight in early summer, when many of the townsfolk dress in the styles of past centuries during Alnwick Fair.

Parts of the old town walls remain and the Norman castle (open) is lavishly elegant within. The life-size statues of soldiers standing atop the walls were put there to fool the Scottish raiders. A riverside path gives impressive views of the castle, which dominates the sloping grounds laid out by Capability Brown.

At certain times the public are allowed into the large grounds of **Hulne Priory,** equipped in the fifteenth century with a defensive tower. The Tenantry Column bears the oddly stiff-tailed lion of the Percy family, which has owned the castle and lands here for centuries. When their tenants erected the column in gratitude for low rents, they revealed that they had money to spare. Accordingly the rents were raised and the column was nick-named the 'Farmers' Folly'.

The stone-built town has some confusing alleyways around the old market centre, and several interesting buildings are described in town trail leaflets available from the information centre. Cobwebs and dust of 150 years festoon dirty bottles in a window of the Cross Keys, where you can discover the reason why. Alnwick has both a cinema and a swimming pool, as well as a fish and chip shop, several cafés and restaurants.

THE ALNMOUTH ROUTE

Alnmouth's red roofs cluster prettily on a ridge between the river Aln and the North Sea. The town was once an important grain port, with a flourishing sideline in smuggling, but a great storm in 1806 broke open a new course for the river, leaving the harbour as a back-water. It has since silted up, its shallow reed-fringed waters now used for mooring of yachts. Alnmouth is popular in summer; meals can be bought here, and the golf-course is one of England's oldest.

The River 'Aln' is pronounced just as it looks. In 'Alnmouth' it becomes lengthened, not quite into 'Allenmouth' but almost, yet in 'Alnwick' it is shortened, the town being spoken of as 'Annick'.

Climbs of 150 ft (50 m) take you out of both Alnwick and Longhoughton, both being long rather than steep. A 100-ft (30-m) rise out of **Lesbury** leads past the radar dishes of Boulmer, part of Britain's system for long-range detection of air attack from the east. Lanes then take you through undulating farm country, and so back to Alnwick.

The Craster Loop

The terrain becomes gentler in this loop, although towards **Craster** some low but cliff-edged hills bring a touch of wildness to the pastoral scenes. Lofty beeches and Scots pines are passed near **Howick**, a pleasing hamlet where doveholes pierce the central tower of a long, stone-built terrace. Howick Gardens (open) are varied, including kitchen gardens and a 'silver wood' planted to mark a silver wedding anniversary. Just beyond Howick you can pause at a little rocky bay, usually quite free of other trippers because it is difficult to park cars nearby.

Longhoughton is rather straggling but **Craster** is a charming fishing village, albeit popular with tourists. It has a tiny harbour where lobster and crab are still landed, and is famous for its excellent oak-smoked kippers. There are tea-rooms, a small tropical shell museum, and a nearby quarry is now a nature reserve.

Dunstanburgh Castle's haunting ruins (DoE, open) stand on a low yet strategic coastal hill and are reached by a pleasant coastal footpath signposted from **Craster**. Surviving fragments hint at the colossal size of the fourteenth-century castle, whose long and bloody history includes five changes of ownership in the Wars of the Roses alone.

At the junction a mile south of **Hocketwell**, is a multi-ovened **kiln** in a field to your right, where each oven helped to keep its neighbours hot.

The Bamburgh Loop

The land becomes ever flatter towards the north, except for a few low hills to the west of **Bamburgh**. Cycling here is easy, unless you have a headwind

217

from which there is little shelter. Although the landscape of fields, scanty hedges and a few woodland patches is not unpleasant, it can eventually become monotonous. If you find it so, or if you wish to shorten your ride and still visit Bamburgh, check the railway timetable for a train to take you from **Chathill** back to **Alnmouth** station. The B roads in the ride are rarely very busy.

On your outward journey you enjoy views of **Dunstanburgh Castle**, the coastal sand-dunes, and the low but cliff-surrounded **Farne Islands**. Accessible by boat from **Seahouses**, these National Trust islands were inhabited by the seventh-century saints Aidan and Cuthbert, and are still a sanctuary for seals and sea-birds.

The red sandstone Castle at Bamburgh (open), with its fine twelfth-century Norman keep looms large on your horizon as you approach, and dwarfs the pretty village below. The church contains the armour of a man who was slain in a feud, the forked beam of Saint Aidan, and a reredos carved with the saints of Northumbria. Grace Darling and her father heroically rescued the survivors of a steamship which ran aground on Big Harcar Rock in appalling weather conditions. Her monument stands in the churchyard so that those at sea can be cheered by the view of it, and there is a museum devoted to her. The village has tearooms and a pub serving food.

Meals can be bought at **Embleton's** Bamburgh Castle Hotel, and a fifteenth-century pele tower stands by the church. At **Preston** Tower (open) you can see how comfort was sacrificed to security in the pele towers, the narrow windows, for example, being easily blocked should attackers try smoking out the inhabitants, a tactic called 'scumfishing' hereabouts. You can climb to the tower roof where the bell of a rare timepiece strikes the hours. Powered by four weights of a hundredweight apiece, its clockwork is open to view.

A 150-ft (50-m) climb out of Bamburgh is the hardest on the loop, bringing you to views over wide and lonely sands stretching for miles towards the unmistakeable silhouette of **Lindisfarne**, where, in the seventh century, monks from Iona settled giving new life to christianity in England.

Beyond Preston sunlight filters through an avenue of gnarled ash trees, taking you on your way to **Rock** with its blacksmith's shop.

THE EDLINGHAM ROUTE

Exploring higher hills inland, this route follows two B roads, but both are reasonably quiet. The first rises and falls gently, flanked by **Hulne Priory's** estate wall for miles. The second climbs 350 ft (100 m) towards heather moors, where the four round **Brizlee** radar dishes, part of the NATO communications network can loom uncannily through the mists that sometimes descend. The freewheel into **Alnwick** enjoys distant views to the sea.

Deserted lanes cross farmlands softened by trees and grazed by sheep, and the clean-lined turf hills both near and distant have an almost forlorn beauty.

Before going to the Battle of Flodden, the Earl of Surrey and his officers prayed in **Bolton** church, which now contains large wall slabs carved with heraldic devices.

Edlingham village was given to the monks of Lindisfarne by a seventh-century Northumbrian king. The church has some Anglo-Saxon fragments, and local sheepskins cover the altar and pulpit floors. A moat probably protected the nearby pele tower which is now being restored by the Department of the Environment; its history is told within the church.

The Rothbury Loop

As far as **Rothbury**, quiet lanes pass through similar countryside to that of the Edlingham Route, except that occasional crags and heather-clad hills add an element of wildness to the scenery. Beech trees betray man's influence near **Callaly** Castle (open), a seventeenth-century mansion with both an elegant plasterwork salon and remains of a thirteenth-century pele tower.

Another battlemented pele at **Whittingham** (one of Northumberland's prettiest villages), was converted into almshouses in the nineteenth century, the cost being borne by the Lady Ravensworth.

For centuries the ancient market town of **Rothbury** was an important stop on cattle-droving routes from Scotland. Although remote, and set below the gaunt edges of the Simonside Hills, it is still a bustling town with several places serving food, and seats on the green. An information centre run jointly by the Northumberland National Park and the Forestry Commission tells of the natural history and forestry work in the area, and you can ask for directions for the three-quarter mile riverside amble to an old mill at Thrum.

Cragside (NT, open) has grounds of over 900 acres, where magnificent trees and rhododendrons are mirrored in lovely lakes. The stream drove a generator in the 1880s, making Cragside England's first house to be completely lit by water-powered electricity. It was then the home of Lord Armstrong, an avid innovator and inventor of the rifle. Much of his apparatus is now exhibited in the Victorian house, together with a collection of Pre-Raphaelite paintings.

This loop is fairly strenuous, with a 350-ft (100-m) ascent up to Cartington, and another of 650 feet climbing out of Rothbury through woods and rhododendrons onto windswept heathery wastes. The few trees sheltering a moorland cottage serve only to emphasize the barrenness, but there are tearooms at New Moor House.

THE WARKWORTH ROUTE

This route can be treated as an extra loop choice to either of the other sets, or it can make a lazy day's outing in its own right, perhaps including relaxation on the sandy beach half a mile from **Warkworth**.

Quiet lanes rise and fall over rolling wooded farmlands. Your longest climb rises gradually from Warkworth at sea-level to Shilbottle at 500 ft (150 m). On your outward journey ascents totalling some 300 ft (100 m) bring the reward of four gentle downhill miles into Warkworth.

Coquet Island's low bulk lies a mile out to sea. It was the home of an eccentric hermit in Norman times, and a garrison of importance in the Civil War. The nineteenth-century lighthouse stands amidst scant remains of a Benedictine priory.

A tight curve in the River Coquet makes **Warkworth** nearly an island, and, with the castle guarding the neck of land, its site is nearly impregnable. Warkworth Castle (DoE, open) stands upon a great earthwork, with a most unusual tall cruciform keep built in the fourteenth century by the Percys of Alnwick. A street of substantial eighteenth- and nineteenth-century houses runs down from the castle to the medieval bridge and gatehouse arch that guarded the other end of the town. A nearby pub serves food.

Saint Lawrence's church is dark; it was built with small windows to serve as a refuge under threat of border raids. It contains the effigy of the knight who gave Warkworth its common, and the room over the porch was once the village school. A riverside footpath below steep wooded banks leads a mile upstream, to a point where a ferry crosses to The Hermitage (DoE, open), which was hollowed out of the rock by a fourteenth-century hermit.

'Bottle' appears in several place-names hereabouts, deriving from the Saxon 'bothel' meaning 'abode'. **Shilbottle's** church has a memorial made of marble from Alhambra, a roof carved with symbols of the Passion, and a twentieth-century *Book of Remembrance* with every page painted by hand. The castellated vicar's pele next door was granted by Henry IV to his son in the fifteenth century.

The Shilbottle area has yielded good coal since the Middle Ages. Your route crosses a mineral railway track, and perhaps you can guess the distance to London given on a huge sign near the British Rail level crossing.

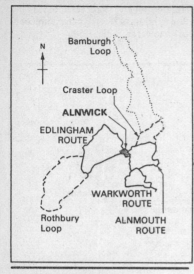

ALNMOUTH ROUTE
14 miles (23 km)
anticlockwise

ALNWICK Leave following
(A1, Morpeth) signs. L (Shilbottle 2½),
to go under the A1 underpass.
R (Shilbottle 2½). L (Alnmouth 3¾).
Cont (Bilton, Lesbury, Alnmouth).
Cont at next junction. Cont (Alnmouth,
Warkworth). Leave roundabout on
B1338 exit (Alnmouth ¾, B1338,
Boulmer 3½). L (Foxton ½ Boulmer 3)
*otherwise detour ¼ mile R (Alnmouth ¼,
Beach ½), for* **Alnmouth**. Cont
(Lesbury, Alnwick). Enter

Lesbury R (Longhoughton 2½,
Embleton 8, Seahouses 15). Reach

a **Longhoughton** *Join the Craster
Loop, or cont.* Leave

a (Denwick, Alnwick). Reach

*d. The Craster Loop rejoins the Alnmouth
Route.* Leave

d (Denwick 1¼, Alnwick 2¾). Cont at
next junction. L (Alnwick, B1340,
Berwick, Newcastle). Cont to pass to R
of war memorial. Cont (Alnwick 1,
B1340). Cont (Alnwick 1, B1340), back
to **Alnwick**.

Craster Loop
adds 8 miles (13 km) and a strongly
recommended 3 mile (5 km) walk
anticlockwise

Leave

a (Boulmer, Embelton, Seahouses).
Cont (Craster, Seahouses, Howick 2¼,
Embleton 5½). Cont at next junction. R
(Howick, Embleton, Seahouses). Cont
(Howick, Craster). R (Howick,
Craster). L (Howick). Pass through

Howick L (Craster). Reach

b. Join the Bamburgh Loop, or cont.
Leave

b (Little Mill Stn 1¾, Alnwick 6½)
*otherwise detour ¾ mile. (Craster ¾,
Dunstanburgh Castle 1¾). R (Craster ½,
Dunstanburgh Castle 1½), for* **Craster,**
and signposted walk to **Dunstanburgh
Castle.** Cont at next junction. Reach

c **Hocketwell.** *The Bamburgh Loop
rejoins the Craster Loop.* Leave

c (Longhoughton, Howick, Lesbury).
Cont (Alnwick). Cont (Longhoughton,
Lesbury). Reach

d. Rejoin the Alnmouth Route.

Bamburgh Loop
adds 23½ miles (38 km)
anticlockwise

Leave

b (Craster ¾, Dunstanburgh Castle
1¾). L (Dunstanburgh ½, Embleton
2½) *otherwise detour ½ mile (1 km), R
(Craster ½, Dunstanburgh Castle 1½), for*
Craster, *and signposted walk to*
Dunstanburgh Castle. R (Embleton).
R (Embleton 1½, Newton-by-the-Sea
4, Seahouses 8½). Cont at next two
junctions. Enter

Embleton L (Beadnell, Seahouses,
Bamburgh). R (Beadnell, Seahouses).
Cont (Beadnell, Seahouses,
Bamburgh). Cont (Beadnell 4,
Seahouses 6, Bamburgh 9, B1340). R
(Beadnell 3, Seahouses 4½, Bamburgh
8, B1340, Swinhoe 1½). Cont (North

221

Sunderland 2½). Cont (Seahouses 2, Bamburgh 5). Cont up a road which has a 2 tons weight limit ¼ mile ahead. R (North Sunderland, Seahouses). L (Bamburgh 2½). Pass views to R of the **Farne Islands** Keep R at next junction, to go towards castle. Enter

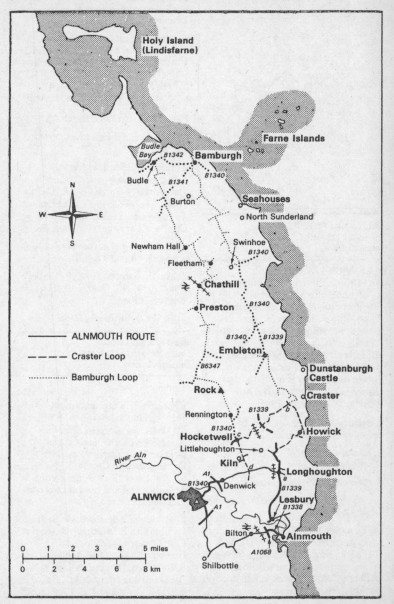

Holy Island
(Lindisfarne)

Farne Islands

Budle
Bay   B1342   **Bamburgh**
                    B1340
Budle   B1341
                              Seahouses
Burton   o North Sunderland

N
W   E
S

Newham Hall   Swinhoe
                              B1340
Fleetham
                    Chathill
                    Preston   B1340

—— ALNMOUTH ROUTE   B1340   B1339
– – – Craster Loop   **Embleton**
.... Bamburgh Loop
                    B6347
                                    Dunstanburgh Castle
                    Rock
                                    Craster
Rennington   B1339
                    B1340
Hocketwell   **Howick**
Littlehoughton
                    Kiln   d
River Aln   **Longhoughton**
          A1
          B1340   Denwick   B1339
ALNWICK   **Lesbury**
          A1   B1338
                    Bilton   **Alnmouth**
                    A1068
Shilbottle

0   1   2   3   4   5 miles
0   2   4   6   8 km

Bamburgh Leave from the bottom corner of the green (Warren Mill 2½, Belford 5¼, Berwick 20). Pass views to R of **Lindisfarne**. L (Waren Caravan Site ¼). R (Waren Caravan Site). Bear L by the site entrance. L (Bamburgh 2, Glororum 1). R at T junction. L (Lucker, A1 trunk road). L (Newhams). L (North Sunderland, Seahouses). R (Coldrife 1, Fleetham 1¼). Cont (Seahouses, Chathill). R (Chathill 1½, Alnwick 11¼). R (Chathill 1, Alnwick 11). Reach

Preston. Cont at next junction. L (Brunton, Failodon, Embleton). R (South Charlton, Alnwick). Cont

(Rock, Rennington. South Charlton, Alnwick). Cont at next junction. L (Rock 1, Rennington 2½). Enter

Rock. Cont (Rennington 1, Little Mill Stn 3, Alnwick 5½). R (Alnwick). R (Denwick, Alnwick). L (Little Houghton, Craster). Reach

c (Hocketwell). *Rejoin the Craster Loop.*

EDLINGHAM ROUTE
**17½ miles (28 km)
anticlockwise**

ALNWICK. Leave from the castle barbican (Eglingham 7, B6346, Wooler 17). R (B6346, Wooler). L (Eglingham.

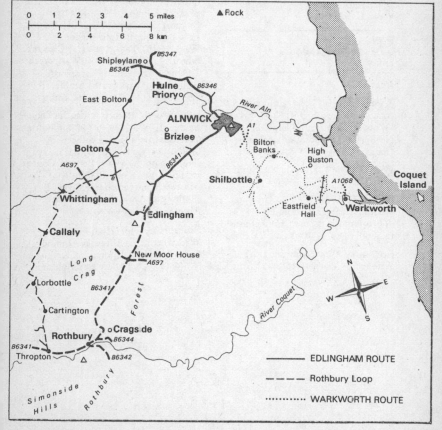

Chatton, Wooler). Cont at next
junction. L (B6346, Wooler). Cont at
next junction. Cont (Eglingham 3¼,
Wooler 12¾, B6346). Cont at next
junction. L (East Bolton, Glanton).
Cont (Bolton ⅓, Glanton 2¾). Enter

Bolton. L (Alnwick). Cont (Bridge of
Aln, Whittingham). Reach

e. Join the Rothbury Loop, or cont. Leave

e (Hill Head, Edlingham). Pass through

Edlingham. Reach

*f. The Rothbury Loop rejoins the
Edlingham Route. Leave*

f (Alnwick). Cont at all junctions,
following (Alnwick) signs, passing
views L to **Brizlee**.

Rothbury Loop
adds 15 miles (24 km)
anticlockwise

Leave

e. Face the (Hill Head, Edlingham
road), and then turn R. Cont
(Whittingham 1½, Callaly 3½,
Netherton 7½). R (Whittingham,
Glanton). Enter

Whittingham. L (Callaly 2, Rothbury
8½). Enter

Callaly L (Lorbottle 2½, Thropton 5,
Rothbury 6¾). L (Rothbury 4½). L
(Thropton, Rothbury). Cont at next
two junctions. L (Rothbury 2). Enter

Rothbury. Cont (Alnwick 11½,
Wooler 20, Morpeth 15½). L (Alnwick

11, B6341, Wooler 19½, A697)
*otherwise detour for 1 mile (1½ km), R
(Cragside), for* **Cragside**. Cont
(Alnwick 10, B6341, Newcastle, A697).
Cont (Alnwick 7, B6341, Edlingham
2½). Reach

f. Detour ½ mile (Edlingham ¼), for
Edlingham. *Rejoin the Edlingham
Route.*

WARKWORTH ROUTE
16½ miles (27 km)
clockwise

ALNWICK. Leave following (A1,
Morpeth) signs. L (Shilbottle 2½), to go
under the A1 underpass. R (Shilbottle
2½). L (Alnmouth 3¾). R (High
Buston, Low Buston). L (High Buston,
Low Buston). R (Low Buston,
Warkworth). Pass views L to **Coquet
Island**. L (Buston Barns, Warkworth
2, Alnmouth 4½). R (Warkworth,
Amble). L (Warkworth, Amble). R
(Warkworth ¼, Amble 1½). Enter

Warkworth. Return across the Coquet
Bridge. L (Warkworth Stn. Shilbottle).
Cont (Eastfield Hall, Brotherwick,
Shilbottle). Cont (Shilbottle). L
(Newton on the Moor, Felton). Cont at
next junction. Cont (Shilbottle,
Alnwick, Newton on the Moor). R
(Shilbottle, Alnwick). R (Alnwick,
Alnmouth, Warkworth). Enter

Shilbottle. Cont (High Buston,
Warkworth). L (Alnwick, Alnmouth).
Cont (Alnwick, Alnmouth). L
(Alnwick 2¾). Follow **Alnwick** signs.

Kilchurn Castle and Ben Donachain

WESTERN SCOTLAND

Soaring mountains, stalwart castles, silent lochs and sombre moors combine here to fulfill the popular image of Scotland, often, it must be admitted, complete with stormclouds rolling in off the Atlantic. The region is notoriously rainy, but even so the dry days out-number the wet.

Exploring the edges of a mountainous area, these rides cross not only some of the grandest scenery in the book, but also lower forested or rough grassland hills, as well as farmed coastal flatlands. With the exception of a few steep ascents the cycling is on level loch-side roads or gently graded passes. This easiness together with the rarity of junctions to slow you down, means that the miles quickly roll away, and the rides are far less arduous than their mileages suggest.

The lesser roads are quiet, but as this is a popular tourist area not far from Glasgow, the A roads can be busy, and it might be wise to avoid doing it in high summer or bank holidays. Midges can be a nuisance too in the summer and it is advisable to take insect repellent. There is a risk of mist in the cooler months, though and as your highest pass is at 1033 ft (313 m), winter brings risk of blocked roads and snow-covered tracks. The best time to do these particular routes is therefore spring or early autumn.

Fairly strenuous, with long easy stretches. Moderate traffic. The two tracks are both quiet and easy but one is very long and desolate.

DALMALLY

Location: 19 miles (30 km) east of Oban, near the northern end of Loch Awe.

Trains: Dalmally Station is on the Oban to Glasgow line. Glasgow: 2 hours 30 mins.

Tourist Information Bureaux: Oban, Mull and District Tourist Association, Argyll Square, Oban, Strathclyde, tel: (0631) 3122 (accommodation service); Tyndrum and District Tourist Association, Tourist Information Centre, Tyndrum, Central Region, tel: (083 84) 246, (summer service only, accommodation service).

Accommodation: Hotel and bed and breakfast accommodation is available in Dalmally. There is a Holiday Fellowship House, and an hotel at Lochawe, and there is more bed and breakfast accommodation in Stronmilchan. There is a YH in Oban, and another in Crianlarich, 5 miles (8 km) from Clifton on the Glen Orchy Route. There is an official camp site at Bridge of Awe on the Cruachan Route, and several on the coastal stretch from Oban to Barcaldine Castle. Camping 'wild' is common in Scotland, and many do so in Glen Orchy, Glen Lonan and by the Black Crofts to Ardchattan Priory road.

Cycle-hire: The Holiday Fellowship House at Lochawe sometimes hires small-wheel cycles to its guests, otherwise the nearest is at Dale's Cycles Ltd, 26–30 Maryhill Road, Glasgow. tel: (041 332) 2705.

Cycle-shop: D. Graham on the Campbeltown road in Oban.

Maps: OS 1:50 000 (nos. 49, 50 and 41 for the Rannoch Moor Loop); Bartholomew's 1:100 000 (nos 47, 48); OS 1:250 000 (no. 4).

Dalmally

The Glen Orchy and Duncan Ban Routes are circuits around **Dalmally**, but the Cruachan Route is linear. Starting at Dalmally and ending at Oban (or vice versa), you can use the train on either the outward or return journey: the directions are given for both ways so that you can suit your plans to British Rail's timetable.

Dalmally is typical of villages hereabouts, having a tiny old part surrounded by newer housing. There is a grocer and a tea and snack shop, and a hotel near Lochawe serves coffee and evening meals to non-residents. Details of private boathire on the loch can be sought at Lochawe post office. No amusements are available for a really wet day when it would be best to take the train to Oban, but if the weather is not too bad you could

make trips to Kilchurn Castle, St Conan's, and perhaps Cruachan Power
Station and Bonawe.

THE CRUACHAN ROUTE

The mountain which towers over Loch Awe and the ancient Campbell
stronghold of Kilchurn Castle is Ben Cruachan; 'Cruachan' was the
Campbell's battle-cry. A tarn high on the mountain is linked to Loch Awe
by a huge tunnel, and you can join a tourist bus drive deep into the
mountain's clammy and echoing halls which contain the machinery of
Cruachan Power Station. It is a pump storage scheme: excess electricity
produced in off-peak hours drives the pumps which force water from Loch
Awe up to the tarn, then when demand peaks, the water is allowed to flow
back down to the loch, driving dynamos which produce electricity fed into
the National Grid.

Loch Awe's waters scarcely rise or fall as this goes on, for it is
Scotland's longest inland loch. A barrage helps to control the water level at
the outflow into the river Awe where you may well see big salmon leaping.

The lochside road is nearly level but busy. The railway opened up this
previously deserted area between Dalmally and Taynuilt. **St Conan's** is a
fascinating post-railway church, designed by a local and with geometric
patterns and animals carved on the walls of local stone.

The narrow, sheer, Pass of Brander could have been created with
ambushes in mind; it was here in 1308 that the MacDougalls nearly took
Robert the Bruce, the thirteenth-century Scottish hero who won his
country's independence from England.

Eighteenth-century Lake District iron masters brought their ore to
Bonawe (DoE, open), building massive stone sheds to house charcoal for
smelting, and diverting waters from the river Awe to power the bellows.
Vicious scars in the hillside across Loch Etive are the old granite quarries
where pavement setts were worked, sometimes with a workforce of 300
men. The detour involves a short climb back up to Taynuilt, but a
home-baking teashop at Bonawe makes it worth-while. There is a café at
Bridge of Awe too.

Reached by a 300-ft (100-m) climb from Taynuilt, Glen Lonan is wild
in places and forested in others. The lichened **standing stone** to the right of
your road is well over the height of a man and must have been important
long ago, but there are no records to tell us why. 150 ft (50 m) of ascent
beyond the standing stone leads to a freewheel into **Oban**, the 'gateway to
the Isles', where a bewildering choice of boat-trips is offered.

Oban is a fishing port of 200 years standing, and the views past
swaying masts over the low green island of Kerrara to Mull's distant peaks
are delightful. There are many cafés and craft shops and you can watch
glass being worked in the Caithness factory. Both the Roman Catholics and

227

Protestants have modern cathedrals here. MacCaig was a nineteenth-century philanthropic banker who started the building of a huge circular hilltop museum to relieve unemployment, but it was never finished and remains an empty folly.

The Lora loop

Looking down from **Connel Bridge** to the surging tidal currents and eddies of the Falls of Lora, you can understand why the ferry crossings here in the olden days were so hazardous. Travellers often had to wait for suitable tides to cross, so an inn was built on either lochside; Ossian Hotel on the northern side serves coffees, lunches and teas.

The grey ironwork of Connel Bridge frames the beautiful view along Loch Etive and its surrounding mountains. Long stretches of level road pass right beside the pebbly shore, where seaweed reminds you that it is a sheltered sea-loch. Thirteenth-century French monks sailed up it to found **Ardchattan Priory**, but their rule was so strict that few Scots joined them, and today the small number of descendants live in the house adapted from the abbey. Well-tended lochside gardens (DoE, open) contain some ruins with impressive tomb slabs often bearing the skull and cross-bones. If you visit the tearoom in Scotland's second oldest inhabited house, ask to see the meeting room where hunting trophies include a 51 lb salmon.

Sheep scurry into the bracken at your approach in the steep, wild little glen beyond Ardchattan Priory. It climbs 500 ft (150 m) in a mile, but descends slowly over 3 miles (5 km) through forests, to lead you back to the coast.

Tiny windows piercing grim walls, slated roofs and turrets make **Barcaldine Castle** (open) a typical sixteenth-century Scottish baronial stronghold. Ruined for many years, it was made habitable again in the early twentieth-century by Sir Campbell of Barcaldine. The lane past Barcaldine Castle is quiet, but the A828 is fairly busy and passes campsites. A farm food bar caters for tourists, and there is a marine aquarium at the Sea Life Centre. If you have a couple of hours to spare, look out for the Ben Lora car park on your left near Ledaig, and take one of its waymarked footpaths to superb, panoramic views on Ben Lora's 1000-ft (300-m) summit.

THE DUNCAN BAN ROUTE

This is a short, and fairly easy route that can be added either to another to make a full day's cycling, or it can be ridden early on a lazy day (the open ground near the Duncan Ban Monument makes a good spot for relaxing in fine weather). If you pass **Glenorchy church** when there is no service, look in to see the octagonal interior with a horseshoe-shaped gallery, and the quaint brass-bound collection boxes on poles.

Kilchurn Castle was built by the Campbells in the fifteenth-century on an island in the middle of Loch Awe, but the waters have gone down since then, and it is possible to (carefully) cross the marshy ground to get to it. Your road through Stronmilchan passes lonely marshes too, and the jagged rim of Ben Cruachan's mountain amphitheatre looms ahead.

The wooded A819 is rarely busy and affords views not only of Kilchurn Castle backed by Ben Cruachan and reflected in the loch, but also the gables and turrets of Lochawe House, which was built as a hotel with its own station soon after the railway made settlement in the area feasible. Look back on your 300-ft (90-m) track climb to Loch Awe's 22-mile (35-km) narrow length winding between low wooded hills. The **Duncan Ban MacIntyre Monument** at the summit commemorates an eighteenth-century poet in the Gaelic language, and marks the start of a scenic and swooping descent back to Dalmally.

THE GLEN ORCHY ROUTE

Fairly busy traffic will accompany you on the A85 to Clifton which climbs 700 ft (200 m) between afforested mountains. Though pleasant in parts, it is the hardest and dullest part of the route but once over, leads you to some scenic and exhilarating riding.

Rocky spoil heaps near **Clifton** show where eighteenth- and early nineteenth-century leadmining was carried out even on astonishingly high, steep slopes. Hotels serve coffees and lunches in nearby **Tyndrum** which is an oasis in this sparsely inhabited area.

From Clifton almost unbroken easy riding takes you past a succession of breathtaking scenes. Beyond the old county boundary summit, the regal sweep of Ben Dorain's cone has an almost hypnotic beauty, so don't forget to pay attention to cars sharing your long freewheel. Duncan Ban MacIntyre lauded Ben Dorain in his poetry, and the mountain is said to have Britain's longest continuous grass slope.

Twisting and peaceful, the road through **Glen Orchy** offers one of Britain's most enchanting riverside rides. The Orchy flows through deep peat-brown pools, or tumbles over rocky shelves and boulders, before flowing more slowly by alders and oaks through green meadows. The natural Scots pine forest was cleared from Glen Orchy in the 1820s at a cost of 6d per tree, but has been replaced in places by conifers. These alternate with the slopes of bracken, heather and rough grass which sweep up from the road.

The Rannoch Moor Loop

This loop is only for the fit for the track is arduous, especially where you have to coax your bicycle over ruts on the first 1½ mile (2½ km) ascent. Rannoch Moor's desolation becomes cruel and dreary in bad weather, and the Kingshouse Hotel is your only hope of food and shelter for miles. If

229

these warnings entice rather than deter you, proceed to enjoy a ride of unsurpassed grandeur, wildness and peace.

Rannoch Moor is a vast, wilderness of sombre moors and ragged and many-isled lochans. Although crossed for centuries by drovers, traders and soldiers, who had to use high roads to avoid marshy ground, the lower sometimes busy A82 is a relatively recent engineering triumph. The older roads crossed the river Orchy at **Bridge of Orchy**—hence the name—and travellers can still break their journeys at the inn there.

Glen Coe's majestic mountains tower beyond Blackrock Cottage, from which the track follows one of General Wade's roads built to aid suppression of highland Jacobites. Made to last, it is firm even when it passes through treacherous marshes. The single stone arch of **Ba Bridge** spans a river, which rushes down from a desolate corrie said to be Scotland's largest. Medieval deerhunters would drive their quarry into the mountain amphitheatre, trapping it for the kill.

Scots pines by Loch Tulla's southern shore, with their distinctive shapes and salmon-red upper bark are remnants of the natural Caledonian forest which once covered much of Scotland.

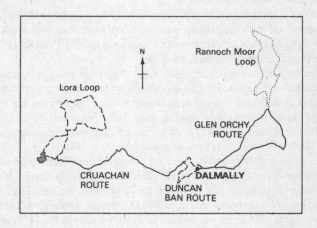

CRUACHAN ROUTE
23 miles (37 km)
(east to west)

DALMALLY. Leave from Dalmally Hotel, passing (A85, Taynuilt 13, Connel 20, Oban 25) sign. Cont past 2 Dalmally turn-offs. Cont (Oban, A85). L (Oban A85). Pass **St Conan's** on your L. Cont at the next junction. Pass

Cruachan Power Station at mouth of Pass of Brander. Cont at next 2 junctions. Cont (Oban, A85). L (Glen Lonan) *otherwise detour 1 mile (1½ km),* R *(Village, B845),* L *(Brochroy ½),* *follow (Bonawe Furnace) signs, for* **Bonawe**. Pass Standing Stone on your R. R (Oban 3). Reach

a. Join the Lora Loop for Cruachan Route (east to west), otherwise cont. Leave

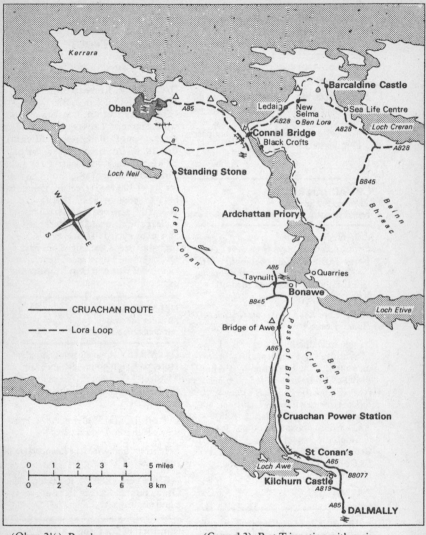

a (Oban 2½). Reach

Oban.

**Lora Loop, for Cruachan
Route (east to west)
adds 24½ miles (39 km)
anticlockwise**

Leave

a (Connel 3). R at T junction with main
road. Reach

b **Connel Bridge**. Leave to follow
northern circuit of Lora Loop. Cross to
north side of bridge, where R (Bonawe
9). R (Bonawe 6). Pass **Ardchattan
Priory**. L (Barcaldine 4½, B845). L
(Oban A85, A828). 1st road R to cross a

231

stone railway bridge with a small AV on its left wall. Pass **Barcaldine Castle**. L by telephone box. *Ignore* 'Shenvallie' turn-off. R (Oban A85, A828). Pass picnic place on your L for walks on Ben Lora. Cont past all turn-offs. R (Oban A85, A828). Regain

b **Connel Bridge**. *Rejoin Lora Loop for Cruachan Route (west to east) or leave for Oban.* Cross to south side of bridge, where second L (Oban, A85). Cont past 2 Dunbeg turn-offs. Reach

Oban.

CRUACHAN ROUTE
23 miles (37 km)
(west to east)

OBAN. *Leave on the Lora Loop as given below, otherwise* leave from near Car Ferry Terminal (Campbeltown, A816, A83). L (Glencruitten). Cont, ignoring 'West Highland Hospital' turn-off. Reach

a. The Lora Loop rejoins the Cruachan Route. Leave

a to go to Dalmally (Kilmore 3). L (Taynuilt 7½). Pass **Standing Stone** on your L. R at T junction by Taynuilt Hotel *otherwise detour 1 mile (1½ km), cont (Village, B845), L (Brochroy ½), follow (Bonawe Furnace) signs, for* **Bonawe**. Cont (Crianlarich, A85, A82). Cont at next 2 junctions. Pass through the Pass of Brander. Pass **Cruachan Power Station**. Cont. Pass **St Conan's** on your R. Cont at all junctions on A85. Reach

DALMALLY.

Lora Loop, for Cruachan Route (west to east)

OBAN. Leave following (Crianlarich, A85, A82) signs. Reach

b **Connel Bridge**. *Join fully written Lora Loop for northern circuit.* Regain

b. Leave to go to *a*. Cross to south end of bridge. L (Barran, Musdale, Kilmore). Reach

a. Rejoin the Cruachan Route, west to east.

DUNCAN BAN ROUTE
11 miles (18 km)
anticlockwise

DALMALLY. Leave from Dalmally Hotel (Stronmilchan 2, B8077). Pass **Glenorchy church**. L at T junction with main road. Cross river bridge. Pass gate on your R to footpath to **Kilchurn Castle**. R (Inveraray, A819, Cladich, B840). 1st track very sharp L (to make sure you have right track, cont on road for about 100 yards (metres) then turn back to see signpost for A819, Dalmally, arrowed half-left). The track is clear and firm and the level parts are able to be cycled. The upward slope probably needs walking. Cont past Dychliemore Forest gate. Reach vicinity of **Duncan Ban Monument**. Cont on surfaced road.

GLEN ORCHY ROUTE
29 miles (47 km)
anticlockwise

DALMALLY. Leave from Dalmally Hotel past sign giving distances to Tyndrum, Crianlarich, Glasgow and Fort William. Cont (Crianlarich, A85, A82). Reach

Clifton. L (Fort William, A82). Pass views R to Ben Dorain. Reach

c. Join the Rannoch Moor Loop, otherwise cont. Leave

c (Glen Orchy, B8074). Ride along Glen Orchy but take care as there are some blind summits. R (Oban, A85).

Rannoch Moor Loop
adds 24 miles (39 km)
anticlockwise

Leave

c (Fort William, A82). Reach **Bridge of Orchy**. Cont (A82, Glencoe, Ballachulish). L (White Corries). At Blackrock Cottage fork L off road onto a track. Do *not* go L to the other cottage.

Soon, where track forks in two, go L. Pass to L of a cairn by summit, then descend to pass L of Ba Cottage ruin. Cross **Ba Bridge**, then, after a further 3 miles (5 km), do not fork L by trees but cont on the more gentle slope obliquely downhill. The track is clear and firm throughout, but crosses very desolate

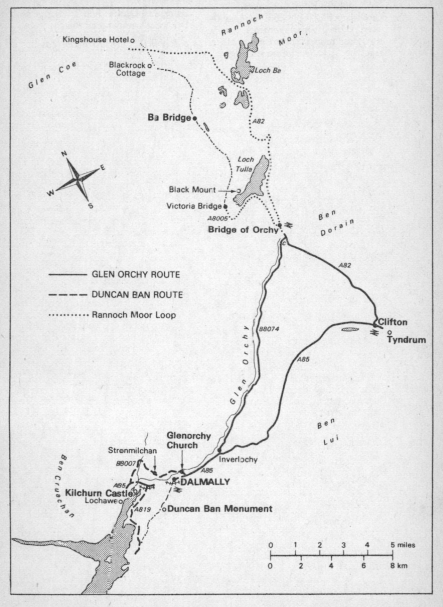

GLEN ORCHY ROUTE
DUNCAN BAN ROUTE
Rannoch Moor Loop

country, and you should have a 1:50 000 map, compass, spare food and clothing with you. First part is hardest, and going up over rough ground you will have to walk. From summit cairn careful cycling is possible nearly all the way. Allow 2½ hours for track at very least, and more if you are unused to track cycling. Reach Forest Lodge through gate with an old road closure sign on it. Cont on surfaced road, soon crossing Victoria Bridge. Follow road around Loch Tulla. Reach

Bridge of Orchy. R at T junction by Bridge of Orchy hotel. Reach.

c. Rejoin the Glen Orchy Route at c.

The Soldiers Leap at Killiecrankie

THE GRAMPIANS

Do not be daunted by the thought of cycling in the Grampians. Although this range encompasses Scotland's greatest heights, it is not so much a collection of towering peaks, but once up there, of relatively low mountains. Schiehallion's 3000-ft (900-m) cone will often haunt your horizon, but more typical are the broad stretches of heathery moorland above wooded lower slopes. There are some big forestry plantations, but there are many beautiful woodlands too. 'Killiecrankie' is an English corruption of the Gaelic meaning 'wood of the aspen trees', and the Pass is famous for its autumn colours.

The river valleys are rich farming country. Cycling with ease past the fields stacked with hay-bales in the summer, you could often think yourself down in the lowlands. The roads beside the lochs, although occasionally undulating, are level for long stretches at a time.

Put in a nutshell, the cycling is easy, except where it is hard, and then it's very hard indeed. There are a few steep climbs of several hundred feet where you will not only be thankful for low gears, but will almost certainly have to walk at times. The long descents are exhilarating, but need great care in wet or frosty weather. Remember too that the higher roads especially, may well be snowed under in the wintertime.

In summer you will share the roads with occasional bursts of tourist traffic, although even the A roads are moderately quiet. Because roads in the mountains are few, very short circuits cannot be made, and so you must have reasonable stamina to cycle here.

The Dunfallandy set of routes have been organised so that you complete your circuit on the Dunkeld–Pitlochry train, or so that you immediately catch a train for home from your end point. The signpost directions are given both ways round so that you can more easily match your ride to the train timetable, although the Aberfeldy and Kenmore Loop passes are better taken from north to south.

Strenuous, with long easy stretches. Very quiet in parts, mildly busy in others.

PITLOCHRY

Location: 25 miles (40 km) north north-west of Perth.

Trains: Pitlochry Station is on the main line between Inverness and Perth, from where there are connections to Glasgow and Edinburgh. Edinburgh: 2 hours 45 mins, (sometimes with a change at Perth); Glasgow: 2 hours (change at Perth).

Coach: A coach runs from Inverness through Pitlochry to Perth, where connections with other coaches can be made.

Tourist Information Bureau: Pitlochry and District Tourist Association, 22 Atholl Road, Pitlochry, Tayside, tel: (0796) 2215 (accommodation service).

Accommodation: Hotel and bed and breakfast accommodation is available in Pitlochry. There is a YH in Pitlochry itself, and another at Garth, 2 miles (3 km) from the Kenmore Loop near Kenmore. The Milton of Fonab Caravan Site is in Pitlochry, but allows campers with cars only. Faskally Home Farm Camp Site is a large site 2 miles (3 km) north of Pitlochry on the old A9. Other official sites on the rides, are at Aberfeldy, Kenmore, Dunkeld, and on the north shore of Loch Tummel. Camping 'wild' is common in Scotland, and many do so south of the loch and river Tummel, west of Coronation Bridge. Prior booking is recommended.

Cycle-hire: Small-wheel cycles are hired by Faskally camp-site to its users, otherwise bikes can be hired at McKerehar and Macnaughton Ltd, 2 Bank Street, Aberfeldy, Tayside, tel: (088 72) 567; E. Yule, Station Road, Pitlochry, Tayside; R. W. Bell, Atholl Road, Pitlochry, Tayside.

Cycle-shop: Mallochs sports shop on Atholl Road stocks a few spares.

Maps: OS 1:50 000 (nos 52, 43 and 42 for the Schiehallion Loop); Bartholomew's 1:100 000 (no. 48); OS 1:250 000 (no. 4).

Pitlochry

Stone-built **Pitlochry** is lively with tourists in the warmer months, and indeed it has many interests to offer. There is a tweed mill which can be visited, and whisky is distilled here. The Festival Theatre has become renowned since its founding in 1951, and presents a performance on most evenings. Faskally Loch provides the nearest of many opportunities for fishing in the vicinity, and there is an observation chamber by the fish ladder in Pitlochry's hydro-electric dam.

A right of way through the golf course climbs to Craigower. The beacon hill's 1300-ft (400-m) summit gives panoramic views over both the countryside and the town, where highland games are held on the second Saturday in September. Pony trekking stables are also nearby.

THE DUNFALLANDY ROUTE

Following the Tummel and Tay valleys, this route has only one significant climb of some 150 ft (50 m) into conifer woods betwen Dunfallandy and Logierait. Otherwise you pass through valleys of farmlands dotted with stone or whitewashed houses.

Trees cling precariously to the craggier hills near Dunkeld: these are the 'Birnam Woods', harbingers of doom to Shakespeare's Macbeth. They tower above the rocky Braan gorge, where nature trails starting from an A9 car park lead to **Ossian's Hall** (NTS, open), an eighteenth-century river-side folly.

The Picts of Scotland struggled successfully to stay free of Roman overlordship, but in the ninth century they were eventually pushed out by invading Irish and Norse. They left stones beautifully carved with designs taken from nature: the **Dunfallandy Stone** is a superb example, and another in **Logierait** churchyard bears a cross on one side and a stylised horse and snake on the other. The three mortsafes nearby were erected to prevent body-snatching, and they gruesomely echo the shapes of the two adults' and one child's coffins in the earth below. Logierait used to be the Regality Court of the Lords of Atholl, and on the wooded hillside above, a nineteenth-century Celtic-style cross stands on the old hanging knoll.

Haugh of Grandtully Farm has one of the circular, slate-roofed outhouses in which horses would walk round and round to power machinery. The National Trust for Scotland have restored the homely, whitewashed houses of **Dunkeld**, and town trail leaflets are available in the centre. A standard 'ell' measure is still fixed to a one-time weaver's shop, and there are tea-rooms, a restaurant, and a regimental museum.

Telford engineered the many-arched bridge over the Tay, which flows past Dunkeld Cathedral. The cathedral (DoE, open) is ruined except for the choir, which still makes a spacious parish church. Inside is an ancient printed Bible, a display depicting Dunkeld's past, and one of Beatrix Potter who spent many happy childhood days there. The 'Wolf of Badenoch' was a knight notorious for his flamboyant and evil life-style, yet his effigy also lies in the church.

The Aberfeldy Loop

Aberfeldy is a thriving town on whose outskirts the distinctive buildings of a whisky distillery contain burnished stills behind big windows. The lovely 'Birks of Aberfeldy' situated by the stream have paths and nature trails that are popular with the tourists. There are several places selling meals, or you can picnic on the riverside green, which is dominated by a monument honouring the Black Watch.

After the first Jacobite Rebellion in 1715, General Wade engineered a network of roads to enable easier suppression of the Scots by the English. He built the pinnacled bridge at Aberfeldy, and the road to Weem which is raised up to cross difficult marshy ground. At **Weem** an old toll-house has windows on all sides to enable the keeper to look along all roads approaching the junction.

The pastoral, gently rolling lane between Logierait and Aberfeldy is in stark contrast to the 1000-ft (300-m) pass rising over bleak moorland to the south. Often following close to the course of General Wade's route, the pass road is best travelled from north to south; one side is a steep three miles (5 km) long, but the six-mile (10-m) descent is gentle enough for you to coast down without constant braking.

The River Braan flows past wooded banks in a broad valley where pastures lie below rough hill-sides. A farm just east of **Milton** has a horse power outhouse like the one at **Haugh of Grandtully. Inver** bridge crosses the Braan, replacing a once-important ferry, and the substantial white-washed building forming three sides of a square was once the Inver ferry inn.

The Kenmore Loop

'Clann' in Gaelic means 'children', and for hundreds of years until the eighteenth century, the clan 'fathers' were a great power in Scotland. The members of each extended family clan showed unswerving loyalty to each other, and nowadays many are seeking to revive that strength. The turreted sixteenth-century **Castle Menzies** (open) is being restored by the Menzies Clan.

The level road from Weem to Kenmore passes two curious buildings of coarsely-hewn rocks. The first has scarlet painted wooden pillars which still bristle with branch stubs whilst inside the ruin of the second, the inside walls of the round tower have been worked smooth in contrast to the craggy exterior. **Kenmore** is a pleasing village where the church and the pinnacled gateway to Taymouth Castle face each other from opposite ends of a street of trim, black and white houses. Lines written in praise of the area by Robbie Burns can be seen above the inn's fireplace, and there are tea-rooms, and boats for hire on Loch Tay.

Broad and fertile, the valleys of the Braan and Tay are divided by a 1300-ft (400-m) moorland pass, which, like the Aberfeldy Loop pass, is best travelled north to south. The ascent from Kenmore is extremely strenuous and long, but as you walk up you have views to Schiehallion's peak seen over **Taymouth Castle**, whose west wing was built especially to accommodate the visiting Queen Victoria. In summer, you may find wild raspberries to eat in the hedgerows.

Amulree was once the meeting place of several drove roads that brought farmers and their cattle down from the harsh highlands to lowland markets. A snackbar caters for modern-day travellers.

THE KILLIECRANKIE ROUTE

The Pass of **Killiecrankie** is a narrow, wooded defile cutting a near-level route through the mountains. Used for centuries by packhorses and drovers, it was improved in the eighteenth century by General Wade, and later by Telford, ultimately becoming the A9 (soon to be rerouted).

At **Killiecrankie** visitor centre, a display tells the tale of the Battle of Killiecrankie, one of the first in the long struggle between the Hanoverian and Stuart Houses for possession of the British throne. A few minutes' walk from the centre takes you to the Soldier's Leap, where a fugitive from the battle cleared the surging river's 18-ft (5½-m) chasm in a desperate bid to escape his pursuers. The centre has a snack-bar.

'Linn of Tummel' comes from the Gaelic for 'pool of the tumbling stream'. Footpaths along the northern side of the tree-clad gorge can be reached by the suspension footbridge named **Coronation Bridge**, after George V, or by the Linn of Tummel Car Park where nature trail leaflets are available. The river has flowed more calmly since the Clunie power station was built to capture much of its energy. The five men who died in that feat of engineering are remembered in the huge section of pipe which forms the **Clunie Arch**.

Beyond Killiecrankie your route climbs steeply up 350 ft (100 m) to a craggy hillside. From here you can see Killiecrankie Battlefield in the foreground and the mountains in the distance. Take care on the descent.

Queen Victoria enjoyed touring in the highlands and they became fashionable because of her travels. A rocky bluff rising from the Tummel-side trees is called Queen's View to commemorate her visit, and commands wide views across the loch. Food can be bought at the snack-bar and meals can be bought at the Loch Tummel Hotel a little further on.

Stretches of the loch-side circuit are level, but others have small but frequent and tiring undulations. Double-arched and making good use of a rocky islet in the river, an old Tummel bridge stands beside the new, whilst the suspension footbridge which takes you back to Pitlochry bears a sign forbidding you to swing upon it!

The Schiehallion Loop

As far as Kinloch Rannoch your ride passes farmlands and level marshes, meeting only one 200-ft (60-m) rise, although mountains slope away on either side.

The lane south-east of Kinloch Rannoch rises 550 ft (165 m) onto moorlands below Schiehallion's soaring flanks. The mountain's shape is haunting: small wonder that its name means 'fairy hill of the Caledonians', and that legend tells of a cave from which there is no return. Cycling by lonely little lochs the only sound is of reeds rustling in the wind; it is here too, that you are most likely to spot both deer and birds of prey. On the lower slopes blanched and gnarled tree-stumps remind us that much of Scotland's moors are not natural, but were deforested by man.

The Dunalastair Hotel serves teas in **Kinloch Rannoch**. 'Kinloch' crops up time and again in Scottish place-names, being an anglicisation of the Gaelic for 'head of the loch'.

DUNFALLANDY ROUTE
20½ miles (33 km)
North to South

PITLOCHRY. From Fishers Hotel in Pitlochry's centre, go downhill to pass the Bank of Scotland. R (Logierait 4¼, Foss 12). L (Dunfallandy ½, Logierait 4). *Pass under the new A9, then soon detour R on a drive, crossing a double-width cattle grid, to go 400 yards (metres) to the* **Dunfallandy Stone**. Enter

Logierait. R (Strathtay 4, Grandtully 4¼, Aberfeldy 9, Killin 32, A827). Reach

a. Join the Aberfeldy Loop, or cont. Leave *a* (Aberfeldy 6, Killin 29, A827). L (Dunkeld 11, Perth 26, B898, A9). Pass **Haugh of Grandtully**. Pass through Balnaguard and Dalguise. R (Perth, A9). Pass a car park on your R for the path to **Ossian's Hall**. Follow Dunkeld signs.

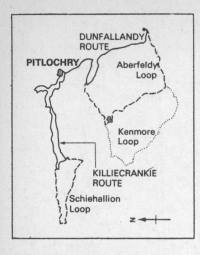

Aberfeldy Loop
adds 11½ miles (19 km)
North to South

Leave

a (Pitnacree ¼, Strathtay 1¼, Weem 6).
Cont (Weem 6). Cont by Spar shop.
Reach

b **Weem**. *Join the Kenmore Loop, or cont.* Leave

b (Aberfeldy ½, B846). Enter
Aberfeldy. Cont at junction just past
river bridge. Cont (Crieff 23, A826,
A822). Reach

c near **Milton**. *The Kenmore Loop rejoins the Aberfeldy Loop.* Leave

c (Dunkeld, A822, A9). Cont at next
junction. Cont (A822, Dunkeld 2½).
Fork L to go obliquely downhill at a
junction where the main road continues
level. R at junction by a river bridge
otherwise detour, L to cross bridge and cont for 200 yards (metres) to **Inver**. L
(Inverness, Perth, A9). Follow signs for
Dunkeld.

Kenmore Loop
adds 10 miles (16 km)
North to South

Leave

b **Weem** (Tummel Bridge 12½,
Kinloch Rannoch 19½, B846). *Otherwise detour for ½ mile (1 km) (Aberfeldy ½, B846), for* **Aberfeldy**. Pass **Castle Menzies**. Cont past 2 turnings to Dull.
L (Kenmore 2½, Duneaves Road).
Cont past the Duneaves Road turn-off.
L by Mains of Taymouth house. L
(Aberfeldy 7, A827). Pass through

Kenmore. At the south-east loch
corner, turn R then immediately L on a
lane which has a 7' 6" width restriction,
except for access. Pass views L over
Taymouth Castle. Follow road over
an 8 ton limit bridge. L (Dunkeld 10,
A822, Aberfeldy 11, A826). Enter

Amulree. Cross the bridge then bear
R. Reach

c near **Milton**. *Rejoin the Aberfeldy Loop.*

DUNFALLANDY ROUTE
20½ miles (33 km)
South to north

DUNKELD. Leave following signs for
(Inverness, A9). Pass a car park on your
L for the path to **Ossian's Hall**. Next L
(Grandtully, Aberfeldy, A827, B898).
Pass through Dalguise and Balnaguard.
Pass **Haugh of Grandtully**. R
(Ballinluig 4, A827, Pitlochry 9, A9).
Reach

*a. The Aberfeldy Loop rejoins the
Dunfallandy Route.* Leave

a (Ballinluig 4, A827, Pitlochry 9, A9).
Enter

Logierait. L (Dunfallandy 3½, Clunie
6, Foss 15). *Just before passing under the
new A9, detour L on a drive, crossing a
double-width cattle grid, to go 400 yards
(metres) to the* **Dunfallandy Stone**. R
(Pitlochry ¾, Perth 27). L at T junction
with main road.

Aberfeldy Loop
adds 11½ miles (19 km)
South to north

DUNKELD. Leave the bridge over the

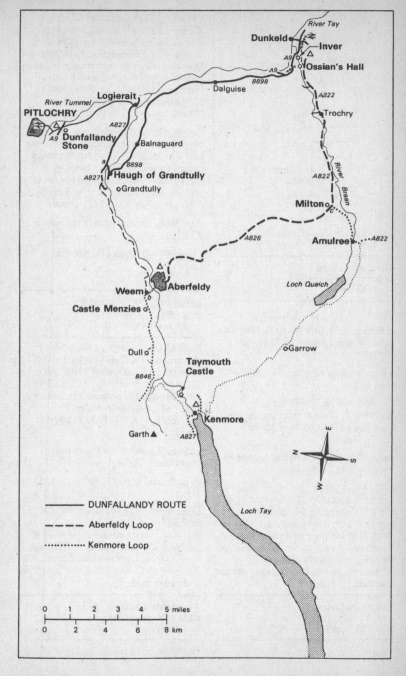

Tay, going away from the Atholl Arms
Hotel. Cont in the Inverness direction
at next junction. R (Crieff, A822,
Crianlarich A85, Inverness A9). L
(Inver, Crieff, Crianlarich, A85, A822).
R (Inver). L at junction by a river
bridge *otherwise detour, R to cross bridge
and cont for 200 yards (metres) to* **Inver**. R
at a T junction with a Give Way sign.
Cont (A822, Crieff 19½). Cont at next
junction. Reach

c near **Milton**. *Join the Kenmore Loop, or
cont.* Leave

c (Aberfeldy A826). Enter

Aberfeldy. Cont (Kinloch Rannoch
20, B846). Cont across the river bridge.
Reach

b **Weem**. *The Kenmore Loop rejoins the
Aberfeldy Loop.* Leave

b (Strathtay 5). Cont by the Spar shop.
Cont (Ballinluig, A827, Pitlochry, A9).
Reach

a. Rejoin the Dunfallandy Route.

Kenmore Loop
adds 10 miles (16 km)
South to north

Leave

c (Crieff, A822). Enter

Amulree. Bear L to cross the bridge. R
on a lane which has a 7′ 6″ width
restriction, and is restricted to 8 tons 6
miles ahead. Follow the road over an 8
ton limit bridge. Pass views to R on
descent over **Taymouth Castle**. R
then immediately L (Killin 17, A827).
Pass through

Kenmore. R (Tummel Br. 11, Kinloch
Rannoch 15). R by Mains of Taymouth
house. Cont past Duneaves Road turn-
off. R (Aberfeldy 4½, B846). Cont past
2 turnings to Dull. Pass **Castle
Menzies**. Reach

b **Weem**. *Rejoin the Aberfeldy Loop.
Otherwise detour ½ mile (1 km),
(Aberfeldy ½, B846). for* **Aberfeldy**.

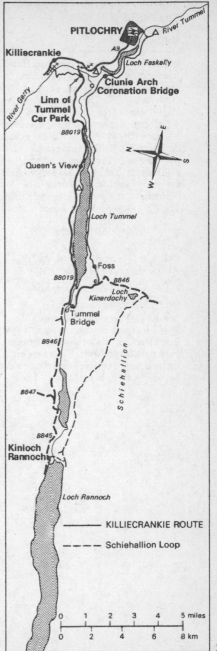

KILLIECRANKIE ROUTE

– – – Schiehallion Loop

KILLIECRANKIE ROUTE
29 miles (47 km)
anticlockwise

PITLOCHRY. From the Fishers Hotel in Pitlochry's centre, go uphill and continue on Atholl Road. Cont (Inverness, A9). This may change with the opening of the new A9 bypass, in which case enquire and make sure that you take the old A9. Pass **Killiecrankie**. At the end of Killiecrankie hamlet, L opposite an Esso garage. L, where the no through road ahead has a speed limit for quarry vehicles. Reach **Linn of Tummel Car Park**. R (Tummel Bridge 10). Pass Queen's View. Reach

d. Join the Schiehallion Loop, or cont. Leave

d (Killin 36, Crianlarich 50, A827, Aberfeldy 13, B846). Reach

e. The Schiehallion Loop rejoins the Killiecrankie Route. Leave

e (Foss 1). Pass views to Queen's View. Pass a footpath to your left leading 100 yards (metres) to **Coronation Bridge**. Pass the **Clunie Arch**. From here on, the ride might change when the new A9 bypassing Pitlochry is opened. Look out for any newly-constructed ways back over the river to Pitlochry. Otherwise L (Portnacraig), into a lane with a sign reading 'To the dam and fish ladder'. In 100 yards (metres) dismount and turn R to walk across a footbridge. R onto Ferry Road. L at the end of Ferry Road.

Schiehallion Loop
adds 16½ miles (27 km)
anticlockwise

Leave

d (Kinloch Rannoch 7, B846, The North, B847, A9). Cont (Kinloch Rannoch 6, B846). Cont (Kinloch Rannoch 3, Rannoch Station 19, B846). Enter

Kinloch Rannoch. L (South Loch Rannoch Road, Schiehallion). R (South Loch Rannoch Road). L just before a sign directing to a camping and caravan site 3 miles away in another direction. Cont at next junction (*not* L to Kinloch Rannoch). Pass L flank of Schiehallion. Pass Loch Kinardochy. L at T junction (*not* R to Fortingall 6¾, Aberfeldy 9). Reach

e. Rejoin the Killiecrankie Route.

In the hills above Loch Ness

NORTHERN SCOTLAND

The area close to Inverness, the 'Highland Capital', is perhaps not quite so mountainous as that nickname suggests. The larger peaks are outside a day's cycling range, but they often dominate the routes, which climb to open moors, silent lochs, and rugged hills. The 1000-ft (300-m) slopes which rise almost sheer on the northern side of Loch Ness, form one wall of the Great Glen, the massive trench stretching right across Scotland caused by the shearing of the earth's crust. At the other extreme, sheltered sea-lochs abut the lower farmlands and woods on the Black Isle.

Generally the roads are very quiet, some being single-track only. The sparse population means there are few places where meals can be bought, but also that the air is clean and fresh, and lichens which will only grow in these conditions can be seen everywhere.

The Culloden Route is unusual, with a large portion of its course being either busy or dull. If you prefer scenic or peaceful cycling, ignore it, but if you cannot resist the fascination of Culloden Battlefield you could spend a day riding that and maybe one of the other short routes.

Fairly easy in parts, strenuous in others. Quiet, with just a few busy miles. One ferry crossing.

INVERNESS

Location: Inverness is a port on Scotland's eastern coast.

Trains: There is a main line station at Inverness. Travel time to either Glasgow or Edinburgh is about 4 hours 30 mins or longer if a change is involved.

Coach: Long-distance coaches link Inverness with Aberdeen, and Perth for Edinburgh and Glasgow.

Tourist Information Bureau: 23 Church Street, Inverness, Highland Region, tel: (0463) 34353 (accommodation service).

Accommodation: Hotel and bed and breakfast accommodation is available in Inverness. There is a large YH in Inverness, but advance booking is necessary in summer. The Bught Caravan and Camping Site, tel: (0463) 36920, is in Inverness.

Cycle-hire: Thornton Cycles, 33a Castle Street, Inverness, tel: (0463) 222810; Balgownie Caravans, Glenurquhart Road, Inverness, tel: (0463) 33051; Bught Caravan and Camping Site, Inverness, tel: (0463) 36920; The YH hires cycles to people who stay there.

Cycle-shop: Thornton Cycles, as above, and Junner, 14 Greig Street, Inverness. There are several other cycle-shops in Inverness.

Maps: OS 1:50 000 (nos 26, 27); Bartholomew's 1:100 000 (no. 55); OS 1:250 000 (no. 2).

Inverness

Inverness has commanded a strategic position at one end of the Great Glen for millenia, but now the only hint of fortification is the clock tower, the sole remnant of Cromwell's fort. The castle is an imposing Victorian edifice, with red-stone drum towers, and beside it stands the statue of Flora MacDonald, the lady who helped Bonnie Prince Charlie to escape after his defeat at Culloden.

Transport has for years used the easy Great Glen route through Scotland; boats travelling the string of lochs connected by the Caledonian Canal, which reaches the sea at the Inverness port basin.

Although much visited by tourists and bulging with craft shops, this is a working city, with all the usual facilities of a swimming pool, restaurants and pubs, cinemas and a theatre. Despite big buildings and bustling crowds, the wide river and views of distant mountains bring a sense of exhilarating country into the city's heart. The museum tells the history of both the city and the highlands, with a special display devoted to the Life of the Clans.

THE CULLODEN ROUTE

On 16 April 1746, Culloden's bleak and windswept moor saw bitter fighting between 14,000 men. The battle was the last to be waged on British soil, and resulted in the final defeat of the Jacobite cause. Decades earlier, when the line of accession to the British throne had been in dispute, the crown had passed to the protestant House of Hanover. The Scottish clans, however, remained loyal to the rival claim from the House of Stuart, firstly from James (hence the term Jacobite), and later from his son, the 'Bonnie' Prince Charles Edward Stuart. In battle each clan fought together as a military unit, bound together by the strong ties of kinship. Today the clan graves on **Culloden Battlefield** are in the care of the National Trust for Scotland, as is Leanach Cottage around which the battle raged. Its rough stone walls and heather-thatched roof now house a museum of the old highland life.

The problem presented to the railway engineers of the Inverness line by the sweeping rise of Culloden Moor was solved by the building of a massive viaduct. It dominates the valley wherein the **Clava Cairns** (DoE, open), are sited. The three prehistoric cairns were probably burial chambers. Kerbed by great boulders and each surrounded by a ring of standing stones, they are still impressive, despite large-scale plundering of their stones for other buildings. Nearby Clava Lodge serves morning coffee.

Much of this route passes through suburbia, yet in its midst is a big **dovecote**, standing beside the road near Culloden House. The walls inside are divided into some six hundred nesting holes. Beyond Balloch a 400-ft (120-m) climb takes you out into unremarkable but pleasant-enough country, where quieter roads occasionally meet with short but sharp gradients. From Easter Muckovie back to Inverness the route is once again busy and not very scenic.

THE BOAR'S STONE ROUTE

Before the Battle of Culloden in 1746 there had been an earlier Rising in 1715, after which the Hanoverians had sought control over the highlands through the building of military roads. The routes chosen then by General Wade are still followed by many modern-day roads, including the lane through **Essich**, where a tell-tale milestone dated 1724 stands near the farm. It rises gradually through low farmlands near Inverness to moorlands at 800 ft (240 m) near Loch Ashie.

Conifer plantations cover parts of the moor. Many Scottish moorlands have been made barren in recent centuries by the felling of natural Scots pine forests, but some fine examples of this rugged tree, with its distinctive irregular shape and salmon-coloured bark, stand by the junction at *a* on the map. Gnarled birches crowd Loch Duntelchaig's lonely shores, their silver softened to grey by lichens.

The kind terrain and strategic position of the Inverness area has attracted settlers for thousands of years, each age leaving its marks on the landscape. The eighth- or ninth-century Picts erected the **Boar's Stone**, the animal carving upon it typical of their style, although worn now and hard to see. Stones of a different kind bear the arms of Scottish clans in **Dunlichity** churchyard, and the nineteenth-century watch house by the gate was built as a guard against body-snatching.

From Balnafoich the quiet B861 drops slowly from the moors back to sea-level, with views over Inverness to the mountains beyond.

The Foyers Loop

Apart from a couple of hard ascents rising a few hundred feet each, the riding is gentle though not flat, and is reasonably quiet even on the B852, since the main Great Glen road runs on the loch's other side.

The loop starts with a hairpin descent from open moorland through woods to the Great Glen Valley. The waters of Loch Ness are nearly as deep as the height of the rock wall above, quite deep enough to accommodate the legendary monster, subject of the Frank Searle Loch Ness Investigation at **Lower Foyers**. There you will also find a tiny museum about the loch, boats for hire and a floating teashop.

Riding beside the loch look out for the stone marking An Ìre Mhór, where gaelic hospitality was offered to Dr Samuel Johnson, and his Scottish companion, James Boswell.

The **Falls of Foyers** rush down a rocky wooded gorge, even though part of their energy is captured by a hydro-electric power station. There are teashops nearby. Later, as you freewheel down **Inverfarigaig** Gorge, you pass the roadside memorial to a geologist who fell to his death from its crags. A Forestry Commission centre nearby has displays about the gorge's natural history, and leaflets describing the Farigaig Forest Trail.

The struggle up steep hairpins beyond Inverfarigaig is rewarded by views over wild, knolly country back to Loch Ness below. From there the lonely road passes farms, wrested in patches from the hostile moors, and takes you through herds of cattle that graze on unfenced land.

THE REDCASTLE ROUTE

The North Kessock ferry runs at half-hourly intervals, the last crossing being at about 10.30 pm on weekdays, but at 6.00 pm on Sundays. A new bridge is now being built to carry the A9, and you can see its span of over half a mile from the ferry. The bridge will carry traffic onto the new course of the A9 over the Black Isle, and it is possible that road construction will alter this route in the busy Tore and North Kessock vicinities. Elsewhere, however, the riding is leisurely, with just a gradual rise from **Redcastle** at sea level to Mains of Tore at 400 ft (120 m), and a 300-ft (90-m) climb beyond Munlochy through the cool grey-green of a beech avenue.

Only pale shingle and, if the tide is low, strands of dark seaweed separates the lane from Beauly Firth. It is nearly land-locked, and the water reflects the low mountains above.

Inland are wooded farmlands where many tarmaced farm drives look like public roads, so be careful not to leave your route. The farmhouses themselves, are often of galetted stonework, galetting being the practise of decorating the mortar between the large stone blocks with smaller chips of stone. It is peculiar to this region and, oddly enough to the Surrey Hills far away in southern England.

The Cromarty Loop

Few tourists venture to the end of the Black Isle, leaving **Cromarty** to enjoy an old-world peace. A number of its sturdy houses of warm reddish stone or whitewash with thick dark lintels, have been preserved by the National Trust for Scotland, which also maintains the cottage (open) of Hugh Miller, the nineteenth-century stonemason, geologist, theologian and author. There are tearooms, pubs serving food, and good picnic spots on the green by the sea, or by the quayside.

The two hills or 'Sutors' of Cromarty guard the firth which provides excellent anchorage for the industrial port of Invergordon. Ships are guided through the strait by the lighthouse at Cromarty, which is opened to visitors in the afternoon at the lighthouse-keeper's discretion.

Near the house called **Shoremill** the level firth-side road passes a yard-tall concrete pillar, one of the triangulation stations in the network covering Great Britain, from which the heights of all other places above sea-level were measured. These 'trig points' are often on hilltops, but this unusual shoreline one stands at 17 ft (5 m) above the zero sea-level as standardised at Newlyn in Cornwall, although it may of course be more or less than 17 ft (5 m) above the firth depending on the tide.

The south-eastern side of the loop is moderately strenuous. The ridge road through Upper Ethie enjoys an impressive view of the long spits and pale ribbon of sand on the far side of the Moray Firth, 400 ft (120 m) below. Beyond Avoch you rise once again to views of Munlochy Bay nature reserve, its marshes attracting many species of wildfowl.

Rosemarkie and **Fortrose** offer afternoon teas, fish and chips and pub food to the hungry. There is a Pictish stone in the grounds of Groam House in Rosemarkie, although it is not open to view at weekends. In Fortrose, scene of the last Scottish witch-burning, are the remains of the cathedral's red ruins (DoE, open), Cromwell having plundered its stones for the fort at Inverness.

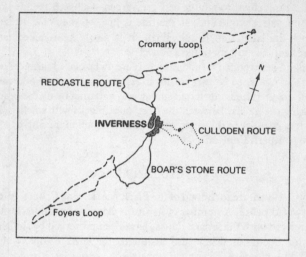

CULLODEN ROUTE
15 miles (24 km)
clockwise

INVERNESS. Leave the city centre following (Perth A9, Aberdeen A96) signs do *not* take the route avoiding the town centre. At the 2nd roundabout, beyond Mercury Hotel, take the (Elgin, A96, Airport, Nairn) exit. R (Smithton 1, Culloden 1¼, Balloch 2). Cont (Culloden ½, Balloch 1½, Nairn 13, A96). Cont (Culloden Moor). Pass the **dovecote**. Cont at the next junction. R (Culloden Moor, Croy, B9006). Cont at the next junction. Cont (Clava Cairns & Standing Stones) *otherwise detour 300 yards (metres), R (Culloden Battlefield)* for **Culloden Battlefield**. Cont at the next junction. R (Clava Cairns & Standing Stones). Pass the **Clava Cairns**. R (Daviot 4, C14). Cross over a railway bridge then turn R by a farm. L at the T junction. 1st R opposite a chevron sign. L at the 'Give Way' T junction. *Ignore* the 'Smithton ¾' turning to the R. Cont

at all junctions in Easter Muckovie. Cont (Inverness 3, B9006 Perth A93). From this point the road system to Inverness was being altered at the time of route-testing: enquire locally for the best route, or follow Inverness signs.

BOAR'S STONE ROUTE
20 miles (32 km)
anticlockwise

INVERNESS. From the main river bridge, walk uphill against the one-way system for a couple of hundred yards (metres). R on Castle Street. Cont on Culduthel Road. R at the traffic lights onto Drummond Road (which had no name sign when the route was tested). L at a 'Give Way' T junction, the first drive on the R being to Bellevue Nursing Home. Cont (Torbreck, Essich, Dores). Cont (Essich). Pass the **Boar's Stone** on your L. Cont to reach

Essich. Cont at next junction *not* L 'Bunachton, Dunlichity'. Reach

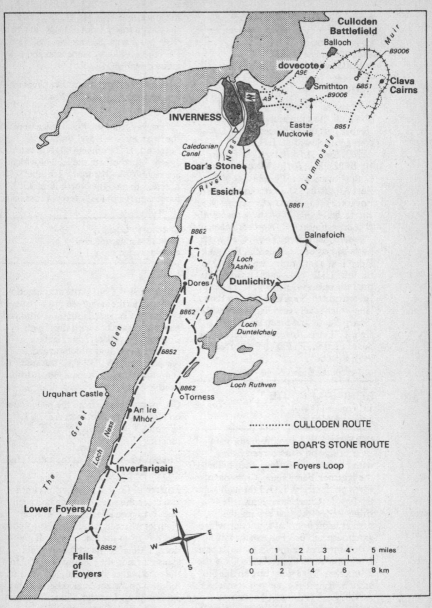

a. *Join the Foyers Loop, or cont.* Leave

a (Loch Duntelchaig, Dunlichity 3½). Enter

Dunlichity. Cont at the next junction. Cont (Balnafoich 2¼). Cont (Daviot). L (Inverness). Cont at all junctions, except at the T junction by a Spar grocers, where you must turn R.

Foyers Loop
adds 27½ miles (44 km)
anticlockwise

Leave

a. Leave on the unsignposted road downhill. At a junction below the steeper part of the descent, bear L to cont going downhill. L (Dores 1, A862). Cont (Inverfarigaig 8, Foyers 10, B852). Pass **An Ire Mhór** on your R. Cont (Foyers 2½, Whitebridge 6½, Fort Augustus 15). Cont (Upper Foyers, Ft Augustus) *otherwise detour ½ mile (1 km) losing 200 ft (60 m) in height, R (Lower Foyers), R (North Highland Charters), for* **Lower Foyers**. Pass the **Falls of Foyers**. L (Glenlia, Errogie). Keep L at a fork near a white house to the left. L (Inverfarigaig 1). Go down the Pass of **Inverfarigaig**. R (Dores 8, Inverness 16). Soon take the first R on a lane which is very easy to miss, passing a 'Sharp Bends and Steep Gradients' sign. L (Dores, Inverness). Cont at the next junction. R (Essich 5¾, Inverness 9½). Reach

a. Rejoin the Boar's Stone Route.

REDCASTLE ROUTE
19½ miles (31 km)
anticlockwise

INVERNESS. Leave from the main river bridge on Bank Street. Swing R with the one-way system, then follow the Kessock Ferry signs. Cross Beauly Firth on the ferry. L (All through traffic). L (Charleston, Redcastle 4). Enter Redcastle. Just beyond the hamlet, cont uphill at a junction with a gatehouse and drive entrance to its R. At another drive entrance to the R, bear L with the road. Cont (Kilcoy). R at the T junction. Take great care on this busy stretch. Roundabout exit (Cromarty A832). Cont (Fortrose, Cromarty, A832). 1st L onto a lane with a 'Lorries over 3 tons unladen prohibited ½ mile ahead' sign. R at the T junction. Reach

b. Join the Cromarty Loop, or cont. Leave

b. Go south-eastwards, (at '3 o'clock' to the Killen road). Cont onto a road wth a 'Kessock Ferry, Service Normal' sign. Pass the Munlochy name sign and cont, going downhill. Reach

c Munlochy Post Office. *The Cromarty Loop rejoins the Redcastle Route.*
Leave

c. Go away from the Post Office to pass the Spar and the Royal Bank of Scotland. L (Drumsmittal, Kilmuir). *Ignore* 3 turn-offs to the L, 2 of which are signposted 'Kilmuir'. L at the T junction to pass the North Kessock name sign. Cont to the ferry. Cross back to Inverness.

Cromarty Loop
adds 28½ miles (46 km)
anticlockwise

Leave

b (Killen 3¾). Cont at the next junction. R then L at the staggered cross-roads (Killin 2). Cont at all junctions until you reach a cross-roads with the (Forestry Commission, Black Isle, Millbuir Nursery) ahead, at which turn L. R (Cromarty 6, B9163). Pass through Jemimaville. Cont to pass **Shoremill**. Cont to enter

Cromarty. Leave from the playground on High Street (Fortrose, A832). L (Eathie). L at the 'Give Way' T junction. Enter

Rosemarkie. Bear R at the end of High Street. Enter

Fortrose. Cont at all junctions until you cross the stream bridge in Avoch, then L to pass an Esso garage. R on Henrietta Street. After turning uphill to go away from the sea, cont at all junctions, following the white diamond signs marking the passing places. After the road makes a right-angled bend L, follow it on a right-angled bend R, do *not* go ahead. L at the T junction with the main road. Cont at the next junction. Pass views over **Munlochy Bay**. L (Munlochy, Kessock 5). Reach

c. Rejoin the Redcastle Route.

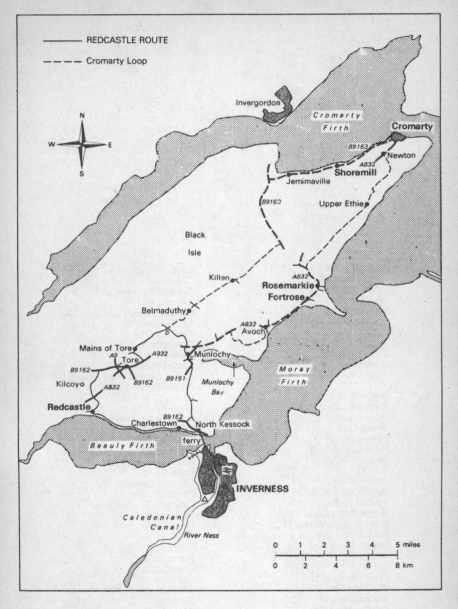

INDEX